T0307608

# VISIONARY

# VISIONARY

## Manchester United, Michael Knighton and the Football Revolution 1989–2019

PHILLIP VINE

pitch

First published by Pitch Publishing, 2019

Pitch Publishing
A2 Yeoman Gate
Yeoman Way
Worthing
Sussex
BN13 3QZ
www.pitchpublishing.co.uk
info@pitchpublishing.co.uk



A CIP catalogue record is available for this book from the British Library.

ISBN 978 1 78531 577 0

Typesetting and origination by Pitch Publishing

Printed and bound in the UK by TJ International

# The Programme of Events

## *Book Three:* The Second Half



## *Book Four:* After-match Analysis

*To Liz, for being there*

*To Eric Brown, best of friends, best of writers*

*To Dale, Carey, Phil, Becky, Lucy, Louise and Sam*

*And to best Spurs fans, Malcolm and Corinne Sell, their daughter Kim, and her husband, Pete*

# Heartfelt Thanks

TO ALL at Pitch Publishing, to Cath Harris for her editorial expertise, to Duncan Olner for his stunning cover design, to Graham Hales for his superb organisation of the photographic section of the book, and to Dean Rockett for his questioning professionalism throughout his proofreading of the manuscript. All have made invaluable contributions to the final version of *Visionary*.

To all my loyal, patient, and critical but supportive readers of my manuscripts, thank you so much: Eric Brown, Leo Moynihan, Pete and Maureen Murphy, Des Vine.

To friends interested in my work: Judith Badr; John and Margaret Cooper; Phyllida Scrivens, Iain Andrews, Kathy Joy and all at the Norwich Writers' Circle; and to Kathy Gale, Juliette Fardon, John Lucas, Ros Senior and Jane Welsh at Writers' Studio.

And, finally, to Michael Knighton, who opened his heart as well as his diaries and private papers.

This book is also dedicated to

*the Covenanter dead*
*the Peterloo dead*
*the Blackwell Colliery dead*
*the Bradford City dead*
*the Hillsborough dead*
*and to the Grenfell Tower dead*

*Victims all*

'But, Edwards, oh dear: the fact is I should never have given him the contract back…'

MICHAEL KNIGHTON

# Matters Up Front

*'It is the business of historians to remember what others forget.'*

ERIC HOBSBAWM

VISIONARY IS the story of the enigma that is Michael Knighton, the man who three decades ago so nearly bought Manchester United, the most famous and most highly valued football club in the world.

He had secured a watertight option agreement to purchase the Old Trafford club, only to abort the deal and hand back the contract to Martin Edwards, the club's principal shareholder, in exchange for a seat on United's board of directors.

The question, why he should have behaved in this extraordinary way, reverberates through the pages of this book.

Had Knighton completed the purchase for the £10m price agreed with Edwards, he might have been the sole owner of an institution valued by *Forbes* in May 2019 at £3.2bn.

Many may judge this maverick man an apparent loser of epic proportions, a here-today-gone-tomorrow phenomenon, but history will surely prove him to have had an outstanding and permanent influence on both Manchester United and the football industry in general. What is often forgotten is that Knighton was the club's chairman elect for sixty-two days, and that those were red hot and revolutionary times at Old Trafford.

*Visionary* is the tale of the wonder and woe that has characterised the life of one of the most influential and intriguing football entrepreneurs of that generation, a man perhaps primarily responsible for the commercialisation of the football industry in England and, through an unacknowledged axis with Alex Ferguson – forged in those sixty-two days – a prime mover in the transformation of United's fortunes on the field of play.

'Give me a trophy every season,' Knighton told Ferguson in the summer of 1989. The manager responded with thirteen Premier League titles, five FA Cups, four League Cups, two Champions League titles and one World Club Cup.

The commercial revolution initiated at Old Trafford by Knighton, and the football revolution supervised by Alex Ferguson, worked together in magical symbiosis to produce hitherto undreamed of profits and Premier League points.

*Visionary* tells the story of an obsessive football man, a prescient and flawed genius, a man unloved and unappreciated by almost all except his family, and of a man who was misunderstood and the butt of both ridicule and venom from many within the sometimes savage confines of the football industry.

*Oi, Knighton, you greedy, fat bastard!*

This was a familiar refrain that greeted him both during and after his years at Old Trafford.

Yet Knighton, in stark contrast to Martin Edwards, never took one penny for any of his work at Manchester United. And in spite of it all, the condemnation and the contempt, Knighton still loves the game, and the industry, too.

Neither his feet nor his brain are ever still. He will talk into the night about any and every aspect of football. His feet still take him to support the team his great-grandfather played for, Sheffield Wednesday.

Recently, too, he has been watching Ilkeston Town and Heanor Town in the Midland League and the East Midlands Counties League, respectively. As a young man in the 1960s, Knighton played for both those teams. He has fond memories of those days and he is fondly remembered, too, and welcomed at his former clubs.

* * *

This book is unashamedly revisionist.

Its original title was *The Truth Game* because so much that is untrue has been written and spoken about Michael Knighton.

*He never had the money.*

*His bid was a front for an anonymous Mr Big.*

*He brought Manchester United and the entire game of football into disrepute.*

Part of the problem for Knighton was his retreat into the silence and the collective responsibility of the Old Trafford boardroom.

Until now, he has held his peace and refused all blandishments to tell his story.

Until now, he has refused to criticise any of his former colleagues at Manchester United.

Until now, he has kept his diaries, his private papers and the documents that prove his determining influence at Old Trafford under lock and key.

*Visionary* sifts the evidence, attempts to set the record straight and preserve the truth for posterity, and aims to place Knighton's remarkable achievements at Old Trafford in true historical perspective.

* * *

This book rewards readers with an explosive and controversial story.

Along the way, *Visionary* provides both the background biographical details necessary for a proper interpretation of Knighton, and all the narrative twists and turns relating to his time at Old Trafford.

It is a book of stories and of stories within stories. And it has enough arguments to start a fight in an empty room. It lights the blue touchpaper and all are advised to stand well clear.

After thirty years, it is time indeed for a retrospective and a reappraisal of Knighton and his place in football's history. Complex, enigmatic, perhaps one of the most misunderstood characters within the industry, Knighton deserves understanding at the very least.

He may well turn out to be a man more sinned against than sinning.

The debates these narratives engender, especially those involving the abuses of the powers of the press – in their hounding and harassment of Knighton – and the complicated web of relationships between sport, money and power, are as fresh and vital in the early decades of the twenty-first century as they were at the fag end of the old millennium.

There is, too, the problem of England that worms its complex way into the plotlines of Knighton's story: England's history, Knighton's history, is a matter of class.

On the positive side, there is the social mobility, the English dream, in which Knighton, a council estate boy from Derbyshire, rose through the ranks, sat within the thick stone walls of his Scottish home, Killochan Castle, the place where the deal to purchase Manchester United was done if not quite dusted, and sat in the boardroom at Old Trafford.

An Englishman's home is his castle indeed.

On the other hand, however, Knighton's story is studded with tragedies resulting from the exploitation of one social class by another.

In 1895, seven miners died at Blackwell Colliery where his great-grandfather worked. In 1989, ninety-five football fans died at Hillsborough, and a ninety-sixth, Tony Bland, died in 1993, as a result of injuries sustained on that fateful day. The home of Sheffield Wednesday was where Knighton's great-grandfather played as a professional for fifteen years.

In both cases the ruling classes of the time blamed the victims.

In some ways, this is the true subject of this book: the dark shadows of England's history.

Certainly, it is the ghosts of English history that have made Knighton the man he is, defiantly socialist, defiantly capitalist too, defiantly iconoclastic.

* * *

These narratives may be thirty years old but their themes, their issues and the sheer bloody intrigue of it all, together make *Visionary* a vital read for the twenty-first century.

As Sam Wallace of the *Daily Telegraph* wrote in September 2017, Knighton's aborted takeover was *one of the great football stories of our time.*

*Book One*

# Games before the Game

## Chapter One

# The Chairman Elect

## *Old Trafford, 19 August 1989*

IT'S HALF past two on the first Saturday of a new football season and Michael Knighton makes what will become his iconic appearance in the annals of football history.

He emerges from the players' tunnel, blinking in the late-summer sunshine, with a football in his hands and resplendent in a brand new Manchester United strip.

He pauses at the pitch edge, as if pondering the enormity of what he is about to do. He jogs on to the hallowed Old Trafford turf, makes for the halfway line, then proceeds towards the Stretford End, juggling the ball, head to knee to foot to shoulder, without once losing control. It is as if the ball is tethered to his body, or part of an invisible aura now made perceptible.

Inside the penalty area, in front of a swaying, cheering crowd, Knighton smashes the ball high and hard into the roof of the Stretford End goal.

He raises his arms aloft and receives the adulation of the crowd.

* * *

Clock hands shift imperceptibly to twenty-five to three on 19 August 1989. All is well with the world and Knighton is heir apparent to the ownership of the most famous football club in the world.

For him, it is a deliberately unorthodox introduction. Not everyone approves, but Knighton would not have it any other way.

Thirty years later he still feels the same, in spite of the spate of shit and spite that follows, in spite of the doubts of Martin Edwards, the disquiet of Bobby Charlton and the disorientation of Alex Ferguson. In spite of the defamations of detractors, Knighton still says he would do exactly the same again given half the chance.

And that is just one measure of the man.

Chapter Two

# Knighton and the Ghostwriter

*Old Trafford, 8 February 1992*

I WAS a tad late arriving on the scene.

I first met Knighton at a more subdued Old Trafford in February 1992. At the time, I was a ghostwriter, doing the rounds of financially challenged chairmen of Welsh football clubs. I was also caring for snotty-nosed kids in a failing Catholic primary school in Holyhead, while attempting to supplement the family income by betting on dodgy racehorses during precious breaks from the tedium of teaching.

There had to be more to life than this, I thought.

Suddenly, there was.

* * *

Ever since those seismic events surrounding Manchester United two and a half years earlier, I had been fascinated by the story of the former schoolteacher, property entrepreneur and fine art collector, whose showmanship on the Old Trafford pitch had been splashed across both front and back pages of the nation's newspapers.

It seemed, soon after, that Michael Knighton had been exposed as a man of straw, lacking the financial substance to bring the deal to buy the club from Martin Edwards, the majority shareholder at Manchester United, to a proper conclusion. According to press reports, he was little better than a charlatan, a showman, a Walter Mitty figure, who had dreamed a dream as chimeric as any in James Thurber's story.

Even so, there were aspects of the story that simply did not add up, that would not let me be.

How had such a man been allowed so very near to the completion of a deal that would have given him control of one of the greatest institutions in British cultural life without proper proof of funding, as many journalists at the time suggested was the case?

What was it that had prompted the sudden turnaround in media coverage of the events, from the euphoria prompted by the release of a national treasure from the widely unpopular Edwards family to the frenzied vitriol against Knighton that foreshadowed and followed the collapse of the deal?

Bar one article, I recalled, in the *Daily Mirror* on the morning before the chairman elect's ball-juggling extravaganza on the Old Trafford pitch, which questioned whether the Manchester United manager, Alex Ferguson, might now be starved of funds for new players, the press coverage initially had been overwhelmingly positive and in favour of the Knighton takeover.

Even the satirical magazine, *Private Eye*, had appeared captivated by this young showman with the balls and the style to do what he did in front of almost 50,000 people on that famous afternoon at Old Trafford.

The questions lay, like an undigested meal, in the pit of my stomach.

* * *

For weeks I intended to contact Knighton. There had to be one hell of a tale to tell.

I felt that the man who had so recklessly courted publicity through his actions on the Old Trafford field of glory had to be a man who would want to share his side of the story with the wider world.

There were lessons to teach, however, and a responsibility to help support five children, rather than waste my time chasing my own wild and fantastical dreams.

In addition, with the shortening of the days, with the onset of winter, the situation surrounding Old Trafford had calmed to an eerie Edwardian silence. Michael Knighton had, to all intents and purposes, disappeared from the face of the earth and certainly from the back pages of the national press. He had become a nowhere man.

He had, I heard, taken a directorship on the board at Manchester United in exchange for returning the ownership of the club to its rightful place, the Edwards family – a dynasty that had been at the Old Trafford helm for the previous thirty years.

Still, though, it was puzzling.

If Knighton really had been an impostor, if he really had nothing more to offer than a circus act, why had he been invited on to the board at Manchester United?

However hard I tried I could not shake the man from my mind. I knew, more than anything I'd known before, that if anyone was to tell the Michael Knighton story I would do my damnedest to make it be me. I had no time, however, what with school reports and a ghosted autobiography of another somewhat less prominent football club owner to write before Christmas. But someone, I thought, had done a job on Knighton, fixed him good and proper, told him to keep his trap well shut. The showman had slipped into a shadow world of secrecy and silence.

* * *

The months passed, the football seasons turned, and Manchester United won an FA Cup and announced a solid profit, both since the new man had joined the board.

In January of 1992, then, in the grip of a New Year resolution, I dusted down my *Rothman's Football Yearbook* and wrote to Michael Knighton, care of Manchester United Football Club, suggesting it might be time to write a book about what had happened back in 1989. Telling the truth, I recommended, was always a boon to posterity as well as to oneself.

It was conceited of me, no doubt, but I wanted to tap into, to rekindle, the arrogance of the mystery man who so nearly bought Manchester United, and I was astonished and delighted in equal measure when the man who had disappeared from public view as suddenly as he had appeared invited me to talk with him at Old Trafford.

* * *

We met in a depth of a late-winter's day, 8 February 1992, but Old Trafford hearts were warming to the possibility of a first league title since 1967; the visitors were one of their rivals for the championship, Sheffield Wednesday.

I was greeted outside the directors' entrance by the burly boss of security who gloried in the name of Ned Kelly. I waved my letter of invitation nervously in the big man's direction. He had eyes that didn't smile and muscles that didn't laugh. I followed him through a maze of brilliantly lit corridors, adorned with images of famous former sons of Manchester United. Old Trafford was a palace of shining steel and glass as thick as ice.

The boardroom door opened and I caught the briefest glimpse of the beating heart of the football club.

'Your visitor, Michael,' Kelly said.

Knighton's features were instantly recognisable. The smile was as wide as a river and as difficult to cross, I thought. The face that had been splashed, and later smeared, across the national press was the same. There was no need for Michael Knighton to wear a red carnation in his buttonhole or carry a copy of *The Times* under his left arm to ensure recognition. His eyes were quick with movement and judgement, and the handshake was warm and firm.

His trademark double-breasted blazer complete with silk, diagonally striped club tie seemed a caricature of the Knighton of the back and front pages of the red-top dailies of three years ago.

Although we had an appointment, although he had invited me to lunch before the game, still I thought I might have only ten seconds to make an impression.

'Come on up,' he said, as he took me by the arm, and we walked away from the boardroom up a shuffle of stairs and entered a small room where fates of nations might have been decided, where ghosts of players, managers and directors might have lingered.

Knighton smiled again and I revised my earlier estimate of ten seconds of opportunity to ten minutes.

'Cup of tea?'

Knighton's voice was plum perfection, ripe and rich, vowels straight from the playing fields of the public schools of England. He might have stepped from the pages of a PG Wodehouse novel.

I began to understand one of Knighton's enviable gifts, perhaps even a key to his rise from prematurely injured footballer to schoolmaster and to head teacher, and from successful serial entrepreneur to the board of directors of Manchester United.

He possessed the ability to make everyone in his presence feel as remarkable as he knew himself to be.

When Knighton was a pupil at school, he told me, his teachers said to him that he would make his mark either in sport or as an artist. But what they did not tell him was how he would make everyone who met him feel special, through the simple trick of giving them his undivided attention for however long he deemed it necessary. I knew, though, he would then dismiss them from his mind as readily as he had welcomed them, but it was enough, this absorption, this concentration, and it was a rare talent in a world of disconnected and feigned focus.

At lunch, in the glass and plush world that was the Old Trafford executive restaurant, I watched as ghosts from the past, from my childhood, drifted by our table.

Bobby Charlton, scorer of a saving grace of a goal against Mexico in the 1966 World Cup, when I was just fourteen and absorbing images that would last a lifetime, appeared now as a god brought down to earth, somehow still substantial, yet drifting by, without a word, subsisting in the fading shadows of his fame. His hair, recidivist even in 1966, was now as thin as gruel.

I also saw Denis Law, Bill Foulkes, Paddy Crerand, an angelic host of household legends from United's glory years. All I needed now was to see George Best stroll into the restaurant to greet his erstwhile colleagues, and the dream would be complete.

By 1992, however, Charlton & Co and Manchester United were perfect partners, both living on memories borrowed from the past. This dependence on a bygone era was what both Alex Ferguson and Michael Knighton, in their different ways, were trying to change. I sensed then, though, what I had already guessed: Michael Knighton was an intruder here, a visitor not much less transient than me.

Since then, I have come to appreciate that Knighton, wherever he goes, whatever he does, will always be an outsider of sorts. It is what he is and what he does. He comes in, he shifts things around, he moves on. Yet somehow, he achieves a kind of permanence in the ideas, the ghosts of energy, that he leaves behind.

* * *

In the plush directors' box, with its padded leather seats, each with a sealed nameplate of the director whose designated seat it was, we took our seats just before kick-off. We discussed the manager's team selection. I ventured to suggest that Ferguson might be getting things wrong with his constant changes to an almost successful side. In those days, it was a hobby horse of mine – that old dictum about never buggering about with a winning team.

Knighton, though, offered merely the possibility of some guarded agreement.

After the match, a disappointing 1-1 draw, I felt just a touch smug, and probably said something that stopped just short of *I told you so*. After reclaiming the championship in the following season, however, and another twelve times since, and earning for himself the mantle of the greatest manager of all time, I suspect it is Sir Alex who now feels rather more vindicated.

His rotation policy, resting key players when necessary, utilisation of a full squad of players, is now copied in every football club in the world. It is easy, though, to forget just how very precarious Ferguson's position still was in 1992, and would be until the league championship was reclaimed.

Like Knighton, the manager was there on sufferance, and there were those at the heart of the club who were far from convinced that the revolution Ferguson was initiating was worth the cost of the upheaval.

* * *

Like any good hack worth his hire, I had done my homework.

'Divided loyalties today was it, then, Michael?' I ventured, as the ref blew his whistle to end the game.

'How do you mean?'

'Well, your great-grandfather played for the Wednesday, didn't he?'

'Yes,' he said, his face consumed by the broadest grin of the day. 'He won the FA Cup with them in 1907, beat Everton 2-1, played at the Crystal Palace in front of over 84,000 fans.'

Also, like any halfway decent journalist, I refrained from saying, 'I know.'

'William Layton was his name. You could look him up.'

I already had.

'An attacking full-back with a crunching tackle.'

Knighton was in full flow, in his element, and I felt as if I had scored the winning goal in that Cup Final, such was my desire to make the right impression on the Manchester United director.

Family, I came to know, was another key to understanding this man and his actions.

* * *

Later, Knighton was struggling to recall someone who had played for United in the 1948 FA Cup Final.

'Charlie...' he said, frowning.

'Mitten,' I said.

'Yes, that's right.'

'Signed for United in 1946,' I said. 'One hundred and forty-two appearances, fifty goals, nifty right-winger, the original rebel with a cause, pissed off with the maximum wage of £12 a week, took himself off to Independiente of Santa Fe in Colombia for a signing-on fee of five grand and weekly wages of £40.'

I feared I might have pushed my luck too far. There was, though, an appreciative smile on Knighton's face. I knew at that moment I had half a chance of telling the Manchester United director's story, and also that my misspent youth reading about nothing much but football had been worthwhile, after all.

* * *

As the crowd began to disperse, Knighton turned to speak to a fellow director, and I sneaked a look at the matchday programme.

The cover showed a murky picture of Andrei Kanchelskis scoring the only goal in a recent match against Everton and an advertisement for Sharp Electronics (UK) Ltd, the main club sponsors.

Inside, there was a picture of Alex Ferguson, who looked young enough to be clipped around the ear by a Glasgow policeman. But there was something in the manager's eyes, something steely and unforgiving, that presaged future success.

In his programme notes, Fergie commented on the fact that there had been no league championship at Old Trafford since 1967.

*It's been so long probably half our support don't even know what the trophy looks like.*

I noted the cast of heroes and villains.

They were all there on the inside front cover, the directors of the club, the power brokers of Old Trafford. Martin Edwards, Michael Edelson, Bobby Charlton CBE, Maurice Watkins LIM, Amer Al Midani, Nigel Burrows, Les Olive.

And Michael Knighton, too, of course.

It was astonishing, though, the coincidence that the visitors were Sheffield Wednesday, fifth in that final season of the old

League Division One. The table showed Leeds United top on goal difference from the United men from Manchester.

Captain of Sheffield Wednesday was Nigel Pearson, later a football club manager whose path of destiny would cross that of my host for the day.

But that was another story for another day, another book perhaps.

Advertisers in the programme included the Lancastrian Building Society and Flight Desk, the travel agency division of the Co-op. Records played during the build-up to the match could be purchased from the HMV shop in Market Street, and the Official Thirst Quencher of Manchester United was Gatorade. The earliest flowering of commercialisation had already begun at Old Trafford.

The Knighton effect was also to be seen in an inserted supplement to the programme headed Pricing and Visitor Policy: the Future.

I turned to the back page to check the names and numbers of all the players and saw scribbled autographs everywhere. I was overwhelmed by Knighton's kindness, thoughtfulness, in arranging for my souvenir programme to be signed by the stars.

* * *

We then retreated to a stark, bare, white-walled room somewhere in the bowels of Old Trafford. It was an alternative universe, in which the deep pile carpets, the shine of stainless steel and glass, and the ubiquitous executive gloss had all vanished from sight.

It was so spartan, so bleak an office, it made me think of a prison cell, a place of solitary confinement. It was where we were going to work and where all of Knighton's charm and ease was replaced by a professional and expectant stare at my tape recorder. It was where I also realised that all of my cleverness would count for nothing if I screwed up now.

It was clear from Knighton's suddenly serious demeanour, his furrowed brow and folded arms, that he had come not only to distrust journalists but maybe to loathe them, too.

'Tell me, Michael,' I said, 'tell me about the most important event in your life.'

* * *

It was a bog standard opening gambit, designed to both relax the interviewee and to stimulate thought as well as talk.

What I expected, of course, was some egotistical recap, claptrap of the ball-juggling extravaganza of August 1989, which I would have then happily rehashed yet again for a delighted audience.

At the very least, I thought, he'll tell me about his time as a young professional footballer at Coventry City, or how he made his millions, but I underestimated the man.

To my amazement, Knighton chose to talk, not about football or money, and not to name drop about Charlton or Ferguson, or any of the current stars at United – Schmeichel, Giggs, Robson, Hughes, Kanchelskis – or a young fourteen-year-old kid called Beckham, who Knighton later revealed might just make a name for himself.

Instead, he told me about the traumatic birth of his son, Mark.

It was another measure of the man. This was someone I was beginning to get to know; he was someone I had underrated by several fathoms of depths.

'Do me a piece,' he said, 'and make it about those who are closest to me and those who are my reason for living. Make it about my son, Mark Knighton, my first born, and a boy who has inspired me in all that I do.'

* * *

I drove home to North Wales, trying to make sense of it all.

I understood that, in talking of his son, Knighton had succeeded both in telling me nothing and yet, perhaps, everything. The only thing I knew with absolute certainty was that the man was a born storyteller, someone with the gift of casting spells. I had not met Martin Edwards but I suspected that the very private public figure that was the chairman and chief executive of Manchester United, with his lean and insubstantial presence, with his grey, shy suits that fitted his personality to perfection, would have been no match for Knighton's clever, charming world of words.

I now know that my suspicions were accurate.

* * *

That day's tape is long since lost but even now, a quarter of a century on and counting, there are elements of Knighton's story that linger in the mind.

The helpless mother, her labour done, the polite husband, unsure of his place in this woman's world, now both dependent on the hapless and incompetent midwife, recreated so vividly through Knighton's mimicry of her West Yorkshire accent.

*Ah says, it's awreet, loove! Yer wife's doin reet well and yer babby's joost champion!*

Except the baby was not champion at all.

The contrast with the storyteller's own accent, refined during his time as a schoolmaster within the public school system, was a counterpoint to the driving narrative.

*Is there something wrong, Nurse?*

Knighton's voice broke with an anxiety born of not knowing.

*Noah, loovey, nah, Mr Knighton, noothing too wrong! The coord, it's round babby's neck, that's all, and Ah can soon sort it owt!*

*Isn't that serious, Nurse?*

*Noah, Mr Knighton, loove, it's noothing too serious, boot Ah'm gooing to coot that coord!*

*Frankly, Nurse, I am a little concerned, a little worried about my son.*

Knighton leaned in towards his new-born son to see for himself.

*With respect, Nurse, I think there may be something seriously wrong.*

Knighton was working hard at not giving in to the alarm that was flooding every cell of his being.

*My child is turning blue, Nurse.*

The nurse, fragile and callow, was frozen in her fright.

*My baby's blue, Nurse, my baby's blue! He's not breathing! He needs oxygen!*

Knighton was shouting now, all ceremony cast aside.

Neither nurse nor child was moving. Everything was as still as death.

*My boy, he's stopped breathing, he's not breathing at all!*

The account of Mark Knighton's agonising birth proceeded to crisis point.

Within the whitewashed walls of an office deep inside Old Trafford, Knighton appeared near to tears as he recalled the traumatic events of that day.

*I'm really getting very anxious here, Nurse!*

Knighton regained a semblance of control over his emotions.

The young nurse melted and her face unfolded into a picture of helplessness, of fear.

*Frankly, Nurse, the situation looks extremely serious to me.*

He paused. Someone had to do something, and soon.

*You're on your own here in this delivery room and surely you must require some assistance, and right now!*

The storyteller paused to comment on the strain of restraint, the ludicrous bounds of English etiquette, the decorum that demanded politeness even while his son was dying.

It also allowed him to regain sufficient composure to conclude his narration.

*Ah think yer may be reet, Mr Knighton.*

The baby lay lifeless, flat on the bed, between his mother's legs, as still as death, a deepening blue in the boy's skin the only shift, the sole movement, in the sickening tableau.

*Quick, Nurse! Oxygen!*

Knighton said he remembered reading that the human brain could survive for only a very few minutes without oxygen.

*Hurry, Nurse, please! My boy needs oxygen!*

Knighton took his time to paint a picture of the oxygen cylinders, four of them on a trolley across the room, leaning together, he said, like old soldiers discussing the war.

*Quick, Nurse, quick!*

He could see no key to free the cylinders, however, and when Knighton eventually found the key, beneath a chipped enamel bowl on the windowsill, there was no oxygen inside the cylinders.

*I think, Nurse, this may now be an emergency.*

Knighton saw a red button on the far wall close to his wife's head, pressed it, and listened to the scream of the emergency buzzer calling for help.

A red light flashed above the exit door.

Knighton ran from the delivery room with one question pounding in his head.

*Where are the doctors? Where are the doctors? Where are the frigging doctors?*

He found them, six of them, in an operating theatre nearby.

*What are you doing? What are you doing in here?*

The doctors screamed at Knighton as he burst into their private domain.

The desperate father attempted to take hold of a couple of the doctors by their white coats.

The medical men were all righteous indignation.

*My baby, doctor, my baby's dying.*

Knighton was dragging two of the medics down the corridor. Understanding eventually dawned on the doctors and they, too, began to run.

Baby Mark was taken to the Resuscitation Unit where his tiny body was pummelled by fists and by electricity.

At last, Knighton saw his son jump-start into movement, his arms jerking in time with the doctor's pumping action.

*Look, baby's colouration is good now! I think we've caught him just in time,* the doctor said.

Knighton's mind was racing, one unanswerable question beating at his brain.

Will my boy's brain be damaged and beyond repair?

He cradled his son in his arms.

It would be six months, the doctors explained, before Knighton would have an answer to his urgent question.

*In the meantime, love him all you can, that's all that you can do, that's all that anyone can do now.*

* * *

I retell the story now because I believe it is key to understanding Michael Knighton, and all his later actions.

I learned subsequently, from his long-suffering former wife, Rosemary, mother of Mark Knighton, that at times of crisis in their life together Michael had always put his family above everything, had always taken decisive action to protect his family whenever required to do so.

*You cannot fault Michael on that score, ever. He is, and always has been, a brilliant father to his children.*

Rosemary Knighton was loyal to her ex-husband, where loyalty was due. In fact, to this day, in spite of a gentle and reluctant separation as a result of Knighton's inability to temper his workaholic nature, Rosemary and Michael remain the best of friends and share regular and frequent family gatherings.

* * *

If he really did have the money to buy Manchester United, I thought, as I neared home, as I crossed the Menai Bridge, travelled deeper into the ancient fortress kingdom of Gwynedd, did he sacrifice it all for love, for Rosemary and for his children?

I laughed at myself for allowing such a thought to intrude into the hard-boiled world of football politics and hack journalism. But the idea would not go away in spite of my ridicule. I also smiled as I recalled a seventeenth-century drama I had studied for A Level, John Dryden's *All For Love; Or, The World Well Lost: A Tragedy.*

It was a tragedy indeed, if Knighton really held one of the world's greatest football clubs in the palms of his hands and then allowed it to slip through his fingers for no apparent or obvious reason.

Other than love?

What price did Edwards name to buy Manchester United?

Ten million, with a promise by Knighton to stump up maybe the same again for the rebuilding of the Stretford End and a few quid for new players?

And what is Manchester United worth in 2019?

With the latest kit deal with Adidas bringing in an annual income of £105m, and with the sports ground naming rights deal worth a staggering £155m, a recent Wall Street valuation of the club suggests Manchester United is worth between £2.9 and £3.2bn.

When I think about it now, it brings tears to my eyes.

All for love?

No, that would surely be crazy.

And yet I could not erase the thought from my mind.

In 2019, Knighton merely smiles inscrutably when I ask the question.

* * *

What Knighton did readily reveal, however, way back in 1992, is that, yes, the six months after the botched delivery of his son was a period of severe doubt and anxiety about Mark's long-term health.

'The birth of my son and the consequent trauma changed my life forever,' he said. 'It was a watershed moment.'

In fact, this time of extreme distress gave birth to a new man walking a path of ambition that led him away from teaching to entrepreneurship. He built business after business, ranging from retail outlets to a sizeable property empire and ultimately to the well-documented £20m bid to purchase Manchester United Football Club.

Knighton, at the tender age of 25, was suddenly a very driven young man.

'How was I to care for a potentially damaged son, especially on a poor teacher's salary?'

The questions found an answer.

* * *

Over the next few days I put together a sample of my writing, one that emerged out of our initial meeting, and which Knighton had asked for in order to evaluate my abilities.

'What do you think, then, Michael?' I said.

The telephone line was like a radio in need of tuning to the correct station, but I heard enough to know I had the job as the author of Knighton's story.

* * *

Over the following months we met several times, on neutral ground in and around the walled city of Chester.

Knighton was mercurial. Some of these meetings took place in five star hotels, others in dark and deserted corners of remote and rural pubs. I went wherever I was told to go and step by step, the story of the most sensational, aborted takeover in British football history began to take shape.

* * *

Then, in June 1992, out of the blue, Knighton offered me the opportunity to work with him full time.

It was only a temporary appointment as a personal assistant but Knighton agreed to match my teaching salary and I decided to take the risk. My wife was horrified at first but was eventually supportive.

'It's my big chance,' I said, 'to really get to know the man, to work closely with him, to see what makes him tick, and what makes him tock.'

One moment I was working on a book about a director of Manchester United and Knighton's takeover bid, and the next I was moving house, wife and children in order to become Knighton's general factotum.

'You're crazy,' my wife told me.

'I know,' I said.

To be fair to Knighton, he had warned me of his impending move away from the glamour and glitz of Old Trafford. He wanted to make a further contribution to the well-being of the football industry and that required an upheaval, a removal, a shift of emphasis.

'Come with me,' he said. 'I need an honest, hard-working man of talent to work alongside me.'

Oh, how insidious indeed were the machinations of flattery.

'What about the writing, Michael, what about the book?'

'It's only a temporary role, Phillip, just until I get things sorted with this new venture.'

And so, what promised to be a brief pause in the telling of Knighton's tale, a comma, turned into a semi-colon, and then a full stop that lasted a quarter of a century.

I left that temporary role with Knighton the following year because of a serious family illness in Cambridgeshire, my home county, and the proposed book then gathered decades of dust in the corner of my study and at the back of my mind.

It was such a shame, I thought, as time accelerated through the years, all that knowledge, all those wonderful stories about Knighton were going to waste. In the end, though, working with Knighton way back when turned out to be an invaluable experience. I saw Knighton with his guard up – and down. And when, eventually, I restarted work on *Visionary* it was with inside information inside my head.

Fast forward from that parting in 1993, twenty odd years, to another New Year resolution to track down Michael Knighton. I knew he had become something of a recluse, licking wounds, I suspected, after the highs and lows of significant proportions that accompanied him through the final years of the old century.

The traditional press and the internet had been crawling with rumours that did not tally with the Michael Knighton I thought I knew. Worst of all were the allegations of some kind of alleged financial irregularities that led to his temporary barring from being a company director.

Michael, I thought, oh Michael, what have you been up to?

I had to find out what had happened.

I had worked with the man, known him to be scrupulously honest and generous to a fault. Even so, I assumed that what I was reading just had to contain some grains of truth. I heard Knighton had been living in the Channel Islands and a letter addressed to *Michael Knighton, Sark* eventually found its way to his home in Huddersfield, Yorkshire.

'Hello, Phillip,' he said. 'Let's meet up.'

We did, in a vegetarian restaurant on King's Parade in Cambridge.

'Very special place for me,' he said, indicating King's College Chapel, the city's and the university's architectural masterpiece across the road.

'I'll tell you all about it later,' he added, in response to my questioning eyebrows.

'We need to finish that book, you know,' he said, after we had ordered food.

'I think we maybe need to start again, Michael,' I replied.

'Why now?' I asked, after the polite preliminaries, after the exchange of news, after the lentil bakes were cleared away.

'Let me tell you a story,' he said, and we began again.

Once more, just as it had been a quarter of a century past, it was not about football, but family.

'Lana, my eldest granddaughter, she's seven now and she's so precocious and internet savvy, like all the kids are these days.'

There was a pause and I nodded encouragingly.

'Have you seen it,' he asked, 'all that ridiculous, absurd, and untrue stuff out there about me?'

'I don't read it, Michael,' I lied.

'Well, she does, my Lana does, and no doubt all my granddaughters will do the same soon enough.'

He was angrier now than I had ever seen him.

'She's the apple of my eye and she only knows me as Granddad Mike.'

'Okay,' I said, more than half suspecting what he would say next, yet still stunned when it came.

'Just this week, as I'm kissing my granddaughter goodnight, she says to me, "Granddad, are you Michael Knighton, that football man, the one on the internet?"'

That was enough for Knighton.

'Let's get that book out there so everyone can read the truth.'

* * *

All those years ago, when I set out to write Knighton's story, *The Truth Game* was the original title I had chosen for our project.

It seemed, at that moment in that Cambridge restaurant, even more important to tell the truth than it did way back then.

And time, great healer or not, all those fat and lean years of it, certainly provided perspective for the task.

The name of the book may have changed to *Visionary* but the aim of truth-telling remains the same.

## Chapter Three

# Going Back

2017, THE first year of Trump and the first year of Brexit, the year of lies.

And I wanted some honesty.

* * *

We were in Huddersfield now, Knighton's place, once a mill owner's fortress, solid as Pennine rock, a brick by bloody brick capitalist's safety of a place, its thick walls now softened by hundreds of books on art, on poetry, on philosophy and, of course, on the beautiful game of football.

We were kicking ideas around.

Like footballs.

'All these years,' I said, 'these past ones that we all live in most of the time.'

Knighton nodded, non-committal.

'They're like long-lost friends.'

It really wasn't very clever stuff, but I was trying to get Knighton to go back.

'Like old enemies, too,' he said, with a face torn between grin and grimace. 'They'll not sit still; they'll not die or rest in peace.'

I waited.

'Okay,' he said at last. 'I'm ready, let's go back.'

'1989,' I said.

* * *

For Michael Knighton, the son of a master baker turned coalminer, and for Manchester United Football Club and its chairman, Martin Edwards, a butcher's boy, this particular year was a date with destiny.

'1989,' Knighton mused. 'That year's both friend and foe.'

I nodded in agreement, encouraging the speech I knew was coming.

'It was a big year in every way, not just for me, but for football, and the rest of the world, the Hillsborough disaster, the launch of Sky TV, Thatcher's poll tax, the fall of the Berlin Wall, the end of the Communist era, the end of history and all that.'

Knighton's eyes narrowed into focus and he looked both wistful and intent.

'In the football universe, 1989, it's the moment when time began anew, when the Big Bang of Money was born, when the first real seeds of financial expansion were being sown, a watershed moment in the history of the game.'

I watched as Knighton's eyebrows arched.

'Of course,' he said, 'I have my own small part in all of that.'

I smiled and the story began to write itself.

As he talked, I, too, remembered 1989, a year of detonations and eruptions, both personal and public.

It was the year I fell, face to face with disaster, after my family's house was repossessed because of a business failure – the demise of a literary magazine that had been set to make my fame and fortune.

If my trajectory was steeply downhill, Knighton's was upwardly mobile and moving. Our paths had yet to cross.

We were both yet to understand that down was sometimes up and up sometimes down.

* * *

Outside of my private hell, in the bright summer of June 1989, Knighton was preparing his bid to buy Manchester United from Martin Edwards.

The rest of the world was as yet innocent of his plans.

In other respects, however, the earth and its most powerful inhabitants were as guilty as hell.

In Beijing's Tiananmen Square, the People's Liberation Army turned its tanks and its guns on civilian protesters, and unknown numbers died.

In the same month, protests in Communist Poland led to elections in which Lech Walesa's Solidarity movement swept their old adversaries from power. By the end of August, just as storm clouds gathered over Knighton's proposed purchase of the most famous football club in the world, Polish trade unionists were heading a coalition government dedicated to the dismantling of the former Russian satellite state.

In the Union of Soviet Socialist Republics, Mikhail Gorbachev, the General Secretary of the Communist Party, was discarding old iron curtain habits as fast as a burglar on the run disposes of his loot.

Everywhere, the Big Bang of unchained Western capitalism exploded and accelerated at the speed of light. Even in Beijing, the tanks were there to defend not socialism but the socialist market.

Francis Fukuyama, a bright young star within the US State Department, declared in an essay in the journal *The National Interest* that the End of History had arrived. He wrote of the universal triumph of Western liberal democracy as the final and perfect form of government.

In England, Michael Knighton, another bright young star, with his radical *Blueprint for the Commercialisation of Football,* full of radical ideas, proposed the End of Football as we knew it, insisting on a new world of corporate branding and exploitation of markets.

No one in the professional football game had ever used the term *brand* in relation to a football club before Knighton appeared on the scene – not even one as big and as ripe for exploitation as Manchester United. His *Blueprint*, however, was all about brand-building and the implementation of the unrestrained commercialisation of the football industry.

Knighton was in tune with the times alright and already far ahead of the field. His ideas would change the face of football forever.

In Russia, future billionaires, Roman Abramovich for one, were moving from the shadowy constraints of the old Soviet Union towards what some observers have described as the legalised robbery of state assets, all in a firestorm of gangster capitalism that would eventually lead Abramovich to the ownership of Chelsea, like Manchester United, a premier brand football club in England.

Throughout the world in 1989, the New Capitalism was the Coming King, spreading to fill the known, expanding universe of time and space.

Even in Britain, formerly the hub of Old Imperial Capitalism, but now a dreary, dingy shrinking land, lost in a twilight world of small wars and small beer, and living on its past in a Thatcherite vision of dog eat smaller dog mentality; even here there was still room for the growing and the harvesting of money.

Michael Knighton had made his, Martin Edwards had inherited his, at least in part.

Soon, they would meet.

* * *

In January 1989, Knighton, at only thirty-seven, was a retired multi-millionaire entrepreneur, and had already moved from his Yorkshire base into tax exile on the Isle of Man. He had made his money through the purchase and restoration of fine period properties and had recently bought a farm which sat high on Richmond Hill and overlooked Douglas Bay.

He was footloose and dapper, slightly softened by the ease of good living, the rough edges of his Derbyshire upbringing smoothed by the years of working in private education, the rough and ready vowels of his youth polished like stones by the subtle movements of the sea, and the sharp elbows and sharp tongues of a footballer's youth replaced by good money and good manners.

He owned a portfolio of properties including farms with fruitful fields, blocks of Georgian property in Edinburgh, Dunbar House in West Lothian, and a magnificent, medieval castle at Killochan, Ayrshire, where great and future events would unfold and where he would meet with the chairman of Manchester United to finalise the biggest deal in football history.

He had a smile that would charm the gods from their heavens.

* * *

Martin Edwards was chairman and chief executive at Old Trafford.

He appeared there every morning, diligent, and ready for work.

He parked his car in his personal garage, walked, slim and trim, to his office at the heart of the football club.

The morning's newspapers were waiting for him there, laid out in their proper order for his perusal by his secretary.

There was comfort in routine and yet was he perhaps living a kind of lie?

Did he tell himself each day I am happy and I am a success?

Certainly, some people wondered whether Edwards ever questioned himself and his privileged position.

If he were living a lie, as some observers believed, actually, there might have been two lies here: both the happiness and the success.

And Edwards was not the best of liars.

Some claimed he was desperate to sell the club his father, Louis, master of the Manchester meat trade and chairman and majority shareholder at Old Trafford since 1965, had, at least in part, bequeathed to him.

Clearly, by 1989, Edwards wanted out.

* * *

In 1989 English football provided a mirror image of the state of the nation.

It was lukewarm Bovril in plastic cups; it was stale meat pies and it was railway sleepers for terracing at some of its Football League clubs. It was unwelcoming and it was unsafe.

It was also Thatcherite in its brutality, Little Englander in its mentality, and it was black and white in an age of Technicolor, a silent movie when talkies had been all the rage for quite some time.

As a nation, Britain was still fighting and still winning the Second World War and, as a footballing power, it was still dreaming of 1966 and all that, when the World Cup win at Wembley was yet another defeat for the Germans.

The national game was haunted by the ghosts of tragedies past.

* * *

Four years previously, on 11 May 1985, a flash fire at Valley Parade, the home of Bradford City, had consumed the club's ancient wooden grandstand after a match or a lighted cigarette had fallen through a gap in the wooden structure on to the accumulated detritus below. Fifty-six died in the fire and a further 265 were severely injured, either burned or crushed in the every-man-for-himself stampede that followed the discovery of fire. It was not just a human tragedy multiplied many times over and captured by the cameras of Yorkshire Television, it was a grim and graphic statement of much that was wrong with English football, and therefore English society, at the time.

The tragedy also provided a ghastly commentary on the capitalism prevalent in the final quarter of the twentieth century. Bradford City's owner and chairman, Stafford Heginbotham, had either owned or been closely involved with eight businesses that, in the space of eighteen years, had gone up in flames and smoke. The fire at Bradford in 1985 was the ninth. Heginbotham benefited from insurance claims of around £30m in today's terms. Money mattered. Lives did not.

* * *

Religion in 1989 had long since ceased to be the opium of the people and had been replaced by football. Curiously, Manchester United, inadvertently, had played a leading role in the creation of such a culture in England and beyond, which had become useful to ruling elites throughout the world.

In February 1958, eight Manchester United footballers, the immortal Busby Babes, lost their lives on the snow and slush covered runway of Munich airport as the British European Airways Flight 608 ploughed through a fence at the end of the runway and into a nearby house, having failed in a third attempt to become airborne in those appalling wintry conditions. Stories of heroism abounded, including that of the United goalkeeper Harry Gregg, who disobeyed orders and stayed at the scene of the disaster to pull survivors, including Bobby Charlton, from the wreckage of the plane. The late Duncan Edwards, at the time thought to be the most precociously talented footballer of his generation, fought for his life for fifteen days in a Munich hospital. The drama only added to the sense that here was a legend building that would provide consolation and comfort in hard times.

Eight years later Charlton provided national cheer, and respite for Harold Wilson's hard-pressed government, with his stunning, sublime, long-distance goal against Mexico, and in World Cup-winning performances against France, Argentina, Portugal and West Germany.

Both 1958 and 1966 were part of a football nation-building tradition that accelerated after the Second World War as organised religion began to lose its hold over votes as well as souls.

* * *

By the time of the Bradford fire, however, working men in Yorkshire and beyond, having been briefly seduced by Arthur Scargill and the romance of high politics and industrial action, were returning to the solace of football after the ending of the miners' strike in March of the same year.

Both pits and pitches in 1985 were symbols of a divided nation.

Flat caps were still the uniform of older fans on the terraces, women still stayed at home to keep their menfolk's fires burning, and on floodlit nights pinpricks of light from a thousand Woodbines and Players No6 cigarettes could be seen on all sides of the stadium like a constellation of distant stars.

These lights, too, were messages from a dying age although at least, at the football, there remained a sense of community and solidarity. After Thatcher's defeat of the miners, it was probably the last remaining place on earth where that community and solidarity might still be found.

* * *

At Bradford City, on that sad Saturday afternoon, a day scheduled to be a celebration of their Third Division championship win, something rotten was exposed at the heart of the nation. Warnings about the state of the grandstand, unchanged since its erection in 1911, had been ignored; the wooden stand had been condemned and was due for demolition in the summer.

Heginbotham's debts, however, would not wait.

The meaning and the message of Thatcher's Britain was that men were expendable, whether they were miners or football supporters or both. Something was rotten in the state of England.

* * *

Most of the Bradford City supporters headed for the regular exits at the back of the main stand as the fire took hold. But the gates were locked and no stewards were on duty to open them to relieve the crush. Some of the crowd escaped by breaking through locked exits, others by making their way on to the pitch. One man was ablaze from head to foot and danced in agony on the abandoned grass. He died in hospital later. The fans behind the goal nearest to the flames, in fear of their lives, broke down the metal fencing that caged them within their section of terracing.

It was a time when men and boys who could not afford seats in the grandstand, or who preferred to stand, were animals behind bars, imprisoned in their own squalid pens of crushed humanity. It was in this year, too, that the chairman of Chelsea FC, Ken Bates, the man who sold out to the Russian billionaire Roman Abramovich, requested permission from the Football Association and the Greater London Council to install electric fences at Stamford Bridge to deter hooligans. It was a time when all football fans were branded by politicians, the press and the general public as hooligans and beyond the pale of civilisation, a labelling that seemed to be confirmed just eighteen days after the Bradford tragedy.

The Heysel disaster, however, was no parochial affair, no third-rate occasion, and, as such, it could not be ignored by the football authorities. But the same abuse of human dignity and human safety was still in evidence at the Belgian ground, venue for the European Cup Final between Liverpool and Juventus.

As at Bradford, the stadium was dilapidated, crumbling even, and many Liverpool fans without tickets discovered they could kick holes in the cinder block walls and thereby gain illegal entry to the ground. The choice of the Heysel Stadium – built in 1930 and unaltered since – to stage such a prestigious match was criticised at the time. It was an accident waiting to happen.

One hour before the scheduled kick-off, Liverpool supporters, many of whom had been drinking all day, as was tradition, charged towards the Italian fans whose only protection was a thin and utterly inadequate separating wall and an equally thin and inadequate line of Belgian police. In the ensuing mayhem, a frenzy of violence led to the deaths of thirty-nine, mostly Italian, mostly Juventus supporters, many of whom were trapped and crushed against a restraining concrete wall which then collapsed and buried many more. Over 600 other fans were badly injured in addition to the deaths. Throughout the ensuing chaos, the natural law of common humanity was in abeyance. Riot police, and reinforcements of riot police, all seemed more concerned with protecting themselves than assist the dead and dying. It was as if some grand scientist had designed a crucible in which to test the reactions of witless and frightened human beings in an experiment investigating fear and panic.

Some Liverpool fans claimed, in mitigation of their behaviour, that they had been subjected to a hail of stones, picked up from the broken terracing and thrown by Juventus fans, before their initial surge into enemy territory. Some might also have said they had learned their behaviour from a long tradition of British military violence over the course of the century and reinforced in recent history by the brutal beating of Argentina over the Falkland Islands in the South Atlantic. There was something oddly reminiscent, too, in the Liverpool charge at Heysel, of British cannon fodder emerging from their trenches in the First World War and charging blindly into no man's land.

There was no official mileage, however, in excuses.

The European football authorities laid the blame squarely on Liverpool fans and all English teams were banned from playing football on the continent for five years.

These were the same authorities who insisted that the game between Liverpool and Juventus should go ahead regardless of the earlier loss of life and limb. What more eloquent testimony could there have been to the expendability of human beings in the minds of those in high places and charged with high responsibilities?

* * *

In June 2017, another seventy-two human beings died in the Grenfell Tower inferno in West London. Nothing changes. Ever. It's the rich wot gets the pleasure; it's the poor wot gets the blame.

* * *

It was in this rancid atmosphere of violence, xenophobia and class war that English football was played throughout the 1970s and 80s.

It was watched by Michael Knighton, an outsider, a man who had dreamed of fulfilling his schoolboy promise as a footballer. He had flirted with the fringes of professional football at Derby County, Everton and Coventry City, before a cruel rupture of a thigh muscle together with a seriously torn cruciate knee ligament when he was still a teenager ended his career before it had properly begun. Having at least begun to play the professional game, he was, however, something less of an outsider than Martin Edwards.

The chairman of Manchester United watched football from behind the corpulent shadow of his father and from the shelter of the façade of the Manchester United directors' box. The glass-fronted restaurant at Old Trafford was as much a barrier between him and the hoi polloi as was the fabled electrified fences in the mind of Ken Bates of Stamford Bridge.

Both Knighton and Edwards were restless men, both aware of the need for change, both needing a catalyst to spark a revolution in English football, but both unaware at the time of that need.

* * *

In 1985 Edwards was halfway through what he regarded as a ten-year project to revitalise Manchester United, to reawaken a sleeping giant.

He was failing miserably, at least by Manchester United's high standards.

Although the Red Devils, under the management of Ron Atkinson, had finished the 1984/85 season in fourth place in the old First Division and had won the FA Cup at Wembley, beating Everton 1-0, the real touchstone of success was the league championship, and that had not been won since 1967 – an amazing statistic for a club the size of Manchester United.

In the year of the Bradford and Heysel tragedies, neither Knighton nor Alex Ferguson were even bit part players in Edwards' life, yet these two men were destined later to become partners in the revitalisation project at Old Trafford, fated to provide answers to the questions Edwards, it seemed, was even failing to ask.

At the beginning of 1985, Ferguson, son of a Glasgow shipbuilder, was still to lead Aberdeen to a second successive Scottish League title. Knighton, growing rich on property investments, was watching the beautiful game from afar with a wistful, sidelong glance and a thoughtful eye and heart.

* * *

If 1985 was a low point in both English football and society, it had not yet reached its nadir.

On 15 April 1989, at Hillsborough, Sheffield, a further ninety-six dispensable human beings, all Liverpool supporters, died during and after the tragic opening minutes of the FA Cup semi-final between Liverpool and Nottingham Forest.

By the time of the scheduled kick-off at three o'clock in the afternoon, there were still over 2,000 Liverpool fans outside the Leppings Lane end of the stadium. When, as a result of a failure of police tactics and police control, these additional souls were allowed inside the ground, the crush was so great that men, women and children were dying of compressive asphyxia as they stood motionless on the terracing. This area of the Sheffield Wednesday ground had been divided into caged pens so that, without carefully controlled entry to the stadium, tragedy was inevitable.

It was not as if the authorities had no prior warning. In 1981, for an FA Cup semi-final against Wolves, Tottenham Hotspur fans were forced to stand and crush in the same notorious Leppings Lane section of the stadium, and there were hundreds of injuries and scenes of chaos and confusion horribly prescient of the tragedy to come.

By the time of the Hillsborough tragedy, the Football Association had known for ten years that Sheffield Wednesday did not possess an up-to-date safety certificate and yet had continued to promote its use as a venue for major football matches.

This was life in England in 1989: nasty, brutish, and, for those trapped in the wrong place at the wrong time in Sheffield on an April afternoon, all too short.

Only *The Sun* newspaper could make things worse, and duly did so with its smeared story four days later. Beneath a banner headline announcing THE TRUTH, editor Kelvin MacKenzie wrote the following bullet points:

*Some Fans Picked Pockets of Victims*
*Some Fans Urinated on Brave Cops*
*Some Fans Beat Up PC Giving Kiss of Life*

Three decades later, the pain was still raw and the insults still added to the injury.

Two years ago, Kenny Dalglish, the Liverpool manager at the time of Hillsborough, spoke out about the intervention of Murdoch's gutter press and the lies of the South Yorkshire Police.

'It was unbelievable. We saw how the Liverpool fans went to help people who were suffering, ripping up advertising boards to use as stretchers, trying to care for them on the ground. How could others have lied? It was unimaginable.'

Dalglish had become player-manager of Liverpool the day after the Heysel disaster and his first official function was to lay a wreath at the city's Catholic cathedral in memory of all those who had died at the European Cup Final in Brussels.

He had been present, too, as a Celtic junior at the Ibrox disaster in 1971, when sixty-six fans were crushed to death on an exit stairway at the end of an Old Firm match. The Rangers stadium was unfit for purpose in 1971, as it had been in 1902 when the rear of a wooden stand collapsed and killed twenty-five people during an international match between Scotland and England.

The more things change, the more they stay the same.

The lack of accountability of those with a duty of care for football fans – and miners and tower block tenants – and the lies of those in positions of power, is a thread that runs through both football and the wider environs of society.

Untruths in the free press, of course, were not exactly news or new, as Knighton understood only too well. The press had their focus fixed on selling newspapers and to hell with anyone whose life they might damage or destroy in the process of that race to turn a profit.

The fact that the Murdoch group thought it could get away with such monstrous lies and sell even more copies of its bestselling rag by targeting football *hooligans* yet again told us all everything we did not want to know about both the state of the nation and of the national game itself at that time.

BBC cameras were at Hillsborough at the time and *Grandstand*, the Saturday afternoon sports showcase programme, provided live and harrowing coverage of the unfolding disaster.

Michael Knighton watched events unfold from his Huddersfield home at Honeysuckle Farm with equal disbelief and distress. Tears rolled down his cheeks as tragedy unfolded less than thirty miles away in Sheffield. His brow was furrowed and his mouth was opening and closing like a fish out of water. He was speaking aloud to an empty room.

'There are people dying … they're football supporters, and they're dying there before our eyes.'

He moved nearer to the television screen, as if closer inspection might prove the impossibility of such events.

'Something must be done, surely, something must be done.'

He was thinking of young lives crushed to oblivion, he was thinking of how this apocalypse must herald fundamental change within the football industry, he was thinking of his great-grandfather, William Layton, who had played his football, plied his trade on this very Sheffield pitch, and tears were falling from his face to the living room floor.

'I will *do* something about this.'

Knighton's voice was raised to fever pitch.

'I am going to do something that will change this game forever.'

Hearing her husband's raised, distressed voice, Rosemary Knighton walked into the room.

'I mean it, I really do mean it, what I'm saying.'

His wife could see the pain and the determination on her husband's face.

'Look, Rosemary, tragedy and farce, human suffering and human incompetence.'

She hugged her man close.

'This great sport, this industry, it's shambolic, it's got to change.'

She wiped the tears from his face.

'And I'm the man to do it, if no one else will.'

Knighton rose to his feet, kissed his wife.

'Just you wait and see.'

* * *

At the time of Hillsborough, Knighton was at the tail end of negotiations with the board of directors at Bolton Wanderers FC for the purchase of that famous old football club now fallen on hard times.

The process had dragged on for months and Knighton was impatient and tired.

Less than one month later, however, Knighton came to understand exactly how he would right the wrongs of English football that had been so cruelly exposed at Hillsborough.

He had been rebuffed at Third Division Bolton, but he would purchase the legend that was Manchester United instead and, through enlightened and revolutionary stewardship, he would not only transform the financial and footballing fortunes of the Old Trafford club, but also save English football from itself by demonstrating a way out of the claustrophobia and xenophobia and class conflict that clung to Old Football and Old Money like an old-fashioned, dirty, pea-soup fog.

Knighton had a plan and he was about to share it with the football world.

He began to write, scribbling down new ideas that were rattling the cage of his brain, adding them to his *Blueprint* for football that was almost complete. It would not only be new money that he offered to Martin Edwards when they met for the first time.

Inside the *Blueprint* was a rattle-bag of ideas, commercial initiatives, which would change the game forever.

With the benefit of hindsight, the result of the Edwards and Knighton axis, forged at medieval Killochan Castle and at Old Trafford in 1989 and which lasted for three fruitful years, would prove to be nothing less than the overturning of the old order in English football.

It would be the beginning of the national sport's commercial Big Bang or Great Leap Forward.

Knighton's plan was Thatcherite, yes, but, ironically, Maoist too, in its simplistic symmetry of both beauty and brutality and in its unleashing of the unashamed potential of the power of commerce.

* * *

After 1989, neither English football nor English society was quite the same again.

The extent to which Knighton was responsible for these social and political revolutions – for football had been high politics since 1966 and all that, not least because of Harold Wilson's claim that the World Cup victory won him the general election of that year – is one of the key themes of this book.

Recovering our histories, telling our truths, is one of the deepest of human needs.

Chapter Four

# Football in the Blood

ONE THING that Knighton always says is that football is in his blood.

And not just in his blood, either, but in his bones and in his every breath.

To start with, there was his famous great-grandfather, Willie Layton of the Wednesday, and of the 1907 FA Cup Final. In addition to his trophies won with the Wednesday, Willie was capped by the English League when he played against the Irish League in 1901. Then there was Willie's brother, Edward Layton, who played for Sheffield United, Rotherham Town, Aston Villa, Middlesbrough, Cardiff City and Stockport County.

Both brothers emigrated to Australia in 1912 and Edward was capped by his state in a match between New South Wales and Queensland in which he scored the winning goal. 'Journeyman-professional,' was Knighton's verdict on his great-uncle, although his judgement might have been coloured by the fact that Edward was an employee of the Blades rather than the Wednesday.

* * *

Knighton, too, almost made it as a top class professional player. No fewer than fifteen professional clubs chased his signature as a schoolboy and only the most serious of injuries when he was an apprentice at Coventry City brought him down, turned his world around within a heartbeat.

As a boy, his father took him to the Baseball Ground to watch Derby County, a club then managed by the legendary Harry Storer, who played 257 games for the Rams and won two caps for England. Storer also played first-class cricket for Derbyshire and later had a dramatic effect on the young Knighton's own football career.

When Knighton was sixteen Brian Clough was appointed to replace Tim Ward as Derby's manager. The young man acquired a new hero as Clough and his sidekick Peter Taylor took County out of the old Second Division, where they had been marooned since Harry Storer's team was promoted from the Third Division North in 1957, and shortly after won the First Division championship.

When Knighton was injured and was told his professional career was finished before it had truly begun, he thought of Clough and how the Derby manager's own career had been cut short by the cruel fates of footballing injury, in a Boxing Day match for Sunderland at the tender age of twenty-nine. At least, Knighton thought, the gods had allowed his hero the time to score 251 goals for Middlesbrough and Sunderland before the snapping of the centre-forward's anterior cruciate ligament in his knee.

*As flies to wanton boys are we to th' gods,*
*They kill us for their sport.*

Knighton knows his poetry, knows his Shakespeare, but it does not make the arbitrariness of it all any easier to bear.

Why did Duncan Edwards die as a result of the Munich disaster, which so clouded and disturbed Knighton's childhood thoughts, whereas Bobby Charlton and Harry Gregg survived to fulfil their footballing potential?

It was the problem of evil writ large in a world either without a god or at least without a deity with any fundamental concept of sporting fairness.

Knighton decided it was dangerous to have either a god or heroes, unless they were either dead or in the family, or both, as was the case with his great-grandfather on his mother's side. He never met the celebrated Willie Layton, a superstar of the first generation of northern professional footballers that straddled the late Victorian and Edwardian eras, but he heard all about him as he sat on his grandfather's knee, ears pricked, mouth agog, as William Layton, son of Willie and Michael's grandfather, puffed at his pipe, mixed heady words with dizzying tobacco smoke, and told his grandson the valiant tales of Willie Layton of the Wednesday over and over and over again.

'Tell me the bit about Great-Granddad and the Cup Final again please, Granddad,' Michael said for the hundredth time in what seemed the same afternoon.

'Just one more time,' the old man replied, 'if only you'll be good from then till teatime.'

It was the sweet summer of school holidays, everlasting days in the 1950s, a time when time stood still, and seven-year-old Knighton was staying with his grandparents in their big house deep in the twisting, turning Derbyshire landscape. The boy's head was light from the buzzing of bees in his grandfather's flower garden of delights, from sweet-pea scent and from the tobacco smoke that swirled like memories in his mind.

Granddad William bounced the small boy on his knee, pocketed his pipe and sent one final smoke signal, saying the story was about to begin, into the hazy upper reaches of the room.

'Listen, Michael,' he said, 'and picture this.'

The boy buried himself into his grandfather's well-rounded body, surrendered to the smoky smells about the old man's clothes, the reek and roil of Robin Redbreast tobacco, the sweet-pea softness and the stillness of the garden that travelled everywhere with his Granddad William, and cajoled the words he heard into pictures for the thousandth time.

'It's such a long time ago now, Michael, it must be hard for a boy to imagine what fifty years is like.'

'Is it like when you die and go to heaven, Granddad, and when you stay there forever?'

William Layton shook his head in disbelief, relit his pipe in place of an answer, began his story with an impossible smile, placed his huge hands around the boy and pulled him even tighter to himself.

'The Cup Final, Michael, all these years later, and it's still the greatest day in the football season.'

Knighton's grandfather tugged at his chin and then at his pipe.

'It's at the famous Crystal Palace, Michael, before cup finals were played at Wembley, and there's 84,000 people packed in there – a massive crowd, that is, my boy.'

'Is that a really lot of people, Granddad?'

'It's like all the people in heaven, Michael, all there together in one place.'

William Layton Junior's eyes sparkled beneath an overgrowth of white eyebrows. He was proud of his famous father, Willie Layton, and loved his grandson beyond words.

'At least,' he said, 'all the Sheffield Wednesday people are in heaven that day.'

'Go on, Granddad,' said the boy, 'tell me about the goals.'

'All in good time, lad, all in good time.'

The old man paused, pulled his solid gold fob watch from his waistcoat pocket, put it to his ear to check it had not stopped, and frowned as if to say there may not be time before tea to finish the story. The fob chain of the watch swung with the weight of history and with the gold medals that his father had won during his outstanding football career. William Layton Junior wore these medals every day, such was his pride in his father's sporting achievements.

'Please, Granddad,' said the young Knighton, who put his hands together as if at his prayers.

There was no danger, however, of the boy having to eat his bread and butter before he heard of his great-grandfather's role in winning the FA Cup for the Wednesday. William Layton loved retelling the story just as much as his grandson loved hearing it.

'Alright, Michael,' he said, 'but not the goals, not just yet.'

The old man was smoking again, each puff of aromatic smoke preceding pearls of words of wisdom. He set the scene at the Crystal Palace, the flat caps in the foreground, the cold April, the bare trees on the far side of the ground behind the bank upon bank of spectators. There were 84,584 of them altogether, stacked like treats in jars on sweetshop shelves just out of reach, the boys and men, down south to see a different world from pits and pubs, to stretch for heaven for their lives. His father was a god in this world.

'The goals, Granddad, please, don't forget the goals.'

The boy's voice was a football spinning in the air waiting for a head to knock it straight into the back of the net.

'It was your great-grandfather, Michael, it was his pass that made the winning goal for the Wednesday to win the famous FA Cup.'

Knighton's grandfather's voice was laden with treasures, rich and full, and as heavy as his garden's bees were fat with pollen.

The boy sat upright, now, clapped his hands in delight.

'There were only four minutes of the game to go and the scores were level, Michael, one goal apiece between the Wednesday and the Everton.'

There was tension, even now, in the old man's voice. He knew the result, of course, yet still he doubted the miracle that was to conclude his story.

His father, Willie Layton, had the ball on the far flank of the pitch near to his own goal line.

'You know, Michael,' he said, 'Willie Layton was famous for the strength and length of his kicking from defence, and he was solid as rock and feared nothing.'

The small boy nodded his encouragement to proceed to the part of the story he loved best of all.

'Well, lad, this one wonder of a pass of that heavy leather football, it flew straight from Great-Granddad's trusty right boot all the way along the touchline, and it was a miracle it never went out of play.

'The crowd on that far side were thinking it was a wasted ball, their voices, Michael, they were going up with the ball, up with their hopes, and then down again, they were going ooooooohhh and aaaaarrrrggghhh, just like that, mouths going flip and flap like fishes out of water.'

William Layton was almost on his feet with the crowd, and Michael Knighton was bouncing to the floor of his grandfather's living room, willing his great-grandfather's pass to stay in play, to be collected by the sprinting, Scottish, Wednesday forward, Andrew Wilson, to be slung across the field of play and to be met by the head of the goalscoring hero, George Stewart.

'Goal,' shouted William Layton.

'Goal,' cried the boy, and he hugged his beloved grandfather as if the old man had scored the winning goal himself.

* * *

There were other stories, too, including one which gave the young Knighton nightmares.

This one was not recounted so often but the ideas of destiny and providence enshrined within the tale of Willie Layton's trial for the Wednesday had a profound effect on Knighton both as man and boy.

This time Granddad Layton's face was a mask of seriousness leavened with an underlying serenity that the young Knighton detected and fed on for reassurance, though he understood already that all turned out well in the end, if only for his great-grandfather.

Destiny, it seemed, was always there to play the hand of fate in the realms of the Layton and Knighton families. Even so, the light was left on in the boy's bedroom through the night when this tale was told.

* * *

Knighton's famous great-grandfather never forgot the day. The trial match he was about to play for the Wednesday was arranged for the afternoon of Monday, 11 November 1895. There was, however, a problem for the young footballer then earning a pittance as a part-time professional at Chesterfield Town FC. He was due to work the Sunday night shift at Blackwell Colliery where he was scheduled to be part of the two dozen-strong team of coalminers responsible for preparing the workings for the following day.

'What's it like down there in the dark, Granddad, down there, under the ground, in the mine?'

'Well, young Michael, just be grateful that you don't have to go down there to find out.'

The old man's eyes fixed those of his grandson.

'That world,' he said, 'that's not for the likes of you, Michael, of that I'm sure.'

The boy was about to protest.

'You'll follow a different path, Michael, you will, if I've got anything to do with it.'

The boy reached for his grandfather's hand in the fading light of the bedroom.

'It isn't all dark, Michael, the men have lamps down there in the mines.'

The old man paused, tucked in the boy's bed sheets as if to keep him safe.

'Does Great-Granddad Willie have a lamp?'

'Yes he does, Michael, but, as you know well enough, lad, he was not there that fearful night.'

The old man's face was like a page torn from a book. Even in the dying light of day, the boy could read his grandfather's distress at the deaths of seven working men and the jagged edge of his emotions that fused guilt and relief at his own father's providential escape from the disaster.

'Tell me again, Granddad, why Great-Granddad didn't go down the mine that night.'

'It was the trial match, Michael, the big match the next day.'

A heavy sigh escaped from William Layton's lips.

'Your great-granddad, Michael, he needed to rest and conserve his energy and strength.'

It was as if the young Knighton needed reassurance that his great-grandfather really had escaped to play 361 games for Sheffield Wednesday between 1895 and 1910, to play every match in season 1902/03 in which his team won the Football League First Division championship, the Midland League, the Sheffield Challenge Cup, the Wharncliffe Charity Cup and the Plymouth Bowl.

'Your great-grandfather, Michael, he understood just how important it would be to be fit and fresh the following day so he never worked his midnight shift.'

There was silence between the man and boy while the import of this decision of Willie Layton's sunk in and filled the space between them.

'What happened then, Granddad?'

The boy wanted to hear about the trial match, wanted to be told again about the famous Cup Final, wanted to squeal with delight when he heard how the Wednesday repeated their league championship success in 1903/04 and how his great-grandfather was part of an invincible Wednesday defence of Layton, Langley and Lyall, dubbed by the press as the Three Ls of the Wednesday. He wanted to listen again to how Willie Layton was so revered by all at the Sheffield Wednesday Football Club that he was inducted into the canon of the 150 greatest Wednesday players of all time.

His grandfather, however, had decided it was time to tell the boy all about the disaster in the Low Main seam at Blackwell Colliery and, this time, to spare no details.

'There were lights down there, Michael,' he said, 'but not the safety lamps this time.'

The old man's voice faltered enough for the boy to understand the need for silence.

'The mine officials, they said there were no problems with naked lights on this shift.'

William Layton Junior paused, gathered himself in preparation for the storm.

'And that,' he said, 'in spite of the fact that gas had been reported in that area of the mine on two previous occasions, and there had been an explosion down there just four years previously.'

He hesitated once more, perhaps unsure whether to continue or maybe to rid himself of the anger that rose in his breast whenever he thought about the loss of his father's friends.

'I want you to understand this, Michael, that death is only part of life, but still it's always very sad when it finally comes to pass.'

The young boy drew his bed sheets closer to his skinny body.

'I want you to picture this, Michael.'

The young boy sensed an in-draught of tight breath.

'Can you do that for me?'

The boy nodded, reached once more for his grandfather's big, strong hand.

'These men, these heroes, Michael, they were deep underground and they all depended on each other for their very lives.

'There were men and boys down there, Michael, there were pit ponies, there were loaded tubs of coal drawn by thick snakes of rope, there was coal dust everywhere, dry as tinder, there was maybe methane gas, there were naked lights, there were tired men and boys down there by four o'clock in the morning.'

'Go on, Granddad,' said the boy, 'I'm grown up enough now for an unhappy ending.'

The old man's smile was thin and sad.

'You know I'm quite brave now, really I am.'

'Well, then, Michael, there was also a spur of rock at a turn in the pit shaft, and the stretched rope between the coal tubs was chafing on it now, and someone said, let's fire us a shot, and someone else packed in the gunpowder, too much, probably, because he had been working down there now for four hours, and maybe he wasn't thinking straight because his wife had been chafing at him like jagged stone on strained rope, and he shouted, stand back now, boys.'

The boy was sitting now bolt upright in bed and the blankets fell from his shoulders. Young Knighton's left hand gripped his grandfather's arm as tightly as a spark took hold of packed powder.

'Above ground, Michael, all that way, up top, they felt that explosion.'

'What did they do, Granddad?'

'They got the manager out of his bed, Michael, all bleary eyed and cross at the disturbance of his night's sleep.'

'Then what, Granddad?'

'Well, Michael, the rescue party had a decision to take.'

The boy's eyes begged the old man to continue.

'The main haulage road to the downcast shaft was completely blocked by a large fall.'

'What did they decide to do?'

'They had no choice really, Michael. They got down the mine through a return airway, and it was difficult and dangerous as it was full of poisonous gases, but these were brave men, lad, such brave men.

'On the way, the rescue party met miners who were carrying one dead colleague between them, and they saw the fear and the exhaustion and the grime of coal dust and death etched in their faces. They carried on, passing heavy falls of rock and broken corpses of tubs, hewed coal flung far from them by the explosion.

'At the scene of the disaster they found the remaining bodies at the foot of the downcast shaft and a dead pony still in harness between the shafts of a tub still full of coal.'

The young boy could see his grandfather was near to tears.

There fell a silence of companionship between them.

'Do you know, Michael, what was said at the inquest?'

The boy shook his head.

'No blame, the coroner said, can be attached to the management.'

Years later, remembering his grandfather's telling of the tale, Knighton thought the families of the dead miners would find that in the following centuries nothing much had really changed.

'Do you know what else he said, lad?'

Again, the boy awaited the news with a tremor of fear in his heart, sensing, perhaps, that the coroner's verdict was somehow worse than the deaths concerned.

'He said, Michael, he believed that all concerned would have benefited from the result of this calamity.'

At the time, Knighton did not understand, but now he thought the relatives of the ninety-six victims of the Hillsborough disaster would comprehend these rules of the establishment cover-up game that always shames the truth.

As, indeed, would the relatives of the victims of the Grenfell Tower fire of 2017.

As truth would have it, the South Yorkshire Police had altered 164 of the initial police statements concerning the events at the FA Cup semi-final between Liverpool and Nottingham Forest, and had threatened officers reluctant to tell lies with retribution including being fitted up with allegations of accepting bribes from fans in return for illegal admittance to the game. One brave copper on duty at the Leppings Lane end at Hillsborough had refused to cooperate and resigned from the force rather than cosy up to the cover-up, but had his signature forged anyway.

In June 2017, following the decision to prosecute those in the South Yorkshire Police involved in the lies and the incompetence, families of the victims of the Hillsborough tragedy hailed the beginning of the end of their twenty-eight-year struggle for justice for their dead relatives.

But by September 2019, however, families of the deceased still await justice.

Knighton wept for all of this. He remembered that these senior policemen, these lying, cheating, corrupt, so-called guardians of justice were from the same police force as those who, just a few years earlier, were ordering colleagues to assault and intimidate striking Yorkshire miners by charging through the miners' ranks on horseback, wielding flailing truncheons, fists and boots. He felt for these beaten men, these hard-working, honest, loyal, proper men, Knighton's own people. He felt the coal dust in his ancestors' lungs and in his own hot blood.

Not only that, but these South Yorkshire policemen then falsified evidence about the pitched battle between police and miners outside the Orgreave coking plant near Sheffield, in May 1984. They had charged and beaten picketing miners with truncheons, claiming, falsely, that the miners had attacked them first. They then provided carefully concocted evidence in court, dictated to them by senior officers.

He felt the force, the violence, of the British state and its political establishment fall on these miners who had nothing but the withdrawal of their labour to protect their livelihoods and their communities. Lying, covering up crime within their own ranks, had become the default position of the English police. Knighton could weep again, for the sheer injustice of it all.

In 1984, even George Orwell would have been surprised at the brazen and brutal conduct of the ruling classes.

'It was ever thus,' Knighton said, his eyes as mournful as the dark side of the moon.

In August 2019 I travelled north to meet Knighton and conversation turned to the 200th anniversary of the Peterloo massacre in St Peter's Field, Manchester, in which fifteen peaceful people, protesting against the lack of English democracy, against unemployment and famine, were killed by the sabre-wielding mounted military authorities. A further 500 demonstrators were injured.

'Peterloo, the Blackwell Colliery disaster, Hillsborough, the Grenfell Tower fire.'

Knighton grimaces.

'Fair play or restitution for the miners and their families who died at Blackwell Colliery in November 1895? Not a chance. It's the powers that be, the establishment jobsworths, representatives of the ruling class, always hard against the people, alright, that's what it is, always has been, always will be.'

* * *

The boy Knighton could not understand all of this at the time, but he knew enough, however, to accept that his grandfather would tell him no more about Willie Layton, the famous footballer, not tonight, at any rate.

* * *

Coal dust is in Knighton's blood, almost as much as the football.

It was not just his great-grandfather who worked at the coal face. His own father, Albert, began adult life training as a master baker, having greased tins in the local bakery from the age of nine. But the real money was to be made grafting amid the black dust of the mine. Like his father and grandfather before him, and like his uncle and brothers, Albert Knighton ended up underground, picking at the seams of coal but also working proudly as a regional branch trade union secretary.

Knighton says that this is where he learned all his values, his life lessons, from these great men, these hewers of coal, with their strong bodies, their strong minds and their strong morals. He was made from these menfolk and he is proud to be so.

Knighton's father understood that there was a living to be made working underground. In contrast, a fortune beckoned for the few who owned the land where all this black gold was buried, and there was a time when Knighton's family, on his father's side, almost joined the wealthy and privileged few.

His paternal great-grandfather, Henry Knighton, was an entrepreneur who owned a frying shop and a horse and carriage for hire. He also organised a discreet private gambling operation, and controlled the labour of a group of local buttymen miners on behalf of the Miller-Mundy family of Shipley Hall, who were mine owners as well as landowners.

Henry Knighton, in fact, was a regular visitor to the Hall. He was often invited by Squire Miller-Mundy to this grand, elegant Georgian pile for drinks and conversation, so much so that it was difficult to comprehend the relative impoverishment and the entrenchment within working class culture of the Knighton family by the middle of the twentieth century. No one can unravel the mystery of the disappearance of the riches that Henry Knighton must have accrued.

At one point, as well as land and property, there was a solid oak roll-top desk in Henry's office, as large as the life its owner led and in which eighteen-inch side drawers overflowed with gold sovereigns. Yet all was gone by the time Knighton's paternal great-grandfather passed away after suffering a stroke in 1933.

Perhaps this was just so that Knighton could do it all again, 100 years after Henry, following in his ancestor's footsteps, chasing the money, wanting to be someone, needing, above all else, in his early years, to be a winner.

Like his entrepreneurial great-grandfather, Knighton was not only destined to make a fortune, but to lose more than one as well.

Football and coal, working class England incarnate, and both in Knighton's blood.

By the middle of the 1980s, however, all was a sea of turmoil and change, both in Knighton's England and in his personal life.

As Knighton turned to football once again, contemplating the finances of the purchase of a Football League club, the prime minister, Margaret Thatcher, was overturning the entire economic foundations of the nation. As she contemplated laying siege about the beleaguered coalfields of middle and northern England and laying waste to the nation's industrial heartlands, leaving precious few mines left, Knighton's dreams of following in his maternal great-grandfather's footballing bootsteps were also in ruins. The serious injury at Coventry City had put paid to that option.

He had dreamed so often of Willie Layton's surging, speed-and-stamina runs from the right wing of the Wednesday's defence, his fearless, limb-juddering tackles, leather against heavy leather, boot against bone, his great-grandfather's thunder and lightning movement, his unique overhead kick that never failed to bring the Wednesday crowd to their feet and cheers to their throats.

He knew he had inherited much of Willie's athleticism, much of his skill, his abilities as an all-round sportsman. Willie Layton had excelled at athletics and cricket as well as football, and his great-grandson shone brightly on the athletics track and on the rugby and cricket fields, too. Like his great-grandfather, though, it was football with the round rather than oval ball that was the prime attraction for Knighton.

At Heanor Gate School, Derbyshire, part of the first wave of new 1960s comprehensive schools, though still sufficiently traditional for its teachers to wear black academic gowns, Knighton won the prestigious School Sports Day Victor Ludorum title for champion track and field athlete every year in which he competed. One of his former teachers, Tom Larimore, provided an interesting insight into the young man's abilities and into his character.

'Michael Knighton?' he said. 'Of course, I remember him. Who wouldn't? He was an outstanding character at school, brilliant at every sport, very talented, and a damn good artist, too. He came top of the class in several subjects, but in art he absolutely excelled, came top every year.'

Larimore leaned forward in his chair, frowned and smiled at the same time, and said something he knew was important.

'In all things at school, he was always so competitive. He was only interested in winning.'

The elderly former teacher was shuffling through his memories, dealing the cards of Knighton's achievements, placing them face up for consideration.

'Knighton was simply the most determined individual you could ever meet, the most strong-willed character I have ever come across in my whole life.'

The cards were aces, all of them.

'He was school cross country champion, the best swimmer, the best gymnast, by far the best track athlete and, in my opinion, the best young footballer in the country at the age of fifteen or sixteen. He played for the school, the Ilkeston & Heanor District Schools XI and Derbyshire County Schools. It was only injury that stopped him playing for the England Schools XI.'

At this point, Larimore rose to his feet.

'It was comic-book hero stuff, really, you know, like something out of Roy of the Rovers. I knew when he said goodbye and left Heanor Gate School it wouldn't be the last we'd hear of Michael Knighton.'

* * *

Knighton thinks a lot about the past, remembers Tom Larimore with affection, recalls the determination of the boy his former teacher talks about and recognises it all as gifts from the genes of his pair of illustrious great-grandfathers, Willie Layton and Henry Knighton. He wonders now how the famous Willie Layton of the Wednesday made it through that day of the trial match at Sheffield, knowing what had happened to his mates back at the colliery.

Knighton, even today, knows the names of the dead colliers by heart, just as some people, including himself, know the names of the England World Cup-winning team of 1966 and the Manchester United 1968 European Cup winners. This time, however, it was not Alex Stepney, Shay Brennan, Tony Dunne, Pat Crerand, Bill Foulkes, Nobby Stiles, George Best, Brian Kidd, Bobby Charlton, David Sadler and John Aston.

At Blackwell Colliery in 1895, it was poor John Jones, blamed for the overcharged shot of gunpowder, and William Martin, the night-deputy responsible for underground safety, Joseph Renshaw and James Fryer, colliery examiners, James Mee and Thomas Shaw, datallers – temporary workers paid by the day – and John Gibson, only a boy, employed as a driver of horses on the main road underground. These are the names recited now, the roll of the dead.

In some strange way, Knighton believes his memory quickens their souls, makes their lives, their sacrifices, worth the while. At least, he says, they are not forgotten. There is the merest hint of familial guilt to assuage here. It should have been his great-grandfather down that damned mine. Knighton, though, does not blame Willie Layton for playing in the trial match, or for refusing the night shift, because he knows him like he knows himself. It was the drive to succeed, the will to win, the blessing and the curse, always.

* * *

Like Knighton, his great-grandfather, Willie Layton, was seriously injured, too.

It was during the final full football season of the nineteenth century, three weeks before Christmas, in a disastrous match for the Wednesday against Burnley. Amid the muck and mud of a wintry Turf Moor, home of Burnley since 1883, Layton launched into a ferocious tackle and almost died as a result, the injury to his abdomen and groin so serious he had to be wheeled across Manchester to the hospital in a folding chair.

The Wednesday lost 5-0 and the full-back missed the next eight weeks of the season, at the end of which his team finished rock bottom of the league.

'But, at least he recovered, at least he played again.'

Knighton cannot help but brood occasionally on what might have been.

As well as the injury at Coventry City, there was the injury at Heanor Gate that prevented his selection for England Schools.

Great-grandfather Willie, though, believed in destiny, providence, call it what you will, as does Knighton, and in thanks for his escape from the Blackwell Colliery disaster and in part as retribution for his guilt, vowed that he would stay with the Wednesday for the rest of his football career. He made that pledge to those who lost their lives that night in the dark hellhole that was the Low Main seam in 1895.

Layton stayed for fifteen years at the Sheffield club until his retirement from the game, resisting all offers of attractive and lucrative moves to wealthier clubs.

Knighton, too, tried to make a successful comeback from his serious injury sustained while at Coventry City, but he had to adjust his sights to the more modest levels of less illustrious relatives.

In addition to Willie's frightening and life-endangering injury in 1883, his brother Edward missed most of the 1903/04 season with Sheffield United through injury. Neither brother's career was ended, however, and Knighton is so glad about that. He just wishes he had enjoyed the same luck, the same recovery.

During his time at Durham University's Bede College, studying to be a schoolteacher in case the football failed, he spent one long summer in the USA waiting for a call from the manager of the legendary New York Cosmos soccer team. Backed by Warner Communications, the Cosmos were about to become the most talked about football club in the world with Pele, Giorgio Chinaglia and Franz Beckenbauer regulars in their starting line-ups. But the summons never arrived and Knighton never joined those famous names, although he did train with them for a short spell.

Instead, Knighton completed his teacher training and played part-time non-league football firstly for Heanor Town FC and then Ilkeston Town FC. In this there were further family echoes, as his great-uncle on his father's side, Albert Holmes, was one of Heanor Town's Midland League legends from the late 1930s to the outbreak of the Second World War. Albert, like his great-nephew, was a prolific goalscorer and it is said that he would often strike the ball so hard it would burst through the tough string netting of his opponents' goal. Locals would joke about Albert's bravery, saying he would head a cannonball if he had to.

It was not Derby County, it was not Everton, it was not Coventry City or even New York, but it was still football, and blood will sing to blood. Knighton was grateful for his time with both Heanor and Ilkeston football clubs.

* * *

In 1976, Knighton married Rosemary, who became his long-suffering and lifelong partner and soul mate. She also had football in the blood. Rosemary hailed from the Edinburgh mercantile class. She was part of the Croan family, whose fortunes were founded in the fishing industry via the long-established family firm of R Croan & Son, formed in 1865. Her father, Robert, together with other members of her family were shareholders in Hibernian Football Club. At one time her family owned ten per cent of the place.

Knighton enjoyed the fact of her family football connections, although he did not marry her for the football. Neither did he marry her for her family's wealth. With Knighton, it is never about the money. Understand this and you understand Knighton.

It might be about winning, or even not losing, but it is never about the money. Even when money might be part of the winning. Of Rosemary's family fortune, he never saw, nor wanted, a penny. Knighton earned plenty of dosh of his own, so much so that, by his mid-thirties, he had become wealthier than the Edinburgh Croans had ever been.

In 1976, both he and Rosemary were teachers, but she was destined to watch hundreds of matches alongside her husband, some in the most difficult of circumstances.

* * *

Just a few years into his marriage, having been a teacher in Warwickshire and Kent, Knighton joined the staff of St David's School in Huddersfield, West Yorkshire, an independent private school, and within three short years he was offered and accepted the post of deputy head and, one year later, at the impossible age of twenty-nine, he was appointed headmaster by the board of trustee governors of this highly reputable school. It was an institution that for generations had prepared boys from Yorkshire for further successes at the great independent schools of Eton, Rugby, Uppingham, Malvern, Shrewsbury and Sedburgh. He was still the youngest member of staff at the school when appointed headmaster, which, surely, must be some kind of record in the modern era of education.

It was a prodigious rise through the professional teaching ranks, made all the more remarkable as Knighton, at the same time, was buying property in the local area. Within a few years he was also able to buy several large Georgian period properties in Edinburgh, building up a sizeable property portfolio stretching from Yorkshire to Scotland. In addition, Knighton rose every day before dawn and went to market to purchase supplies for the florist's shop that he owned and ran with Rosemary. All this, and teaching, and while he suffered from periodically acute depression as a result of concerns for his baby son's well-being following the trauma of Mark's terrifyingly botched birth.

By 1983, Knighton had made sufficient money to purchase the school of which he was headmaster. It was a story the entrepreneurial Henry Knighton could only have dreamed of. Knighton knew in his heart how proud his forbear would have been of his youthful achievements. Football, though, was in his blood and, although there was honour, there was neither romance nor swashbuckling heroism in running a private school, albeit a very successful one, in the backwoods of Yorkshire.

And this was why, in June 1989, Knighton was on his way to Old Trafford to meet Martin Edwards, to try to put together the biggest deal in football history.

## Chapter Five

# The Blood in the Butchery

ONE THING Martin Edwards must surely think is how lucky he is that he never sold Manchester United to Michael Knighton.

And no one could ever argue with that.

In 1989, Edwards and Knighton shook hands on a deal that would have paid the butcher's boy £10m for his controlling shareholding in the Old Trafford club. Ten years later, Edwards accepted a bid for his club – later blocked by the Monopolies and Mergers Commission – from Rupert Murdoch's BSkyB for a reported £680m. In 2005, the former railway works team from Newton Heath was eventually sold to Malcolm Glazer & Sons from Florida for £790m. Edwards' sale of the remaining 6.7% of his Manchester United stock to the Glazers realised £22m, making a total of £107m trousered cash for the former Old Trafford chairman.

Surely, however, he must have regretted selling the majority of his shares in 2002 to a Scottish entrepreneur, Harry Dobson, at a bargain basement price of £1.27 a share, when the mining investor sold his stock to the Glazers at £3.00 less than three years later.

Edwards' undervaluing of Manchester United shares in 2002 was reminiscent of his inability to see the true and potential value of his football club way back in 1989.

Even so, returns of £107m from sales of his shares in 2002 and 2005 were not to be sneezed at when they might have all disappeared into Knighton's pockets for £10m a decade or so previously.

It was, though, back in 1989, a damn near-run thing, both for Knighton and Edwards, the major players in this drama.

So, questions, undoubtedly, need to be asked.

Judgements, too, may be made.

Who, then, played the innocent, the dreamer in this play?

Who was the black-hearted villain?

Would a hero appear in the final act to save the day?

Naturally enough, though, in real life, no man is wholly hero, wholly villain.

What then may be made of the opening scenes from a time before the twin protagonists, Edwards and Knighton, ever shook hands?

Only, tentatively, this.

The retired schoolmaster, the man with football in his blood, appeared at first an open book, pages well thumbed and browsed, whereas the Old Trafford man may have been more of a closed book, his secrets less easy to read.

Furthermore, even though Edwards was the son of a butcher, and even though he was chairman and chief executive of Manchester United, it seemed he might be neither red-meat man nor football man. The blood was in the butchery but the butchery was not in his blood.

Not like the coal and the football in Knighton's veins.

Butchery, though, was a useful enough trade to be apprenticed in.

Sharp knives were essential tools in business and butchers have always provided an indispensable service to the public, that of killing and cutting in private, doing the dirty work behind the scenes, away from front of house.

Not that Edwards was an uncivilised man, quite the reverse, in fact. He had a suavity, a touch of the debonair.

It was the Old Trafford owner's gentility, moreover, combined with a shared public school accent and background, which might have allowed Knighton one foot inside the Old Trafford door in the first place. Edwards was shy, retiring almost, the very image of a company clerk or an accountant, surprising for the head of England's most prestigious football club and as different from his father, Champagne Louis, as lamb from pork.

His father was a socialite in the heady days of the 1950s and 1960s, a friend of Matt Busby, United's manager since 1945 and legend and ghost ever since his retirement in 1969. Some said Louis Edwards rode to power and prestige on Busby's back; some said Champagne Louis stabbed Busby and his family in the back, sidelined the great man when he was no longer of use; some said butchers' knives were used; some said that Martin Edwards, allegedly, carried on his father's work in this respect in the way in which he mistreated the Busby family, if only in small yet significant things, like moving Sir Matt's office from the hub at Old Trafford to the periphery. So the stories go, although it has to be said there appears to be no proof, certainly nothing that would stand up in a court of law. Rumours, however, of shabby treatment and ill usage of both Sir Matt and his son, Sandy, by Martin Edwards, persisted as strongly held views by many in and around Old Trafford throughout the Edwardian era.

Louis Edwards was a man whose corrupt business practices of bribery and insider trading of shares, widely reported in the public domain, helped him gain control of both Manchester's meat trade and one half of the city's football business. His son always says that his father was killed by the 1980 *World in Action* television programme that exposed Champagne Louis for the unprincipled and unscrupulous adventurer the documentary showed him to be. The younger Edwards would never admit to his father's deficiencies or dishonesties, although it is easy to understand and empathise with any son who defends a much-loved father.

Indeed, shortly after the death of Louis Edwards in February 1980, the younger Edwards appeared on the front cover of the United matchday programme, feet astride, defiant face, as if saying, we're still here, we Edwards, and we're still in charge.

And to be fair, there is something to admire in such a determined stance in the face of equally strong criticism of his family and its ongoing control of Manchester United.

Objectivity in the business of the Edwards' family firms is difficult to come by with regard to the ethics according to which these businesses were managed, but it is probably true and fair to say that Louis Edwards enjoyed a good run for his money, having been caught out as early as 1966 by the local council for delivering the lowest quality meat to the schools in Manchester's poorest districts. In the fifties and sixties, Louis Edwards was perceived as a social climber within the tight-knit world of Manchester's sporting community, even rediscovering his own Catholic roots on finding out that Busby was a staunch Roman.

Martin Edwards had no such need to fawn or grease the palms that crossed his path. The profits from the butchery business funded his private education, and the profits from his father's alleged manipulation of Manchester United shares bought him a place on the board of the club at the age of just twenty-four.

* * *

Knighton, though, regularly says that Edwards is a gentleman and that they have never had a crossed word in all their dealings.

The pair of them were never anything other than civil and polite to one another, even during the period of extreme pressure at the height of the takeover saga in the summer and autumn of 1989. Knighton enjoyed Edwards' company and always felt he was a man he could do business with. He was certain, in those heady days of initial meetings and negotiations, that his feelings were reciprocated.

What happened in the autumn of that year, however, changed the relationship between the two men, inevitably in view of Edwards' role – both in the open and behind closed doors – that led to Knighton's resignation as chairman elect at Old Trafford, after his decision to abort the option agreement to purchase the club. Yet the two men remained on cordial terms throughout Knighton's time on the board at Old Trafford.

To this day, Knighton remains reluctant to criticise Edwards, although his patience was sorely tried by some distortions peddled by the club's former chairman and chief executive in his 2017 book, *Red Glory – Manchester United and Me*. That is not to say that Knighton approves of everything Edwards has done in his career in football, or that he approves at all of the Edwards' model of football club stewardship.

Nor, indeed, of the darker side to Edwards' personality.

In August 2002, the chairman of Manchester United received a police caution after an incident at Mottram Hall Hotel in Cheshire. Edwards had been caught in the ladies' toilet, peeping under the cubicle door at a woman he had followed in.

Knighton was reluctant to comment on the chairman's conduct, but did admit that rumours that Edwards was a sexual shark were widespread within the Old Trafford community and hierarchy for many years.

In November 2002, Edwards was allegedly forced to resign from the Manchester United board as a result of the Mottram Hall incident, though whether the two affairs were connected is still a matter of conjecture.

There was no hint in *Red Glory – Manchester United and Me* of anything untoward in Edwards' departure from his position of authority at the football club. In an interview with the *Telegraph* at the launch party of his apparently ghostwritten book, he joked, 'I don't kid myself I was popular at Old Trafford.' Not a single member of the football club's then current administration made it to the party. Neither did Sir Alex Ferguson.

What Edwards failed to get is that neither sexual nor financial predation is much appreciated by most football men and women.

* * *

One thing that Knighton does commend Edwards for is his determined facilitating of the full implementation of Knighton's *Blueprint* for the commercial future of Manchester United, which he gave to Edwards at the same time as he joined the board of directors of the football club.

In the early months of 1989, both Edwards and Knighton were civilised men, courteous and cultivated, both public school, both men whose word was their bond and for whom a handshake was a deal done. Both had outgrown their backgrounds, emerging from different shadows to become men that could do business together.

They appeared a good fit.

In Knighton's case, he had left his roots far behind.

He tells a good story against himself, a disarming and common characteristic of both his public and private persona.

As a schoolmaster, freshly graduated from Bede College, Durham, in 1974, he was about to make his way in the world of education. His first teaching post was at Eversfield Preparatory School in well-heeled Solihull, gained after seeing off the challenge of more than forty other applicants. He was to teach geography, English, maths and PE. Eversfield was an institution similar to St David's, the school Knighton would own just fifteen years later. He had not yet learned, however, to unlearn his Derbyshire drawl of an accent.

'I enjoy all regional English accents and local dialects,' he said, 'but, if you are in a different part of the country from your own roots, it pays to be able to instruct pupils in clear, plain, Queen's English – as I soon found out in my very first teaching post.

'I'm teaching a first year class of 7/8-year-olds how to control themselves on a trampoline for the first time. I'm shouting, *on yer 'eels, lad, on yer 'eels, bounce only on yer 'eels.'*

There is one boy, however, who appeared deaf to instructions.

*'Don't bounce on yer toes, yer silly boy. That'll shoot yer straight off trampoline and yer'll seriously hurt yourself.'*

Knighton paused to note the effect of his pearls of wisdom.

*'So only ever bounce on yer 'eels, lad, on yer 'eels.'*

The small boy was Simon Abbott, all of eight years old, and this young Eversfield pupil provided Knighton with a memorable lesson in elocution for which he is eternally grateful.

'With respect, sir,' said the boy, 'eels are fish.'

The youngster paused, trusting he had not overstepped any invisible mark between man and boy.

'I think you may mean *heel*, Sir.'

Knighton smiled broadly at the sheer impertinence of young Abbott.

*'You're quite right, Simon, I apologise, and now please bounce on your heels.'*

It was a lesson that Knighton has never forgotten.

* * *

Martin Edwards needed no such instruction, and neither does he give any teaching to those whose etiquette or elocution may fall short.

In 1984 he was dining with a man who gave no hoots to manners – Robert Maxwell, global entrepreneur, publishing bigwig, proprietor of national and international newspapers, and owner of Oxford United and Derby County. They met in Maxwell's plush London offices.

The story goes that Edwards arrived by helicopter and landed on the roof of Maxwell's penthouse suite atop the Daily Mirror Group headquarters, Maxwell House. Edwards had in tow his usual trusted entourage of accountants from KPMG, together with Maurice Watkins, the Manchester United solicitor.

Maxwell was playing the role of international entrepreneur, and was up to his elbows in trickery and up to his neck in deceit, wallowing in his own bubble of fawning adulation. There were six telephones on the table, all different colours, and Maxwell had arranged for the business lunch with Edwards to be interrupted by a call from the Russian prime minister.

'Tell him to hang on,' said Maxwell in his rich swindler's baritone voice.

Only those present at this meeting will know whether or not this part of the Maxwell story is genuine, or whether it is just another of the many myths surrounding the publisher and his bizarre and sometimes unpalatable antics.

The tale, though, was told to Knighton by Edwards, and related with great relish.

It was a late lunch with all the trimmings, including smoked salmon for starters. Edwards' fascination with and revulsion for the prospective purchaser of Manchester United increased equally as their meeting went on.

Maxwell's face, with its folds of fat, was crawling with the juice and torn pieces of flesh from the fish he was cramming into his wide open mouth. Slivers of salmon dangled from Maxwell's bottom lip and chin. 'He was eating like a Czech peasant,' Edwards told Knighton.

The Manchester United man's own sleek frame contrasted markedly with the publisher's exuberant celebration of obesity.

Five years later, Knighton was dining with Edwards in an upmarket Manchester restaurant.

'Michael, I must tell you,' Edwards said, 'I could never sell Manchester United to a man like Maxwell, a man with such appalling table manners.'

At that point, civilised behaviour mattered more to Edwards than the money he needed to pay off his allegedly fattening overdraft. In 1984, Edwards turned down Maxwell's millions, feasibly all eight to ten of them, figures that were tossed off in the press as attainable prices for the sale of United. It was perfectly possible, however, with Edwards' reluctance to mention anything so sordid as cash, that money was never brought to the bidding table at all, or at least not until the very conclusion of their negotiations. Similarly, in the preliminary negotiations relating to the sale of Manchester United between Edwards and Knighton in 1989, it seemed to take two men's lifetimes before a price for Manchester United was mentioned by either man.

Maxwell never forgot or forgave his rebuff by Edwards, just as the press baron neither forgave nor forgot Knighton after his appearance on the Old Trafford pitch prior to the new season's kick-off in August 1989.

'My football club,' was how Maxwell referred to Manchester United, as his journalists at the *Daily Mirror* fawned and scraped and prepared to do whatever was his bidding in the business of bringing down the upstart Knighton. Maxwell's fury, as it turned out, was to be the Manchester United chairman's good luck and Knighton's bad luck.

After his dalliance with the devil in the shape of the rotund and devious – and later found to be utterly corrupt – Maxwell, Edwards resumed the stewardship of his father's football club and continued to try to make ends meet. He waited for a change in fortune that came with Knighton. But by the summer of 1989, Edwards had no suspicion of the storm that the man hitherto unknown to the public and the press would bring with him.

## Chapter Six

# Away Games

### *Halifax Town, Sheffield Wednesday and Bolton Wanderers*

BY 1986 Knighton was in a position to indulge his frustrated passion for football, but the vision was not yet crystal clear, the strategy perhaps bearing more relation to scattergun activity and chaos theory than his usual rational planning. He was now a successful businessman with the Midas touch. He owned a sizeable property portfolio in England and Scotland. He was headmaster and owner of St David's School in Huddersfield and had transformed the school financially and further improved its already outstanding academic record and reputation. The number of pupils had risen from 275 to 516.

In the depths of his heart, however, Knighton was beginning to comprehend that his destiny was to become the chairman and owner of a professional football club. He talked to Rosemary, with whom he now had three children, Mark, Chevonne and baby Rory. She was supportive, as always. She knew her man better than he knew himself. The one thing Knighton did understand better than his wife, however, was the perilous financial pitfalls of football. This is not a game, he repeated to himself, as he pondered what to do next. Even some of the most successful businessmen, having bought into the football industry, seemed to leave behind the sound sense that had won them success in the first place, to fall into the fiscal traps with which the game was fraught for businessmen turned dreamers. Knighton did not intend to be one of them. This was not a game; this was football business. This was Knighton's mantra.

* * *

A mere five miles from Huddersfield lay Halifax, famous for its former prominence in the woollen trade, for its building society, now part of the Royal Bank of Scotland, and immortalised in the disparaging ditty, 'Hull, Hell, and Halifax'.

The song, indeed, refers to a Gibbet Law of 1280 which permitted the lord of the manor of Halifax to condemn to death by decapitation anyone stealing goods worth in excess of thirteen pence.

Knighton was aware that Halifax was hardly fertile ground for medieval theft or for his attempts to revolutionise football, but he was either keen or desperate or both to begin and made his move when he heard that the local football club, Halifax Town, was about to go into administration.

A sum of £200,000 was needed urgently to prevent the club going belly-up. It was not a lot of money – Knighton, by this time, had purchased many properties for much larger sums – and yet it was a lot of money, too. It was a very large sum to invest with no guarantee of return.

The difference, Knighton reminded himself, between buying a medieval castle in Scotland or a Georgian town house in Edinburgh and buying a football club without the freehold to the land and the ownership of the stadium, was like the difference between buying money and giving it away. Nevertheless, in early 1987, he met the Halifax chairman John Madeley, who had already displayed some of Knighton's later propensity for courting publicity.

In October of the previous year, Madeley had announced that Halifax were close to collapse, with debts of £350,000 including a most pressing demand from the Inland Revenue for £76,000. In early November, their home match against Exeter City was billed as Halifax Town's final match at their traditional home, the Shay.

The chairman himself ran around the speedway track that encircled the football pitch sporting a billboard that pronounced to the world that 'Halifax Fans Are The Best'. It was not quite on a par with Knighton's 1989 efforts, juggling a football in front of the Stretford End at Old Trafford, but it was a valiant effort.

In December 1986 Madeley had trumpeted an agreement he claimed would safeguard Halifax until at least the close of the season, but this arrangement foundered when it was discovered that the prospective purchasers – prior to Knighton's appearance on the scene – were planning to use the club's ground as a building plot. After Knighton and Madeley had exchanged opening civilities, the Halifax owner explained to Knighton that Calderdale Council owned the lease for the Shay and so any purchase of the club would require its approval.

Knighton knew the deal he had planned was dead.

He understood that the chairman was desperate to dispose of his failing football club but he had nothing really to sell. Still, Knighton arranged to meet the town councillors. They were men in denial of capital, he thought as the meeting started. They had already seen too many speculators who wanted to feather their own nests and deprive the community of their football club. Everyone in the room of polished oak and marble had read the recent press reports about the proposed merger of Fulham and Queens Park Rangers. If that deal had gone ahead, already very rich men would have built big houses on football land and made even bigger bucks. It was the unpleasant spirit of the age and Knighton was damned by implication. These town councillors were having none of it, either inside the Victorian town hall or at the dilapidated Shay.

'That, though, with respect, gentlemen, is not what I want, what I am about,' Knighton had said through clenched teeth and an exasperated smile.

'In order to consider the implementation of these ambitious plans, if I am preparing to invest £2.5m to benefit your local community, I need, in order to protect my investment, to secure the freehold on the land.'

Eyes were averted among the gathered councillors.

'Is this obstacle insurmountable?'

It was, and Knighton always knew it would be.

'You have, gentlemen, the biggest building society in the world.'

Still, he continued to try.

'Why not the biggest football club in the world?'

Of course, Knighton knew this was but a dream. But he was, like all would-be owners of a football club, a dreamer. If football was a business, he thought, it was in the business of selling dreams.

For a few moments, at least, Knighton really believed he could take a football club from the bottom of the old Fourth Division, a team with a history only of mediocrity and with a stadium that was a dangerous and ramshackle blot on the landscape, into the upper realms of the football firmament. It was the first time he had dreamed such a dream and it would not be the last. The Halifax councillors were not, however, of Knighton's world. They were men whose hair and teeth had fallen out and who slept secure at night without the wonder or fear of dreams.

'Gentlemen,' he said, 'I am offering you cast iron guarantees that the Shay will remain in perpetuity a community asset, that there will always be a football club here.'

They were deaf as well as sound sleepers. They did not like men like Knighton, the smooth talkers, the whizz-kids, the new men of a new age.

'We are custodians,' they said.

'For our future generations,' he heard one of the heads whisper.

That's exactly what I thought I was about, he nearly but did not quite say, because he knew it would be an abuse of good breath. He walked away, frustrated, amazed at the lack of vision of the men with whom he had just shared such wasted time, yet knowing in his heart he should not have been surprised. He never stood a chance.

* * *

Those short talks, though, were an opportunity to refine a more coherent strategy, and Knighton had already identified several essential criteria for the purchase of a football club. Firstly, there had to be a strong core of traditional and paying support which would later come to be called a fan base. Secondly, a good freehold had to be available to buy, preferably with surplus land, to provide an extension of the club's facilities. Thirdly, the club must have the potential to develop peripheral income streams with which to generate profit from sources additional to the traditional gate receipts. It was this latent potency that would provide the value in any purchasing equation. It would be the core principle on which Knighton's financial strategy would be based; these criteria provided a simple and effective model for the future of football.

Knighton laughs as he admits now that Halifax Town passed none of those tests. He began to look elsewhere for an opportunity to put theories into practice.

* * *

If Halifax Town provided Knighton with an antithesis to his thesis, Sheffield Wednesday appeared to possess all the necessary possibilities. There was also the little matter of his romantic attachment to the club.

Knighton's family had a 120-year-old connection with this famous Yorkshire club and because of his great-grandfather's success there as a player, the club held a special place in Knighton's heart; Sheffield Wednesday was in his blood but was not, however, within his reach. He knocked once on the doors and met an official.

'Are you looking for directors?'

The response was polite but in the negative. At the time, the ownership structure of the Hillsborough club was complex and recruitment to the board of directors was via a nominations process only. The club, in spite of their placing in the lower half of the old First Division, were happy enough with their leadership structure.

Knighton was rebuffed once more, but understood that what does not kill you makes you stronger.

* * *

As 1988 became 1989, Knighton was distracted by the purchase of a farmhouse and a sizeable piece of land on the Isle of Man. The move into tax exile and retirement had been planned for some time, at least by his long-suffering wife, Rosemary. It had not been an easy journey for her, being married to an incurable, restless workaholic. For a brief period at least, Knighton's wife had won the day.

Through the cold of that January, he and Rosemary busied themselves with delights and domesticity relating to the ninety-two-acre property set in dizzying, undulating countryside overlooking the Isle of Man capital, Douglas. But into this emerging idyll in the following month came the hardly earth-shattering news of the resignation of a football chairman, someone formerly presiding over a browbeaten club languishing in the lower reaches of the third tier of English football. There was something about a dispute with fellow directors over the future of the team's unsuccessful manager. Knighton's ears pricked up. They were tuned specially to receive news like this.

'It's Bolton Wanderers,' he told Rosemary, as if this explained everything.

She sighed and shrugged her shoulders.

'And you're Michael Knighton,' she said.

* * *

The chairman's name was Barry Chaytow, a clothing manufacturer specialising in school and scouting uniforms and fancy neckties. His was a club, Knighton told himself, for whom the phrase sleeping giant might have been invented, and one that ticked all the boxes according to Knighton's criteria for potential success.

Another card was about to be dealt by the devil, and would be played later in the game.

It was Chaytow, a few months later, who provided Knighton with an introduction to Edwards, and to the keys to the kingdom of Old Trafford.

There was great history here – Bolton were four times winners of the FA Cup including iconic finals in 1923 and 1958. In the first they defeated West Ham United 2-0 after chaotic scenes in the inaugural final at Wembley, when a crowd possibly as large as 300,000 overflowed on to the pitch and was kept in check by one policeman on a white horse. In 1958 the remnants of Manchester United's Busby Babes were beaten 2-0, with Nat Lofthouse scoring both goals and, for the second, bundling both ball and United goalkeeper Harry Gregg into the back of the net, using physicality that today would have seen both the goal disallowed and the goalscorer sent off.

There was also great potential.

Before the Munich crash made a legend of an already famous football club, Bolton Wanderers were the Manchester United of English football. Now, though, in the first months of 1989 they were sinking towards relegation from the old Third Division. They had been stagnating there since 1983, apart from one season when they fell even further into the Fourth Division. In charge of the team in 1989 was Phil Neal, hero of Liverpool and England, but, according to Barry Chaytow, not hacking it as a coach or as a manager.

Attendances at the louring, cavernous and ancient Burnden Park stadium were threatening to dip below 4,000 and it seemed to the chairman that more ghosts were pressing through the turnstiles and standing on the terraces than real men with real money in their pockets.

'In the final analysis,' Chaytow said to his fellow directors, 'it comes down to paying players' wages.'

There were murmurings of agreement around the boardroom table. Chaytow could see his own furrowed brow and those of his colleagues reflected in the polished surface of that table. He looked for inspiration from the black and white photographs of heroes past that lined the walls around him.

'Look,' he said, 'the manager may have a half century of England caps in his attic, he may have played 650 times for Liverpool and won four European Cups, but none of that makes him a good manager.'

'He got us promotion last year, Barry,' a fellow director proffered.

'But only from the Fourth Division.'

Chaytow knew he was losing the argument. He understood it would be pointless cataloguing the endless list of top class footballers who had failed as coaches and as managers. He had Bobby Charlton's recent dismal failure just up the road at Preston North End particularly in mind, but he said nothing. Instead, Chaytow resigned from the Bolton Wanderers board. He met Knighton while he was still licking his wounds.

* * *

It was ten in the evening and it was a Bolton night, brass farthing cold and nothing to welcome or warm the soul. Knighton delivered a letter to Chaytow, strolled the streets, breathing in the history of the place, smiling at the ghosts, studying the bricks and mortar of the home of Bolton Wanderers.

The stadium was embedded in the past, part of the Victorian landscape of terraced houses from which working men emerged for work or drink or football, a shrine of buried memories, the Lowry painting, *Going to the Match*. As Knighton turned a corner of the stadium, he was confronted by a bold as brass supermarket.

'This is sacrilege,' he said, although there was no one there to listen. 'This is where once there were banks of terraces of sound, where fathers gathered on a Saturday, passed down their sons, working hand by working hand, above their heads, so boys could take their places at the foot of the terracing, behind the goal, where they could see their heroes and grow to be fathers and, like them, take their sons to see the match.'

Knighton recalled his own childhood visits to the Baseball Ground, Derby, and the kindness of strangers who permitted a boy to find his way to the front of the crowd.

'This is an utter abomination,' he said.

It was, too, an aberration, a denial of all that the working class culture he grew from once stood for. It was not that Knighton was against change. Far, far from it. Or against football clubs turning an honest shilling or two. God forbid that anyone could lay that charge against him. It was just that the past deserved respect and supermarkets should know their place.

Knighton says he isn't sexist but felt there was something approaching an unholiness there, with women trespassing on their menfolk's sacred territory. Shopping, he thought, was okay in its place, a necessary evil even, but it became a profanity once inside a football stadium. Aesthetically, too, this was desecration, disfigurement.

'And I know a thing or two or three about architecture,' Knighton told himself. In fact, it was a passion.

He was not, and never could have been, a property developer in the strict sense of that term. He had made his money buying the most beautiful period buildings that he could afford, working men's Victorian terraced houses in Yorkshire as well as the fine Georgian town houses of the moneyed classes in Edinburgh.

He would never despoil the symmetry of a football stadium by replacing its heartland with a supermarket. He wondered what sort of people would do such a thing. He looked forward to finding out.

* * *

Some weeks later he met Barry Chaytow.

The former chairman of Bolton Wanderers looked like a man betrayed by his lover, Knighton thought, a man clearly troubled by the goings-on at his football club.

But Knighton liked him, and that was important, indispensable, really, if they were going to do business.

He listened attentively to Chaytow's accounts of the Bolton boardroom shenanigans over the proposed sacking of Phil Neal. Knighton empathised, and a rapport was established.

'In the final analysis, Michael, it's a matter of self-respect, principle, honour, even, if you like,' Chaytow said. His voice was soft, bruised fruit. 'I suggested the manager's position should be tabled; others on the board thought not.'

The former Bolton Wanderers chairman was tall, 6ft 2in, yet seemed reduced. Knighton, at 5ft 10in, felt himself the taller man.

'Tell me about your business, Barry.'

Knighton knew that his new acquaintance's business was in textiles, clothing, and that Chaytow's firm was called the Manchester Tie & Scarf Co. He was not surprised, as the Bolton man was dressed immaculately, polished and pinned, with a smile that was now beginning to win over the rest of his face.

'Debonair,' he told Rosemary when he returned home. 'Barry thinks I should buy the club; says I should speak to Nat Lofthouse.'

* * *

The telephone was ringing and Knighton bubbled with excitement and anticipation. When you are a football fan, and of a certain age, and you have been weaned on tales of great men of the fifties – of Ferenc Puskas and his Hungarian compatriots who came to Wembley and taught England a footballing lesson as they scored six goals; of Stanley Matthews and his club's eventual 1953 FA Cup Final triumph, a 4-3 victory against Bolton Wanderers after being 3-1 behind and deep into the second half; and of the magnificent and tragic Busby Babes, the teenagers Duncan Edwards and Bobby Charlton, one dying in a Munich hospital, the other dragged from the wreckage of the stricken aeroplane and living on to win World and European cups – you are allowed to be a touch star-struck inside when you are about to speak to the president of Bolton Wanderers, the immortal Nat Lofthouse.

On the outside, however, Knighton allowed himself no betrayal of emotion.

Lofthouse was due to speak at a sportsman's dinner in Accrington.

'You're a legend,' Knighton said, because it was not just banal, it was true.

What else can you say when you introduce yourself to the Lion of Vienna, the man who scored the winning goal in a 3-2 England triumph over Austria after being tripped and hacked from behind by the home side's defenders, after being elbowed in the face and, clattered by the goalkeeper, and still holding his nerve and keeping his feet to slide the ball into the gaping net?

'I want to meet your directors, Nat, I'm interested in buying the club.'

Lofthouse had been Bolton's president since 1986, having been a one-club man with the Wanderers, playing 452 games and scoring 255 goals, having captained them in both their cup finals in the 1950s, and having been chief coach, chief scout, caretaker manager, and administrative manager as well as president.

'Please telephone your colleagues and explain to them that I would like to meet with them to discuss the future of this great football club.'

'Come to the club tomorrow at nine in the morning,' said the legend, 'and I'll be there to meet you.'

When Lofthouse spoke, his voice was dark brown and as rich and welcoming as a coal fire in winter. The accent was Lancastrian and full of round-mouthed vowels.

* * *

Knighton arrived early, 8.45. He is never late. He was confident the Bolton board would listen to what he had to say. He had done his homework and knew the club was in serious financial distress. He knew, too, that the supporters had been demonstrating against the Warburton family, famous for bread and pies but not for running football clubs. These bakers had run Bolton Wanderers as a family fiefdom since the years before the Second World War.

One of the senior members of the board, George Warburton, was a descendant of Henry Warburton, former Liberal mayor of Bolton, who became the club chairman in 1930. Knighton smiled as he recalled a story he has read about Henry's feisty and footballing wife, Rachel. While her husband was politicking, Mrs Warburton would take herself to Burnden Park to watch the weekday training of the footballers, in those days in the capable hands of George Eccles.

'Eccles,' she said one day, 'one thing I just cannot understand is why your players miss so many penalties when it should be so easy to score.'

'Ah, what you don't understand, Mrs Warburton, is the difficulty of the situation.'

'Well,' the chairman's wife replied, 'I think I could score three times out of six myself.'

'Do have a try, madam.'

Knighton pictured the lady in her finery and the trainer – the hired hand in flat cap and football boots, all mud and leather, up to his ankles in both boots and mire. He imagined the trainer beckoning the chairman's wife on to the pitch, smiling with condescension, a chance in a lifetime to patronise his master's eyes and ears on the training ground. Eccles walked into the mouth of the goal and the lady shot and scored. The contest was abandoned when Mrs Warburton placed her third successful shot wide of the diving and despairing Eccles and into the back of the net, a hat-trick for an indomitable woman.

* * *

Sharp at nine, Knighton saw Lofthouse walking towards him, striding rather, with the confidence born of having scored thirty goals for England in only thirty-three appearances. The legend stepped straight out of a monochrome photograph from the fifties, from Knighton's childhood, or from one of his grandfather's cigarette cards. He was powerfully built, athletic and slim, muscled beneath the tailored suit, stocky and an inch or two shorter than Knighton. His trademark slicked-back Brylcreemed hair, parted to the left of centre, was thinning now and silver grey, and his forehead was marked and mottled like a duck's egg. Knighton almost expected to be able to read there the imprint of the laces of the heavy leather footballs that Lofthouse had headed so often past flat-footed goalkeepers in the mud and grime of now forgotten games.

The president of Bolton Wanderers was warm and welcoming. He introduced Knighton to his companion, the chairman, Sam Jones. He was not on the board of directors himself, Lofthouse explained to his visitor. Too nice, Knighton thought, much too nice to run a football club of this kind. He knew already that Lofthouse was a figurehead, a man of straw within the moneyed structure of the club, a man he wished to appreciate rather than needed to negotiate with, a straightforward soul with the heart of a lion that would also lie down with a lamb. He shook Knighton's hand and left him with Jones outside the boardroom.

There was something about the chairman's manner that Knighton disliked. He did not appreciate dealing with brokers with clammy hands and unhealthy complexions. Jones, too, was clearly less than enthusiastic about this meeting arranged by Lofthouse.

'Mr Jones,' Knighton said at last, 'I am not a time-waster. I have serious proposals to put before your people.'

He watched as Jones nodded with grudging acceptance.

Knighton's eyes swept around the walls and furnishings of the Bolton boardroom. It was sadness for his soul, this dour 1960s refurbishment, all Formica and tat; this tawdry disavowal of both style and tradition.

'I want no publicity,' Knighton said immediately, almost as if he wanted no association, no public acknowledgement of any connection with any of this malaise, this complacency, this cheapskatedness, this lack of vision.

'I'll come to the home match against Swansea on 11 February, and, if you would be kind enough to call a board meeting for after the game, I will then outline my proposals for taking this great club forwards.'

In response, Jones mumbled, muttered, as if his tongue could not shake the lethargy from his words.

'Mr Jones,' Knighton said, 'please do not prevaricate.'

* * *

It was not long before he concluded that the chairman was no less a cipher than Lofthouse. Jones was indeed George Warburton's man and had worked for him all his life, both in the football club and in the bakery that had made the Warburton family its bread, and jam and butter, too. Knighton was good at working these things out – he enjoyed the analysis of power and where it hid and where it lay within organisational structures. He liked to know with whom he was really dealing. Sam Jones was overweight and lightweight at the same time; he carried excess baggage but no clout.

Bolton Wanderers, Knighton understood, was a family affair. Warburton himself was a cheery man, hiding, perhaps, behind his ready smile. Or, maybe, Knighton thought, he only permitted his mask to slip when his football team won 1-0. Or when someone visited his boardroom to offer him money for his shares.

Knighton glanced at the rogues' gallery of ill-placed photographs of the current board of directors, and back at the faces that surrounded him, with suspicion and perhaps resentment. There was no reassurance to be found either in mug shots on walls or in dreary fleshy countenances around the table. Uninspiring surroundings, he thought, uninspiring people. He knew he was arrogant but he knew no other way.

'Gentlemen,' Knighton heard himself saying, 'I'm here with both my skills and my money.'

Warburton's smile was fixed, like a freehold asset.

'I have £1.5m to put on the table.'

He heard a collective intake of breath but the Bolton directors were merely drawing in the stale air of mediocrity that pervaded the room.

'In return, I require the majority shareholding in this football club.'

Knighton looked around the table to gauge reactions. Jones looked to his master. Warburton smiled at one of his relatives, Brett, a scion of the family already in place for when the old man was gone. Someone called Ball spoke and Knighton quickly saw that this man was the most pompous human being he had ever had the misfortune to meet. Throughout the next months of negotiations and prevarications it was Gordon Ball, an infuriating know-all, according to Knighton, who did most of the talking and who appeared to be making most of the decisions, all of them negative. For now, though, Knighton looked to the head of the Warburton family who wiped sweat from his spectacles to avoid the difficulty of framing a response.

It was Ball who first talked of custodianship. It seemed he had no interest in the creation of new revenue streams, nor in the saving of his football club, only in the preservation of the cosy mediocrity of the present situation. He not only pontificated on the subject of custodianship but lectured the prospective investor on the subject. Eventually, Knighton snapped.

'Please,' he said, 'by all means, remain true to the noble traditions of custodianship.' Knighton's voice was cold, calculating the cost and benefit of every word. 'What I suggest, then, is that I will utilise my investment to pay off the company debts and to purchase players. If you are here as genuine custodians of the good health and prosperity of Bolton Wanderers, there can be no doubt you will prefer this option to my original proposal of purchasing your shares.'

There followed a stunned silence unbroken even by Ball's nauseating platitudes.

'Mr Warburton, you own a company with an annual turnover of £80m and with a workforce of 2,000 and a profit of £10m.'

Knighton preferred to speak to the organ grinder and not to the organ grinder's monkey.

'And here am I, with not a tenth of your wealth, willing to invest it all in this football club. Yet you allow your colleague to harangue me for what seems like hours on the subject of custodianship. I am the outsider here, but still I am the only one around this table, it would seem, who is prepared to put his hand into his pocket.'

* * *

When Knighton first appeared at Bolton Wanderers, the team had won only one of their previous ten games and the club's misfortunes on the field of play were well matched by both maladministration and increasing debts off the pitch. Knighton sensed the directors were desperate to sell in spite of their apparent reticence and suspicion of his motives. He recalls speaking to them as if he were already the owner and chief executive.

'Gentlemen, this club can now move forward with confidence; your problems are over.' He truly believed in the idea of destiny and in his own destiny in particular. 'Go down to the dressing room, talk to the manager, to the players, nurture confidence, become a family.' It was Henry-V-before-the-battle-of-Agincourt stuff, but Knighton really did believe in its powers to motivate.

He was, however, defeated by his own success, and it was a curious, inexplicable sequence of events that brought about that reverse. From the moment of Knighton's first arrival on the evening of the Swansea match, the fortunes of Bolton Wanderers began to turn around. There were two more defeats, it is true, when Warburton and Ball seemed most interested in Knighton's proposals, but then Bolton Wanderers began a record-breaking run of twenty matches without defeat, stretching until the end of the season and finally culminating, not merely in staying in the Third Division, but in a top-half finish and a Wembley triumph over Torquay United in the unfortunately named but halfway prestigious Sherpa Van Trophy.

As Knighton had predicted, the troubles of Bolton Wanderers were indeed in the past, and, as results improved, and attendances and income increased, so the desire to sell the club to anyone at all diminished, and then disappeared entirely. Knighton's proposed deal was as dead as a dodo and he wrote to the club withdrawing his offer.

'I shall leave,' he wrote, 'and take my Lady Destiny with me.'

He paused, considered the possibility of over-writing, the uses and abuses of purple prose, and allowed his phrase to be because he liked words and he loved the way they played together, like a team of the best footballers.

'Yes,' he continued, 'and she will weave her magic web of silver and golden threads at the next football club I go to.'

* * *

What hurt Knighton most of all in the Bolton saga was the press conference, presided over by chairman Sam Jones.

When Jones was asked about Knighton's one-time bid to buy Bolton Wanderers, he admitted to only one cursory discussion and not the series of lengthy meetings that had actually taken place.

'It was nothing serious,' Jones said. The meeting with the press then concluded with a blatant and damaging lie. 'In any case, Knighton only offered us £50,000.' It was a callous and careless attempt to save face by writing off Knighton as nothing more than a dreamer. Knighton was already learning hard lessons.

There were men in football, as in other walks of life, who had no sense of honour, who spoke with forked tongues when it would be to their advantage. Ugly lies, Knighton thought, disfigure this beautiful game. It would not be the last time he would be forced to confront them.

Knighton telephoned Jones to vent his anger.

'Sam,' he said, 'this is just not true what you said to the press. This is not fair, it's just not cricket, old boy.'

It wasn't football, either.

There was an embarrassed silence on the part of the Bolton chairman.

'Why on earth did you feel the need to tell lies about my dealings with you and the Bolton board?'

'Oh,' said Jones. 'Oh dear, I'm sorry Michael.'

'We had serious discussions, Sam, over a period of four months and I put £1.5m on the table in cash and with proof of further funds for you all to see.'

'Sorry, Michael, I don't really know what to say to you, but I'm very sorry,' Jones said. 'I got it wrong.'

Later in 1989, at Knighton's press conference when he appeared as the new owner elect of Manchester United for the first time, he was asked about previous attempts to purchase football clubs.

'Was it Bolton Wanderers?' he was asked.

'I'm sorry, but I have no comment on this matter,' Knighton replied. He stayed true to his word to the Bolton directors about the confidentiality of the negotiations. He might so easily have exacted his revenge on Sam Jones, George Warburton and Gordon Ball, et al, and he might have caused them considerable embarrassment by the publication of his farewell letter, but it is another measure of the man that he did not do so.

In spite of his warning to the Warburtons that he was taking his Lady Destiny elsewhere, Knighton takes no pleasure from the tragic current state of Bolton Wanderers, formerly owned by Ken Anderson, the latest in a line of disastrous owners.

In late August, 2019, Bolton was on the cusp of liquidation, only saved at the last minute by a takeover bid from Football Ventures Ltd.

As Knighton said recently, the donation of the tiniest fraction of Manchester United's annual wage bill of almost £300m would have been sufficient to save their Lancashire neighbours, Bolton Wanderers, from extinction. Even individual United players could help as the average yearly earnings of a first team player at Old Trafford now weighs in at £6,534,654.

Solidarity and community, however, are words that are now as obsolete as coal mines.

* * *

Through those dark days of the Bolton–Knighton imbroglio, Barry Chaytow stayed in touch with Knighton.

The clothier was honest in his motives and told his friend that he was interested in returning to the Bolton boardroom, should Knighton buy the club. He also supplied uniforms to the school in Huddersfield that Knighton owned. It was just business and the business of scratching backs for bucks. He knew Knighton had moved to the Isle of Man, with the stated intention of writing poetry and painting pictures and relaxing in his studio in the peace of the Manx countryside. But he also knew exactly what Knighton really craved.

Several months passed, then Chaytow called.

'Michael,' he said, 'I have a football club you might be interested in and I really do think this one is perfect for you and your ideas.'

Knighton's ears were all ears.

'Yes,' Chaytow said, 'this one might just meet your criteria.'

The former chairman of Bolton Wanderers paused for what felt like an age to Knighton.

'Go on, Barry.'

'Yes, it has a fine tradition and a very strong base of support, and just a little more than your minimum requirement of a few thousand hard core fans, not to mention a real history.'

Knighton disliked guessing games but played along as he sensed the suppressed excitement in Chaytow's voice. He reeled off a few names of possible clubs.

'Grimsby Town? Huddersfield? Swansea? West Brom? It's not my beloved Sheffield Wednesday, is it? Or my home town Derby County?'

He rattled off more than a dozen more football club names, but was wrong every time.

'No, Michael, you'll never guess this one.'

'Please,' Knighton said.

'I was with someone last night who is very close to the club. It might even soon be reported in the *Manchester Evening News* that it's actually for sale.'

Knighton's pulse quickened.

'Some board members are reported as trying to buy the club, Michael.'

'It's not, surely, it's not ...'

'It is, Michael, it's Manchester United.'

Knighton took one deep breath.

'And, I firmly believe that you are just the sort of man who could strike a deal with the current owner. He'll like you, Michael, and with your great ideas on how to run a football club, he's bound to be interested.'

Chaytow knew Martin Edwards, the majority shareholder at Old Trafford, well enough to introduce him to his friend Michael Knighton.

Knighton understood he had to act and fast.

'I'm due on the UK mainland next week, Barry, but I'll bring it forward.' Knighton's pulse was racing as fast as his thoughts. 'Let's get together tomorrow, Barry.'

* * *

By the time the two men met, Knighton had done his homework. Meticulousness was always his method. There was now almost nothing that he did not know about Manchester United. He had made up his mind. The Old Trafford club was a perfect fit for his *Blueprint*. Knighton was used to doing deals but this one would be the biggest of his life.

'I can buy that football club, Barry, I really can.'

Chaytow nodded, supportive.

'Call him now, please,' Knighton said. 'Phone Edwards and say you want to meet him for lunch with a close friend of yours.' Both men were smiling, their food untouched. 'Tell him your friend knows a bit about football.'

*Book Two*

# The First Half

## Chapter Seven

# Pre-Match Meal and Meeting ...

### *A Home Game for Edwards*
### *Old Trafford, 20 June 1989*

ANOTHER DAY, another lunch, this time chicken and seasonal vegetables, early new potatoes, carrots, broad beans and peas, a sauce Edwards may not even have noticed, for one simple reason.

He had other matters on his mind.

This time, he was on his home turf and this time, Edwards must have hoped there would be no bad manners at the meeting Barry Chaytow had organised. Edwards knew Chaytow from his time as chairman of Bolton Wanderers, well enough to be sure he would not be bringing Robert Maxwell to Old Trafford. Chaytow had told Edwards he wanted him to meet a business associate, a colleague and friend, and knew that Edwards was looking to sell his shares in the club. Edwards was guarded, his face and body language prepared in advance. He was hopeful this would not be just another day in the close season, just another dog day before his holiday in Greece, before the players returned for pre-season photo calls and sweaty training, and before his employees left Old Trafford once again for their tour of Thailand and Japan.

Knighton watched as Edwards smiled a greeting at Chaytow, saw the chairman and chief executive of Manchester United sneak a look behind him, saw his grey eyes sweep all four corners of the restaurant. The newcomer was not about to think Edwards paranoid. Knighton understood well enough this was a delicate situation, knew only too well the probability that Edwards' colleagues on the board at Old Trafford might well be watching the majority shareholder's every move, waiting perhaps to make moves of their own.

Secrecy was king for at least a day.

Edwards had put it about that he was meeting a potential sponsor. The other directors at the club – Amer Al Midani, Michael Edelson, Nigel Burrows and Bobby Charlton – might be potential conspirators, possible predators for his shares. Edwards suspected there might be innumerable insiders, prospective plotters, confederates, who would unseat him if they could, persuade him to sell the club to them, perhaps as a consortium, if only they could catch him somehow, could somehow force his hand.

* * *

Edwards, though, may well have had no intention of selling his shares to those inside the club, to those he might have regarded as rivals and potential conspirators, determined in their plans to own the club themselves.

But who could really know what was inside the chairman's head?

From his table, Knighton could see Edwards was putting his best face forwards, but the chairman of Manchester United was sure he did not know the man accompanying Chaytow.

He had never seen him before in his life, not even in a photograph in the local press.

* * *

Knighton and Chaytow had waited fifteen minutes, seated at a table in the glass-fronted executive restaurant overlooking the Old Trafford pitch. That was fine, though. Knighton knew the score. He was not born yesterday. They chatted and admired the view over the lush summer grass, the stadium which was to become Knighton's Theatre of Dreams. He knew everything he needed to know. He had been hard at work, researching every facet of the club, examining all areas of the business that he could capitalise on and grow.

Once more he calculated the value of it all, the Old Trafford stadium and its footprint, the Cliff training ground facilities in Salford, the restaurants and the car parks. The players alone must be worth at least twice the top whack valuation of £8m placed on the club by the bankers Kleinwort Benson around the time of the Robert Maxwell fiasco. Knighton had also been secretly assessing the club's talent at youth and schoolboy level. He always said he could spot a proper footballer in a crowd, even from a couple of pitches away. He had visited the United training ground at Salford and the various schools of excellence. If anyone asked, he was just another punter watching the kids training, but he had already identified several future stars: Giggs, Neville, Martin, Scholes, Sharpe, Butt, and a skinny 14-year-old kid called Beckham. All of them thoroughbreds in the stable, all prized assets that could bring future success to the club. All of them valuables on the balance sheet.

The previous season Manchester United had underperformed and finished a hapless and hopeless eleventh in the league championship. This was a travesty, a betrayal of the Busby legacy of success and legend. Knighton knew in his bones that a return to the top table was long overdue and well within reach, with only a little loosening of the purse strings by the man in charge at Old Trafford required.

'I could be that man,' he said to himself.

'What did you say, Michael?'

Chaytow was on edge too.

'Nothing.'

Knighton was too busy reviewing the prime playing assets of the club to care for any more inconsequential chatter.

Under contract to the Old Trafford club were the England captain Bryan Robson, great strikers such as Brian McClair and

Mark Hughes, joint top scorers in the previous season with sixteen goals apiece, and stalwart and much-prized defender Steve Bruce. And rumours were swirling around that manager Alex Ferguson was about to sign Neil Webb, another England midfielder.

'That is,' Knighton said, 'if he can persuade the chairman to part with the money.'

'Michael?'

Edwards had entered the restaurant and was spotted by Chaytow, who hoped his two friends would get along, that his newest friend would impress. Knighton saw the chairman, too, and smiled. He understood Edwards was not a natural spender of money and realised that this parsimony was madness if the club was serious about winning titles and cups.

Knighton had a deal, a price in mind and knew an agreement was possible. He was aware that the land and property alone – Old Trafford and the Cliff – was worth a conservative £26m. Neither was Knighton guessing: the Manchester estate agent Suttons had already completed an evaluation on his behalf. There were spin-offs, too – the contract with Sharp, the Japanese electronics giant, worth £800,000 a year, the perimeter advertising at £200,000, the shirt manufacturing deal with Adidas which brought in £350,000 – all of which he added to the scales of commercial values. Calculations filled Knighton's head as he had waited for Edwards. He also recalled that United had won seven Football League championships, six Football Association Cups and a European Cup, and that the club had become a leading *brand* in the worldwide football industry. Knighton was shameless – proud perhaps – of cornering the word *brand* in conjunction with a football club. Brands were licences, if not to print money, at least to rake it in. He foresaw the building of a football team and a football club that would return Manchester United to its former glories.

There would be richer pickings from sponsorship, too, for multinational corporations that were set to play a profitable role in the globalisation of the sporting entertainment industry that he predicted was only just around the corner. All this was part and parcel of Knighton's philosophy of success within the football industry, opulence, extravagance even, not for its own sake but to ensure the club at the core of this enterprise could purchase the best players in the world, so that that club, Manchester United, could win matches, win more championships, win more cups, and rule the roost of planet football.

Knighton suspected that Edwards was utterly ignorant of this brave new commercial world that was there for the making and the taking. Otherwise, why on earth was Edwards considering the sale of his assets at Manchester United at such an opportune time for their exploitation?

* * *

Knighton watched Edwards as he saw the chairman of Manchester United studying him.

How does he see me?

Edwards, he thought, might have taken note of the newcomer's sleek clean-cut dark hair, his fashionable moustache, his wide, dimpled smile. He hoped he might have paid attention to his athletic frame, less so to the tad of fat about his middle, thought Edwards too astute to be fooled into thinking his guest might be soft on the inside.

He thought Edwards might be something of a ladies' man, wondered whether the Manchester United man might think the same of him.

Knighton tucked away his thoughts, deep inside his blazer pockets.

Chaytow made the introductions and withdrew to the shadows of the conversation, and Knighton saw his friend smile as the gentle sparring began between the owner and the would-be purchaser of the Old Trafford empire.

Knighton heard the words tumble from his mouth.

He knew his voice was deep, rich, public school correct, and he wondered if Edwards might be thinking, thank God, he's one of us, one of our special, privileged breed of expensively educated men.

For his part, Knighton was keen to get beyond the pleasantries. He had seen pictures of Edwards but was still surprised by the man's stature and trim, his sporting build. He was almost handsome in a debonair sort of way – a looker, for a certain type of lady.

He must know why I'm here, Knighton thought. He studied Edwards more closely, saw the neat parting in the slightly foppish hair, heard the clink and chink of the silver spoons chattering in Edwards' mouth, and thought, yes, this is a man I could do business with.

'Well, Martin,' Knighton said, after a drawing in of breath whose depth he hoped Edwards had not noticed, 'I won't beat about the bush. Let me come straight to the milk in the coconut: I'm here to discuss the future of Manchester United Football Club on the basis I understand it could be purchased. I'm the man that you need to sell the club to, and I'll tell you why that is, too.'

The words tumbled one after another, the metaphors were mixed but the message was loud and clear. Knighton knew that Edwards' interest had been piqued, even though nothing was discernible from Edwards' mask of a face, nothing was betrayed.

Knighton thought he heard Edwards speak.

'Well ...'

He watched Edwards' mouth open, poised to speak, but the newcomer reckoned the chairman of Manchester United would be relieved to find he was not permitted to finish a sentence he had no desire to complete.

'I'm here to tell you why I'm the man you should sell this club to, and that is because I can take it to a place where I believe it needs to be, strutting in the super-glory zone, in the highest echelons of world football, and that is where I believe that I can take this great club, and I have my own, original ideas on how to achieve this goal.'

Knighton said all this as if he were Zeus pronouncing divine edicts from his throne atop Mount Olympus.

'I know I can make this happen, Martin, I'm a doer not a talker.'

Knighton thought Edwards' face betrayed surprise, agitation, perhaps unused to such hyperbole.

'I have a business model, Martin, like no other, and Manchester United is the perfect football club for the implementation of my plan.'

Knighton busied himself during the brief pauses from speech in trying to read the runes in Edwards' face. The Old Trafford man's expression was quizzical. Knighton hoped the chairman would respond to the charm in his voice, would believe his words were like honey from a rock.

* * *

Knighton always says he knew the deal was done right at the beginning of his first meeting with Edwards. Ten seconds was the time, he claims, it took to sense that the business was there, waiting for him to win it for himself, although he understood it would take a while longer for the pact to be acknowledged – for Edwards himself to understand and agree that the deal was done.

Edwards said nothing, though, but Knighton could see he was thinking deep and hard for what seemed an eternity. Chaytow, too, was silent, knowing there was nothing more for him to say, that he had already played his role in this momentous occasion.

Knighton sensed there was something inside Edwards, somewhere just beneath the skin, that he was scratching – a man inside the man looking for an honourable exit, a man whose finances were under pressure. Knighton had been that squeezed man himself, once or twice, someone who had to sell in order to survive or thrive.

Manchester United, Knighton thought, had not won a league championship for twenty-two years and official attendances in the season just ended had been the lowest for twenty-seven years. Supporters were not just on the chairman's back but trying to get to his neck to string him up too. The noose was swinging for Edwards; the Manchester United chairman was loathed by many of the Old Trafford faithful. Knighton could see that Edwards had endured more than enough of these troubles and was certain that Edwards both wanted out and needed out. He believed he had the perfect exit plan to lay before him.

* * *

Knighton knew Edwards had tried everything to make United successful and profitable. In desperation, four years earlier, Edwards had even launched a basketball club.

Knighton, though, doubted Edwards had either the knowledge or the energy after almost ten years at the helm, after almost a decade of trying and failing, of hiring and firing, of Dave Sexton, Ron Atkinson and Alex Ferguson, of Inland Revenue investigations and of massive fan discontent. He thought Edwards was just too tired and was sure he now needed someone to tell him exactly how it might be done, how he might leave with dignity, with honour halfway intact. Knighton would whet his appetite, permit him to tease out some of his secrets, show him the colour of his money and bide his time. Then he would invite him to Scotland, seal the deal within the thick walls of his sixteenth-century castle at Killochan.

In these early talks, who knew whether Edwards was thinking of his bank overdraft, his borrowings now totalling around £900,000, or how to play his cards closest to his chest?

In 2017, in his book, *Red Glory*, Edwards admitted as much. Knighton was 'offering to wipe out the debt I had carried since 1978'.

* * *

The lunch was superb and lasted three hours.

Chaytow was a vegetarian and played with his meal nervously. Edwards was lean and narrow and could take or leave his food. Knighton was hungry and not just for his lunch. There seemed enough mineral water on the table to flood a football pitch.

At some point, between courses, Knighton took the trouble to explain that he was not a Robert Maxwell, nor a Richard Branson.

'I must tell you now, Martin, that I do not have that sort of wealth. But what I do have, that neither Maxwell nor Branson possesses, is a genuine love of the game combined with a business model that is genuinely innovative.'

Knighton studied Edwards' mask of inscrutability, certain already of what lay behind that grey façade.

'Martin, I can make a commercial success of this great football club. Please trust me when I make this bold assertion.'

Knighton had no idea at that moment how important it was to Edwards that his guest knew how to handle his knife and fork, understood the difference between a fish knife and a steak knife, and that he did not dribble his food down his shirt front. But he did know how to conduct himself. And it was good for both parties that he also knew a man who wanted to sell his shares when he saw one.

'No,' he said again, 'I'm no Robert Maxwell, nor Richard Branson.'

These declarations seemed to be well received, so Knighton continued.

'I've made a few bob, hard earned, but I'm just not in their class of money. I'm a million miles away from their kind of wealth.'

Knighton saw Edwards nod his head, perhaps encouraging the spillage of more information.

'But you should know, right from the outset, that I do possess sufficient wealth for the purpose of purchasing this great football club.'

The subject of money was never broached again between them until the day the deal was finally agreed. Edwards knew his price, Knighton thought, but it would be unconscionable to mention it now, uncouth to descend from principles to practicalities, the worst of form. To negotiate now would be as shallow, as common, as sex on a first date.

Edwards was pulling hard on a Benson & Hedges tipped cigarette and Knighton watched him relax. He reached deeper into his bag of goodies.

'First,' he said, 'we must develop the Stretford End, complete the Old Trafford development, make this stadium one of the very best, not just in England but in the world.'

Knighton watched a smile unfold across Edwards' face.

'The stadium,' he continued, 'needs to reflect the glory years that are to come, and it's a crucial part of my overall plan for the future.'

Knighton knew the development of Old Trafford was key to Edwards' acceptance of his proposals, the legacy the chairman wished to leave. Edwards was impressive, Knighton thought, and yet somehow unremarkable.

Edwards had survived as Manchester United's leader for over nine long years, amid palpable lack of success. He had become chairman after the sudden death of his father at the still tender age of thirty-four. He had needed such sheer thick skin, operating in the dark shadow of his heavyweight father, Champagne Louis, who had wined and dined with the Busbys and chaired United to triumphs at home and abroad. He had survived his father's shame and his father's death, and yet, Knighton felt, still Edwards could not see what the newcomer could see in plain sight.

Edwards, the newcomer concluded, had no idea of the intrinsic value of the business he owned. The name alone, Knighton estimated, was worth at least £10m. The stagnation, the lack of vision seemed a criminal dereliction of the duty of care of this national treasure.

Knighton was first to his feet.

'Perhaps, Martin, we can meet again.'

* * *

Afterwards, Knighton confided in Chaytow.

'Barry, I know he will sell and I know he will sell the club to me.'

He enjoyed the smile on the face of his friend.

'I know it in my bones, Barry, and I can see it in his eyes.'

Chaytow laughed.

'What you can see, Michael, what you can see in Martin's eyes, is a great fat cheque for many millions of pounds and a sign above the Old Trafford door marked *EXIT*.'

Knighton shared in the laughter.

'Next time,' he said, 'it won't be an away match.'

'Michael?'

'Next time, Barry, I'll meet Martin on my home ground, and that's where the deal will be done.'

## Chapter Eight
# Attack, Attack, Attack

*A Home Game for Knighton*
*Killochan Castle, 21 July 1989.*

ANOTHER THING Knighton says is that he is a quick learner.

Football, teaching, business, and back to football, anything you like.

After selling the goodwill in his florist business in Huddersfield, while retaining the freehold of the premises from which he could command a useful rent, Knighton developed a strategy for increasing his wealth, for providing security for Rosemary and his children, and by the early 80s was already well on his way in business.

He was a driven man and property acquisition was his driver. He loved Edinburgh, his wife's home town, and it was here where his property empire rapidly developed; there were masterpieces of architecture to be purchased in the capital city's Georgian New Town.

To understand Knighton, however, one must accept that he does not merely love the work of Robert Adam and William Playfair, but that he also loves the thread of history that runs through their bricks and mortar, that links building to man and man to building.

There were no thoughts then of Manchester United.

In the season 1984/85, Ron Atkinson's Manchester United won the FA Cup and Martin Edwards dreamed of emulating his father's success at Old Trafford, and of imprinting his own authority on a boardroom now containing an assertive and allegedly concerned Bobby Charlton. Insiders have suggested Charlton was having disagreements with Atkinson over signings, indiscipline, and a drinking culture among the players. If true, Knighton thought later, Bobby was spot on in his demands, but also wondered why Edwards had not asserted himself in these matters in support of his fellow director.

At the same time as these Old Trafford shenanigans, Knighton purchased his first block of exquisite, and profitable, town houses in Edinburgh.

Knighton had always swooned over fine period buildings. Indeed, his passion for architecture encompassed both the work of the ancients of classic culture and the cutting edge contemporaneity and modernity of the twentieth century. He had, though, always favoured the masters of the neo-classical eighteenth century, and so it was easy to understand why he fell in love with Edinburgh, the Athens of the North.

As a boy, Knighton's imagination skipped between times and between places, from his home in the Derbyshire pit village of Loscoe to the ruins of Codnor Castle, a twenty-five-minute hike across the county's green fields. Another attraction was Chatsworth House, home of the Dukes of Devonshire for the last six centuries. The young Knighton was fascinated by its deep pile carpets, its period furnishings and the manicured grandeur of its gardens.

Closer to home, another great Georgian house, Shipley Hall, drew him too. Knighton walked there across another deep pile carpet, this time of abandoned horse chestnut leaves. The mansion house, which is now a mere footprint of a building having been demolished in the 1940s due to chronic mining subsidence, was where his great-grandfather, Henry Knighton, had met Squire Miller-Mundy, whose home it was in the early years of the twentieth century.

As a teenager and young footballer, apprenticed to Coventry City, Knighton sometimes found himself alone in the ruins of the old bombed-out cathedral, where he gazed in rapture at the new adjacent architecture of Basil Spence, his mind shifting like a ghost through time, through civilisations and their art and artefacts, through the pomp and circumstance and pride of man. Through it all, he saw man's need to build, to leave behind a record of his birthright, to create and to construct.

* * *

Fast forward now to 1989, and Knighton thought of Edwards, a fellow builder, and the light that he had seen in the chairman's eyes when Knighton explained his project to redevelop the Stretford End.

In one sense, Knighton's desire to purchase Old Trafford was a mere continuation of his obsession with the beauty of building and buildings.

Recently, Knighton had purchased Broxmouth House, a magnificent Georgian mansion, for £350,000, and sold it six months later for more than twice the price.

He found it difficult not to smile at those memories, not just because of the money – because it was never just about the money with Knighton – but also because he liked winning, always has done, always will do, too.

* * *

Killochan Castle was a grade A listed baronial pile complete with fairy-tale pepper-pot turrets that rose high into the Ayrshire sky.

Its stone walls were sixteen feet thick.

That's not falling down anytime soon, he thought, the first time he saw the castle.

He felt something similar, too, about Old Trafford when he first met Edwards. Although he understood he was a gambler, Knighton liked solidity and thick walls in his gambles.

Most of them, anyway.

* * *

Knighton smiled as another interesting episode was called to mind, his meeting with Graham Sharpe of William Hill, that firm's master of specialist bets.

Knighton had an agreement with Sharpe to place a bet that would net him a cool £1bn. It would gross him the biggest ever betting payout in history. It reminded Knighton of the old music hall song, 'The Man Who Broke the Bank at Monte Carlo', and of George Soros, the man who broke the Bank of England by short-selling sterling on Black Wednesday, 1992, and making a £1bn profit during a few days of rampant currency dealing. Knighton's bet would probably bankrupt William Hill, that well-known High Street gambling business.

It was a simple wager.

'What odds,' Knighton asked Sharpe, 'would you give me about me being picked to play for Manchester United?'

Sharpe was young, smart, suspicious, his eyes full of this ridiculous thirty-seven-year-old man, already overweight, running to seed, unknown and arriving from nowhere in particular.

'Let's make it more interesting still,' Knighton said. 'Let's say I would also have to play in an FA Cup Final.'

Sharpe's smile widened.

'Have you played professional football before?'

Sharpe was performing due diligence. Sharpe by name and sharp by nature, this man was considered the best in the business at his job.

Knighton told him the truth, about his brilliant schoolboy career, but also about his career-ending injury at Coventry City before he was 17 years old.

'Wait a minute,' said Sharpe, and he disappeared from view.

Knighton knew the bookmaker was checking whether anyone with his name was a marked man on Hill's lists of big-time punters. He looked around Sharpe's London office. It was small and untidy for such an important person within the bookmakers' executive stable. But it was functional, like the man himself. Sharpe was known as a shrewdie in the trade.

The odds compiler returned to his seat, eyes still fixed on the mug-punter before him. He sharpened his pencil before speaking.

'I will lay you 100,000 to 1 against such an event ever happening.'

He put down his pencil and relaxed into a smile of such serene confidence that it encouraged, almost begged, Knighton to place the bet. And why not? Knighton asked himself. After all, there's a good hundred grand of loose change rattling around in my pockets.

'How much,' said Knighton, 'would you allow me to bet at those odds?'

Knighton's smile was now almost as wide as Sharpe's.

'No limit,' said the bookmaker.

'Are there conditions of any kind?'

'No conditions whatsoever,' said Sharpe, 'other than the game you play in must be part of a properly recognised, professional competitive fixture.'

The odds compiler leaned back in his chair.

'Not a charity match or a friendly game.'

'That would be the FA Cup Final then,' said Knighton.

Both men laughed as if they had gambled away the world, then rose and offered each other their hands.

'I think,' said Knighton, 'I may well even put on £100,000, perhaps even £200,000.'

'No problem,' said Sharpe.

Knighton was amused by the thought that Sharpe was thinking he was at least ten pence short of a shilling.

For a while, Knighton kept his plans for the bet in his bag of secrets, sharing it only with Rosemary and the thick walls of his magnificent medieval castle home.

Killochan, he thought, this castle must keep as many secrets as there are stones in its walls. What was one more confidence to all that stone and all that time?

For the moment, at least, there were more pressing things to do than place bets with Graham Sharpe.

* * *

Knighton steadied himself as he descended the turnpike stair inside his castle home, aware of the importance of the day.

He looked up as if to ascertain the value of each cloud and each stretch of blue sky, glanced at the nearby Girvan river and headed for the main gate. Life was as it should be, pregnant with so much possibility.

He considered Edwards, and paused at the thought of their conspiratorial meetings, their whispered telephone calls, their scribbled notes, each one a staging post on the road to today's meeting at Killochan Castle, each one bringing them to this point in the shaping of football's future. He recalled the code words *Rider* and *Rugby*, which he and his accountancy and legal teams had used in their correspondence with Edwards. Both Knighton and Edwards were desperate for secrecy in their negotiations.

Knighton laughed, a sound carried far away on the Ayrshire winds. His fortunes were now in the ascendant, and the future was his. Edwards, in contrast, was a man in decline, a thin man, almost a ghost, already a diminishing part of the past. Knighton believed that in the depths of his bones.

* * *

Before he left Killochan, on his way to meet and collect Edwards from Glasgow Airport, Knighton turned to read the inscription above the castle's ancient entrance.

*This work was Begun the 1 Marche 1586 by Ihone Cathcart of Carlton & Helene Wallace his spous*

John and Helen, 1586, and Michael and Rosemary, 1989. Life had been glowing then, for John and his good wife.

'Marriage,' Knighton said to the winds, 'is a blessed estate, and my marriage is blessed, mine is wonderful.'

* * *

There was a time when Knighton was more lithe of foot, when life was more open to myriad and unforeseen possibilities, when less of his body was more, and when there was time for dancing.

In the autumn of 1973 Knighton was beginning his final year at Durham University when his life was changed forever by the appearance at a freshers' ball of Rosemary Croan, scion of the Edinburgh fishing dynasty founded in 1865 by her great-grandfather, Robert Croan, which later became part of the Christian Salvesen shipping and logistics conglomerate.

After the dancing, Knighton walked Rosemary back to her digs in Gilesgate, kissed her on the eyes, nose and cheeks and said, 'You are the girl that I will marry.'

He stepped back to judge the effect of his words.

The eighteen-year-old Rosemary, caught in the chiaroscuro of street light, shadow and moonlight, looked both beautiful and bewildered. She had been a student at St Hild's for only one week. She heard Knighton's soft voice as a charm, a mix of magic, black and white.

'Rosemary,' he said, 'I am poor, a working class boy with no money, but I will become a millionaire, and you will be the mother of my children.'

Knighton's words were hurrying now, sprinting for the finish line, hoping for the prize, desperate to win the race for her heart.

'Three children, that's what we'll have, two boys and a beautiful daughter, lovely as her mother.'

Knighton paused, breathless with agitation and excitement.

'I will make you very happy.'

* * *

Almost sixteen years later, as Knighton examined the legend above the gates of Killochan Castle, he realised he had kept most of the promises he had so wildly yet sincerely pledged, including the hat-trick of children – two boys and one girl. Life was full, he thought, overflowing, as it must have been in 1586 for John and Helen, the builders and the proud owners of Killochan, whose land had been gifted to them by Scotland's greatest king, Robert de Brus.

He continued to read the inscription.

*The name of the Lord is ane strang tour and the rychteous in thair troubles rinnis unto it and findeth refuge*

And here, within the runes of the stone, lay Killochan's dark and secret heart, the gift and grace of asylum.

Between the sarking and the roof were hiding-holes where, in the seventeenth century, Scots Covenanters were provided with refuge from the rampaging forces of the Stuart crown and from Cromwell's republican army of orthodoxy. There were tunnels elsewhere in the building, too, Knighton had been told, though he had not yet found them.

The tragedy of happiness, he thought, is that it has to end.

John Cathcart was the man responsible for the building of Killochan Castle, and his family members were legal advisers to the Scottish royal court.

Later, though, Covenanters, men who refused to yield to the brutal power of the state or to bend their knees before anyone but their god, used the castle as a secret meeting house. These men were rebels who had covenanted their independence as presbyters from both king and kirk.

Ayrshire, including the wooded pathway down to the river, and including the green sward about the castle, was the very heartland of resistance and repression throughout the Covenanters' fifty-year struggle against authority. Knighton walked down the hill and across a field that sloped to the Girvan Valley. He paused at the Barons' Stone, a boulder of grey granite that weighed thirty-seven tons and was thirteen yards in circumference.

Here was the meeting point of the barons of Killochan, where armies were mustered, raids planned, booty shared and unrepentant prisoners hung by the neck until they were dead. He grappled with the understanding of it all, the stomach of it all, the very innards of the castle, its wild speech, its arms outcast, and knew that nothing or no one could escape the past.

Knighton enjoyed his history and made sure he could recite it to impress Edwards during his visit. Knighton says one should know other people's history, but also make one's own history, make one's own slice of special time that will, in its turn, become the glorious past. He knew them, these Scottish martyrs, as well as he knew the dead miners from the Blackwell Colliery, as well as he remembered the Hillsborough dead. One of them, John Brown of Priesthill, a stutterer, was shot dead at his own front door in full view of his wife and children.

The Wigtown Martyrs were Margaret Lachlane and Margaret Wilson, who were tied to stakes on the beach and left to drown. It was rumoured one of the king's soldiers cut the sixty-year-old Margaret Lachlan's throat with his halberd to ease her ending.

James White was another to lose his life. He was preacher to a conventicler at Little Blackwood Farm, near Moscow in the parish of Kilmarnock. His head was severed from his body by his own farmyard axe and used as a football in a friendly game for soldiers on the burgh green close to the garrison at Newmilns, for the amusement and edification of a large crowd gathered to see the execution of the Covenanters.

And, despite the sacrifices of James Renwick's family, their scrimping and scraping and working overtime to ensure the teaching of their son at the universities of Edinburgh and of Groningen, Renwick went to the scaffold, the king's soldiers beating on their drums to silence the young man's dying words.

The brutality and callousness sent shivers down Knighton's spine.

As with the miners, as with the Liverpool supporters at Hillsborough, as with the Covenanters, it was the waste, the sheer bloody waste of all those lives, young and old, that was so appalling.

Knighton thought of his own parents, Albert and Barbara, his own education, his good fortune to escape, like Renwick, from his humble origins, the sheer bloody chance of it all, the building of the new school at Heanor Gate, just in time to prevent him continuing his lack of real education at the William Howitt School in Heanor, where he was forever naughty and where Mrs Fowler called him 'that silly boy'. In front of the rest of his classmates, this primary school teacher had humiliated him time and time again.

'The naughtiest boy in the whole school, that's Michael Knighton,' she told his parents. 'He looks intelligent, but he's not, he's just a very, very naughty boy.'

Knighton hoped his parents were proud of him, though he had moved far beyond their narrow worlds of work and sacrifice.

He hoped, too, that Martin Edwards would be impressed by Killochan.

He just knew he would be.

The land on which Knighton stood, waiting for the hired helicopter to take him to Glasgow where he would collect Edwards, was granted to the Cathcarts by Edward Bruce, King of Ireland, in 1317. The legal entitlement was confirmed by his brother, Robert Bruce, in 1324, on condition that the king was furnished with 'three sufficient spears on Christmas day at the head manor of Turnberry'.

It was early morning, a fateful Friday, and Knighton smiled at his own alliterative wit – something to calm the nerves, he thought.

He had organised his regularly used McDonnell Douglas 500E helicopter for Edwards' transport. He wanted nothing left to chance.

* * *

Knighton greeted the Manchester United chairman and chief executive in the arrival lounge. It was all very public school, and it was very significant, the idea that our words are our bonds, our handshakes are our contracts.

The two men walked to the waiting bird and in twenty-five minutes saw below them the spectacular manicured lawns of Killochan, the blaze of colour from the hibiscus borders, the castle's parkland with its 500-year-old hardwood trees and the more recent additions of eighteenth-century giant Douglas firs. It was a soft landing on the front lawn of the castle and Knighton smiled as he saw his youngest son, Rory, running to greet his returning father and the very important visitor. The boy had broken ranks from the welcoming party, who were standing, politely, restrainedly, at the edge of the lawn.

Knighton saw Rosemary, Mrs Haggerty the housekeeper and Maxwell the head gardener of the Killochan estate, and was grateful for their presence. He took Rory in his arms and introduced him to Edwards.

* * *

The tour of the castle was designed to impress and provide Edwards with the comfort and reassurance he was probably seeking in respect of his new friend. Knighton had not merely been purchasing property. The interior walls of Killochan were dressed with Scottish Old Master paintings depicting hunting scenes and Scots royalty. The staterooms were charged with fine period furniture, and one wing of the castle was devoted entirely to the style of the Adam brothers, Robert and James. Knighton loved all this stuff and had been buying fine old master paintings and period furniture for years. It was remarkable how useful it was now in proving to Edwards that he was not only a man of substance but also a man of exquisite taste. Edwards could not but be impressed.

The two men strolled through the rooms and around the grounds. Knighton led the way, through the wine cellar, through the medieval kitchen with its ancient roasting spit, and on to the secret passageway that brought the two men to the bottleneck dungeon with its ghostly guardroom.

He saw Edwards shiver.

Beyond the castle walls, Knighton showed the man from Manchester the river Girvan and the estate's two and a half miles of double bank salmon fishing. He pointed out the deep pools in which the salmon rested. He paused by the Barons' Stone, speculated as to the number of men condemned to death at this spot by the lairds of Killochan, mentioned the inalienable rights of the lairds to the local lasses living on their estate. All day, talk ran like babbling brooks through the Ayrshire countryside. It was getting to know and trust each other time.

The setting, amid the exquisite French and Italian baroque furniture, the Georgian sideboards, the gilded frames of fine paintings by Robert McGregor, John Opie, Sir Joshua Reynolds and Allan Ramsey, all within the breathing, listening but uncommunicative stone of the original castle walls, was so different from the glass, brick and steel of Old Trafford. It was the first time Knighton had had the chance to play at home in this pre-season of negotiation. He felt at ease here, surrounded by such beauty, such perfection.

He had loved art since his childhood and had collected art from the first moment he could afford to do so. It had become a private passion, and Knighton's was both as collector and as painter and sculptor. He saw his guest begin to relax.

* * *

It is easy to think that Knighton hoped he liked it here, the Manchester United majority shareholder.

Perhaps Killochan's owner thought Edwards might think well of him too, might be impressed by Knighton's discerning taste, the castle, the magnificent art and antiques, the helicopter flight, the cultured wife who loved and knew her theatre.

That there was the smell of money here, without a stench of the stuff.

It was even possible, Knighton thought, that Edwards might admire Knighton, his ability to attract a fortune or enough at least to buy a Scottish castle and a football club in Manchester. There was, too, Knighton's apparent capacity to remain free of the dirt and dreariness of money, the grubbing around for the cash, the greed for its possession.

Many believed Edwards' father had cheated for his profits, that he had sent the boys around to pressurise old ladies into selling their shares in Manchester United.

Knighton's heart went out to Edwards whenever he thought of these matters. He did not know the truth but understood well enough how wounded the son of the father must be, how he thought Edwards must wish it had not been like this, the exposure of his father in a trial by television, how the son must wish he could uphold his father by shrieking his defence from the rooftops.

What loyal and loving son would not feel this way?

Knighton also understood Edwards' protestations would fall on deaf ears because so many Manchester men and women believed the stories about his father's behaviour.

God knows, Knighton thought, Edwards had worked hard enough, tried everything to replicate his old man's success, but he didn't have as much of the grit and the graft. Throughout the eighties, Martin Edwards had endeavoured this, undertaken that, and none of it had worked quite as successfully as he would have wished.

He had regularly increased his own annual earnings as chief executive from an initial £15,000 to a current £95,781. He had essayed moneymaking schemes in partnership with Glasgow Rangers; Sunday markets had spread across Old Trafford car parks; and pop concerts had played out on the pitch. He had cut expenditure across the board including dismantling the United fourth team and curtailing some overnight hotel stays for the first team. He had paid himself dividends, which many had said should have been used for the purchase of players. Yet, through it all, Edwards must have been concerned for the weight of the personal debt incurred through the purchase of his own shareholding in the club.

Knighton understood how Edwards surely dreaded the prospect of failure at Old Trafford. He did not want to let his father, his family or himself down, but perhaps, deep down, he understood his time as supremo of Manchester United was coming to an end. That may have been why he met Knighton at Killochan, why he was in Scotland to sell his shares for the best possible price.

The lack of success on the playing field and his own inability to bring about financial prosperity had long troubled him. Perhaps he lacked vision, enjoyed merely a succession of ideas he worked hard at but which failed. The botched attempts to follow Tottenham Hotspur's lead in floating the club on the Stock Exchange and to switch his allegiance to basketball were among them.

He had rearranged the human furniture in the boardroom, allegedly easing out traditionalists such as Alan Gibson, son of the man who had saved Manchester United from oblivion in the 1930s when the club's bankers refused to allow them to draw down the players' wages. He had replaced them with younger men, some of whom might have had more pliable personalities more sympathetic to Edwards management style, and brought in United legend Bobby Charlton, whose appointment was seen by some as a public relations exercise to appease supporters, many of whom had come to hate the personal stewardship of the club by the Edwards family.

Fans had been calling for Martin Edwards' head to roll for years.

According to Michael Crick in his book, *Betrayal of a Legend*, written with David Smith, Edwards paid himself a percentage of transfer funds received. In addition, the chairman and chief executive had, allegedly, signed cheques in 1987 for the payments of dividends to shareholders after this had been voted down in a show of hands at the annual general meeting.

Edwards, too, was the first ever paid director at Old Trafford.

Knighton guessed at the financial pressure Edwards was under.

Why else was he trying to sell the football club his family had been associated with since the day following the Munich air crash in February 1958 when his father, Champagne Louis, purchased ten shares in United at £1 each and joined the board of directors?

Knighton studied the man now seated opposite him deep within the heart of Killochan Castle. He thought Edwards might be a man who may have felt he would never make ends meet, who knew there was always too much month at the end of the money. Knighton sensed, too, a suspicion of fear, of the demands of the interest payments on Edwards' rumoured debt, and a tired resignation, an understanding that, after all his efforts, he might never be loved or appreciated by the fans at Old Trafford, those who maintained their steadfast support despite another defeat, another disappointing season that failed to match their high expectations.

Now Knighton looked even harder at Edwards, decided that the man with whom he had shared a delightful day might be concerned lest he lose it all, lest his shares might become worthless, that he was ready now to exit.

He must be a desperate man, Knighton concluded, to be on the brink of cashing in his investment in a football club that was clearly still dear to his heart.

It seemed clear to Knighton that here was a man who wanted out and that he was the man to show him the way.

* * *

It was approaching midnight, the witching hour.

The two men had enjoyed their walks and their talks and they had luxuriated in the salmon starter – 'fished from our very own river, Martin' – and in the slabs of prime Scottish beefsteak that followed. Their conversations had been washed down by the finest wines from Knighton's impressive cellar. They then retired to the Great Hall and to their bottles of Bordeaux and Glenfiddich single malt.

They had been negotiating through most of July and early August but money had never been mentioned. It was so public school, this refusal to countenance the existence of the crude power that money might bring to the relationship. It was like two sweethearts playing circle games, round and round and round, all the while pretending that it was not sex that would bring them together but love.

The time was coming, though, and neither Knighton nor Edwards were virgins. They had feasted well and the fire was roaring and crackling in the massive hearth. Knighton had chosen an eighteenth-century baroque throne chair and offered Edwards the smaller Turkish red silk-clad ottoman stool. He watched as Edwards pulled yet another cigarette from his shiny, golden Benson & Hedges pack. Cheap, Knighton thought, but not quite tawdry.

There were beads of sweat on Edwards' brow. As well as the blazing fire, the central heating was cranked to maximum. It was warm enough, Knighton admitted to himself but not to his companion. Knighton put down his wine glass and heard its protest as it jarred on the expensive walnut of the coffee table. He leaned forward ever so gently, ever so persuasively.

'Martin,' he said, with all the seductive power and aura of a king in his castle, 'we've been talking and talking now for weeks and weeks and we've discussed everything that one would have expected us to discuss, all save for one critical thing.'

Knighton watched, Knighton waited, Knighton smiled, as he saw more small bubbles of perspiration break on Edwards' forehead, saw them coalesce and trickle slowly down the sides of his new friend's cheeks.

'And that,' Knighton said, 'is money.'

He swirled the claret in his glass and took a measured sip of the burgundy wine.

'And you know, Martin, throughout all the weeks we have been talking, you've never told me how much you want for your shares.'

Knighton's eyes were wide, fixed in a gambler's stare.

'So the time has come for you to name your price.'

Edwards looked down at the floor, studied the rich colours of the Turkish carpet beneath his feet. He drew long and hard on his cigarette, and Knighton waited, for numbers, pounds and maybe pence, to be exhaled from Edwards' mouth. He raised his tumbler of whisky to his lips as a poker player raises his cards to cover his face. There was silence as deep as doubt which seemed to last into another age, and yet it lasted only seconds. Knighton knew the stakes had been raised.

He glanced at the heavy, ornate French gilt clock to his left, the one decorated with nymphs and swans, the one that sat high and proud on the mantel of the great fireplace. It was 11.55. His confidence, his certainty, returned. It would be nice, he thought, if this deal could be done by the stroke of midnight. He looked at Edwards, watched him draw once more on his cigarette. The pressure, Knighton thought, he is under the most extreme pressure.

He reminded himself that the secret of successful negotiation was to insist that the other person named the price. He waited for Edwards to speak, understanding all too well the man's almost certain desperation to unburden himself of his shareholding; his imperative and impatience to sell oozed from his body like the sweat that now washed his face.

'Michael,' he heard Edwards say, 'I want £20 per share, £10 million clear, and I will not take less.'

The Manchester United owner's voice betrayed the quality of a painted porcelain vase, slightly cracked, slightly chipped and cheapened.

Now it was Knighton's turn to let the seconds of silence tick by before he showed any signs of responding, one way or the other. He knew Manchester United shares were changing hands at £5 or £6, and on the face of it Edwards' valuation of £20 per share appeared excessive. But Knighton had his independent valuation of the club and would have paid twice as much, or even £60, £70 or £80 per share. This was unbelievable; this was the deal of the century and it would be the deal of all deals in football history.

He waited for precisely twenty seconds, playing Edwards like a fish on the end of a line. He guessed that maybe Edwards could not see the wood for the trees with respect to the true future value of Manchester United. Some said Edwards rarely, if ever, visited the Cliff training ground where youngsters such as Giggs, Sharpe, Neville and Scholes were already strutting their stuff. Knighton would have been there, appreciating their talent every day, had he been the owner of Manchester United.

In his *Football Blueprint,* Knighton had already valued Manchester United at £150m, so an asking price of £10m together with a further £10m commitment to redevelop the Stretford End and a few quid for buying players was a bargain of the highest order. But he had still not replied to Edwards' asking price. He preferred to watch the profusely sweating Edwards for a little longer.

The hiatus lasted only a moment but Knighton deliberately made it a tad longer than Edwards' earlier pregnant pause. It seemed a lifetime. He swirled the wine in his crystal glass, cast another glance at the huge French mantel clock, then rose to his feet and shot out his right hand.

'Deal, Martin, we have a deal, the deal is done,' said Knighton.

'Deal done,' replied a smiling and relieved Edwards.

The two men grasped each other's shoulders, like brothers, rather than clumsy lovers, and Knighton heard the gilded French clock on the mantelpiece chime midnight, as if sealing the gilded deal to end all gilded deals.

An essence of any successful deal, Knighton knew, was that both parties be deliriously happy. Both men were: Edwards because he had secured his escape from the trap of personal debt and from the pressures of coping with a toxic combination of disgruntled fans and suspected boardroom conspirators; Knighton because he had secured his ownership of one of the greatest institutions in world sport. And at a truly bargain-basement price. The two men continued their talk into the small hours before climbing the ancient spiral stone staircase to their respective sleeping quarters for the night.

The castle walls breathed in more history.

* * *

In the morning, Edwards was still glowing. After a long lie in, and a hearty full English breakfast, he was happy. He would be debt-free for the first time in his adult life, and a multi-millionaire. Edwards had possibly been expecting Knighton to haggle, to barter and batter him down, and he may well have taken considerably less than the agreed price in spite of his avowed intent to take not a penny less. For him, £20 per share represented an extremely handsome premium price. He was still hoping not to wake from a dream and find Knighton negotiating him down to a tenner a go.

The only blip on Edwards' horizon was the members of the Manchester United board. All save one, Maurice Watkins, the football club's lawyer and close confidant of Edwards, had been kept in the dark about the chairman's negotiations with Knighton. And all bar Watkins would be devastated by the news of Edwards' apostasy, his betrayal.

Edwards was not looking forward to the inevitably angry reactions of Midani and his cohorts who had hoped, some claimed, to win control of the club for themselves. In the final analysis, however, Edwards had found an exit strategy that he believed was an honourable one, and, in the nicest possible way he told himself, he little cared for what the other United directors might think about him selling his shares without consultation. They were, after all, his to dispose of in any way he saw fit. The problem was no longer his problem. Before he left Killochan, Edwards hugged Knighton close and shook hands once again. That was how public school gentlemen did their deals.

* * *

Some time later, the paperwork was drawn up by the parties' respective lawyers, and both Edwards and Knighton signed the binding option to purchase agreement. It was done and it was done well. A few days later, Edwards handed Knighton the keys to the kingdom, including those to the chairman's office and all other areas of Old Trafford. He was even given the keys to the underground garage that had always been Edwards' private domain.

* * *

As for the other deal, the one with Graham Sharpe at William Hill, agreed and confirmed in writing, it was never followed through by Knighton – he didn't place the bet. Perhaps he was too busy. Perhaps, like Don Quixote, he merely enjoyed the tilting at these windmills of power and had no use for razing them to the ground. Winning the bet would have destroyed both Sharpe and William Hill. Knighton said he had no stomach to bring a good man like Sharpe and his family to their knees, or the desire to bring the game he loved into disrepute. After all, as the new owner of Manchester United, he now had propriety to consider.

Eight years later, Sharpe claimed in his book *Gambling on Goals* that he unmasked and foiled Knighton's betting coup. Knighton was saddened by Sharpe's recollections, which were so different from his own. He immediately telephoned the odds maker, and once Sharpe was reminded of the facts, he apologised and confessed to his inaccurate memories.

'Thank God, though, Michael, you never placed the bet,' Sharpe said. 'It would have ruined me and the company too, bankrupted them.'

Knighton agreed to let the bookmaker's errors now die, but he kept a tape recording of their conversation, just in case his truth-telling concerning this episode was contradicted again.

He is a stickler for all kinds of truths, is Knighton.

Curiously, however, even in 2019, the unplaced bet remains one of the regrets of Knighton's life.

'You know, I could have ended world poverty at a stroke, fed the starving millions with the winnings, at the very least provided clean drinking water throughout Africa.'

These are big regrets. I asked Knighton whether he thought Alex Ferguson would have allowed him to don a Red Devils shirt and step on to the pitch in an FA Cup Final.

'Seriously, I think Fergie would have agreed if he had been told the proceeds were all going to charity.

'Just think of it, it's the last minute of the Cup Final replay against Palace. It's May 1990, it's Wembley, it's magic, it's wonderful. It's 1-0 to United and we can't lose it now, even if Knighton comes on just seconds before the final whistle.'

I smiled indulgently.

'If Fergie had allowed me to take just one step upon the pitch, the bet was won and the winning cash comes raining down, and it would have been an even bigger story than Knighton buying Manchester United.'

'It doesn't bear thinking about, Michael,' I said.

Of course, the whole of that shebang depended, not only on Knighton placing his bet, but also on his completion of the deal to buy Manchester United from Edwards.

Chapter Nine

# Problems at the Back: Moles and Leaks

## *Old Trafford, Thursday 17 August 1989*

EVENTUALLY, ON 17 August, Edwards told his boardroom colleagues of his intention to sell the club to Knighton. He explained that the die was cast and the deal was done and dusted, right down to all the legal stuff, too, in respect of signing and exchanging the option agreement. There was a watertight option to purchase agreement in Knighton's favour. The sole task remaining was for the new man's accounting and due diligence teams to inspect the club's books and property title deeds. It would take a few more weeks but this process was a mere formality.

'The deal is irreversible,' Edwards told his disgruntled colleagues.

He had, though, left his confession unconscionably late and only decided to summon his fellow directors when he was warned that the news was out. That delay may have caused the trouble that followed the announcement of the deal.

Michael Edelson and Bobby Charlton were unavailable for the initial meeting and were briefed only minutes before the storm broke. There would be a formal press conference the following day, Edwards said.

In fact, in spite of all their self-righteous protestations and indignations, the news was probably not news to some members of the United boardroom, and certainly not to one of their number, Nigel Burrows, who feigned ignorance. There was allegedly a coterie of four directors – headed by Midani – who may have already been scheming to buy the club for themselves.

These men, it seemed likely, had their ears close to the ground, although it was possible that Charlton was caught unawares, as he had been on holiday at an inopportune time.

It was also possible that Burrows and Midani were hoping to proceed independently of the absent former footballer, or maybe to have presented the returning Charlton with a *fait accompli* and used him as a publicly acceptable figurehead for their own ambitions.

* * *

Edwards had insisted on secrecy throughout his dealings with Knighton but had spoken often of his fear of a mole inside the boardroom.

He did not suspect Maurice Watkins, however, who had been on the inside track with Edwards from the beginning. The football club's solicitor was someone the chairman appeared to trust with many of his inner secrets. Watkins had been involved with the minutiae of the deal, with dotting i's and crossing t's and with providing access to enable Knighton's team to perform the preliminary due diligence on the club's finances.

Watkins had been Edwards' right-hand, go-to man since he was invited to join the board on the same day as Charlton, in May 1984. The move had been part of the young chairman's putsch against his father's old guard, the old-timer allies that also included Sir Matt Busby, who resigned from his directorship.

Both Edwards and Watkins were smooth men, hair neatly controlled or, in the lawyer's case, prematurely vanishing. Watkins was a Manchester Grammar boy with a law degree from University College, London. His academic success contrasted with that of Edwards who gained his six O Levels after multiple sittings at Cokethorpe, a minor public school in Oxfordshire.

Watkins was a partner in the prestigious Manchester law firm, James Chapman & Co, and had worked for the Edwards family since 1976 when one of his first real jobs was to smooth the sacking of Tommy Docherty following the manager's affair with the club physiotherapist's wife. Curiously, as a footnote to that sordid business, it was the young Martin Edwards who dealt with the initial confessional call from Docherty at his father's home in Alderley Edge.

Now Edwards was fielding questions from his fellow directors about his proposed sale of the club to a man whose name was unknown to all bar Watkins and Burrows. The lawyer was silent and the former Stretford Ender was garrulous. All of these shareholders, however, stood to make fortunes if the deal was concluded as Knighton was required to make the same £20 per share offer to all shareholders.

None of the directors admitted to prior knowledge of the deal with Knighton.

The source of the leak, however, was impossible to locate, although Burrows, according to Edwards, had to be a prime suspect.

Burrows, a fanatic from the terraces, was seen by some as a rough diamond, a wide boy of the board. To Knighton, at least, and probably to any prospective purchaser of the football club, Burrows was not one of its obvious assets. Knighton thought him anathema, an unfathomable loose cannon, unprofessional and lacking in integrity, a bruising brute of a man. Years later, after he had resigned as a director, as reported on both television and in the press, Burrows was arrested for alleged fraud.

Edwards told Knighton that he suspected the former Stretford Ender had overheard a conversation in which his wife, Susan, had been talking about the purchase of an expensive house in the Lake District, which Burrows would have known that Edwards could not afford, as the chairman had repeatedly complained about the state of his overdraft. Burrows, Edwards surmised, would have guessed that Edwards had agreed a deal to sell his shareholding.

But, in fact, it was worse than that. Edwards had not told Knighton the truth.

On the club's summer Far East tour, he had revealed to Burrows the outline of the forthcoming deal and had sworn him to secrecy.

It seemed an extraordinary thing to do.

Knighton even wondered what kind of hold Burrows might have had on the United chairman, what knowledge Burrows might have possessed that Edwards did not want made public.

So much for Edwards' apparent desire for secrecy and for his integrity.

Knighton, in contrast, had told no one bar his wife and the professionals working with him on the deal, including Bob Thornton, a respected City figure and former chairman of Debenhams, and close friend of Knighton's to boot.

Whatever their respective grouses, Burrows and Midani were seething with anger when they realised that Edwards had done the deal with Knighton behind their backs.

It is easy to imagine cries of *Why not sell to us? You knew we wanted to buy you out!*

This was precisely why Edwards had tried – and failed – to conduct the negotiations with as much discretion as possible. The previous day's final edition of *The Sun* had run with the story of a possible sale of Manchester United and, inside its pages, it was Burrows, and then Midani, who were shouting the loudest, protesting the hardest.

Why not sell to them indeed? God knows, Edwards might have thought, Midani has the money. Or, at least, his father and family may have. Not Midani, though, not with his gambling losses at the casino. This was the man who had lost more than £20 million at various roulette tables.

Edwards really had made some questionable appointments as fellow directors of Manchester United.

'Why not sell to these people?' Knighton asked.

'Propriety perhaps,' Edwards explained. Knighton had become, if not exactly a friend, an ally in the breach.

'Midani,' Edwards says, 'he's not one of us.'

Knighton was uncomfortable with Edwards' prejudiced explanation. Less propriety, Knighton thought, more squeamishness, more old school English and implied racism, even if it had been unintentional.

Later, Knighton would speak highly of Midani as he came to know him better as a fellow director.

'I could never sell Manchester United to a foreigner – well not an Arab anyway – if you see what I mean, Michael. Please don't get me wrong, I like Midani, but they, the fans and the press, would string me up if I let the club go to a foreigner.'

You were happy enough to talk to Maxwell, Knighton thought, until you discovered his bad table manners. But he held his peace. In times to come, Edwards would show fewer scruples concerning the selling of shares to foreigners. The irony of Manchester City's second consecutive Premier League title under Arab ownership, in 2019, may not be lost on Edwards. In fact, since the takeover of City in September 2008 by the Abu Dhabi United Group headed by Sheikh Mansour bin Zayed Al Nahyan, they have won four Premier League titles, four Football League Cups and two FA Cups.

* * *

Burrows was easier to dismiss as a potential recipient of Edwards' shares.

Knighton thought the man a chancer, a guttersnipe never to be trusted, and Edwards said nothing to signify disagreement with this view. Burrows was 6ft 2in and burly, and was later to become the rabble rouser of the anti-Knighton brigade, a fanatic in the worst senses of the word. He was a man, Edwards told Knighton, who always put self-advancement first.

Burrows' rant, following the leak of Edwards' deal, showed him to be a man watching his power base, built up over the previous year since buying a place on Edwards' board, disappearing over the horizon.

'Who is this man?' Burrows demanded, meaning Knighton.

It was a question everyone now wanted answering.

## Chapter Ten

# The Press Conference

*Old Trafford*
*Friday 18 August 1989*

THE LIGHTS in the Old Trafford trophy room were blazing and there was not a seat left in the house. The rumours of the sale of the most famous football club in England, were, it seemed, about to be confirmed. The conference started inauspiciously with Edwards introducing Knighton as Michael Whetton, who was the Old Trafford catering manager.

'Get it right, Martin,' Knighton hissed.

The new man still smiled, however, eager to cover for Edwards' nervous incompetence. There were muffled guffaws and whispered sniggers among the grizzled hacks who spotted the gaffe before the clearly nervous Manchester United chairman corrected his error.

Curiously, and laughably, this would not be the only time Edwards got names wrong.

Ten years later, while introducing Steve McClaren as Ferguson's new assistant manager to the press, Edwards called him Steve McClaridge.

* * *

The press now knew Knighton's correct name but still, understandably, the first and last questions were lightning strikes in the stormy air.

*Who is this man?* Who *is* this man?

This was the burning question on all minds.

'Where has he come from? What is his background?'

Since reports of the possibility of an impending sale had reached the mainstream media via both BBC News and ITV News at Ten the previous evening, there had been frenzied speculation. Many thought the Kelly dynasty at Celtic Football Club was involved, a rumour Manchester United's Catholic roots did nothing to dispel. The one person no one had mentioned, because no one had heard of him, was Knighton.

*Who is this man?*

Knighton was keen, anxious perhaps, to answer this question, and any other questions the media had prepared for him. To the surprise of most of the hacks in the room, he came across as an accomplished public speaker as he announced exactly who he was and why he was there. He was confident, self-assured and, as the press conference progressed, began to enjoy himself. He was unblinking in the lights, polite in the face of persistence, articulate in giving information.

He was asked about previous connections with Manchester United and understood the need to establish his credentials. But he would not reinvent his past to please the media.

'I am a football fan but not a fanatic.'

He paused, and the assembled press waited, already hanging on his every word.

'There is a difference between someone who is a fan and a lover of the game and an obsessive who believes football to be the most important thing in the world, which it most clearly is not.'

'How many times have you seen United play?'

Knighton smiled, aware of the journalist's attempt to put him down.

'Only a few times, alas, but please understand I am a fan of football in general, I am not a fanatic of just one club.'

Still he smiled, but the lights were bright and the cameras were popping, and he could not really see the people he had hoped to charm with his honesty.

'Fanatics,' he said, 'are sometimes dangerous.'

He turned for support from Edwards, but the chairman was sweating profusely under the lights and under pressure to compose his own answers.

'I have always appreciated Manchester United,' Knighton said, 'the way they have played their football, the traditions of the club.'

'But who are you?' a hack shouted from the back of the room.

'I remember,' he said, 'my father taking me to the Baseball Ground to see Derby County in the FA Cup. We were thrashed 5-2 by United; George Best was the inspiration of that United team and scored two magnificent goals.'

It was Knighton's way of answering the question.

All eyes were on him.

'It will be my privilege,' he continued, 'to restore this club to greatness, to compete each year in Europe, to win a trophy every year. But, in order to ensure this, there has to be commercial success, too.'

Knighton was already starting to give away his secrets, his strategy.

'We have to start winning trophies.'

'What about the manager, Mr Knighton?'

'Who am I,' he replied, 'to question a man like Alex?'

'Is Ferguson's job safe with you?'

'Look,' Knighton said, 'Alex Ferguson was the man responsible for breaking the mould of Scottish football. With Aberdeen, he demolished the domination of their game by Celtic and Rangers.'

Ferguson had managed Aberdeen from 1978 to 1986 and, allowing him a couple of years to get his feet under the table and his ideas across to his players, in the seven seasons from 1980 he won three Scottish League championships and four Scottish FA Cups. Prior to 1980, the Old Firm of Rangers and Celtic, the Glasgow giants, had won the previous fourteen championships between them. Since Ferguson's departure, the Scottish championship has returned to either Celtic Park or Ibrox, the home of Rangers, for thirty-four consecutive seasons.

'For me,' Knighton said, 'the manager has nothing to prove.'

'But is his job secure?'

Hacks from all directions were asking the same question.

'Alex has come,' Knighton continued, 'to the greatest football club in the world and he knows that people are expecting trophies in the cabinet.'

'Would that be the end for Fergie, then, if he failed to deliver those trophies?'

'He has 250 per cent support from me,' the new man said, in order to emphasise the complete support he wished to offer the manager.

Aside from the dodgy mathematics, which Knighton hoped the press would excuse as the enthusiastic exaggeration of a newcomer to this kind of thing, he could not, he thought, have been clearer.

'But I will require a trophy every year and Alex Ferguson knows that.'

The situation was now 250 per cent clear.

* * *

Knighton had already met Ferguson forty-eight hours earlier and had said he was very much looking forward to working with the manager and to taking the club forward.

At their meeting, Ferguson had been polite, listening rather than talking, assessing rather than judging. This initial encounter was the beginning of a remarkable collaboration, an axis of outsiders and of revolutionaries, both accidental and unacknowledged but real enough, nonetheless. Over time, it would produce one of the greatest partnerships in sporting history, though it was destined to be unappreciated for the best part of the next three decades.

After his initial introduction to Knighton, Ferguson told the press that the newcomer was an impressive young man with confidence to burn.

Given the outstanding successes that followed at Old Trafford, both on the field of play and on the financial balance sheet, it is easy to forget how precarious Ferguson's position was in the summer of 1989 and how ill-conceived and unimaginative was the club's commercial base, how relatively cheapskate and penurious it all was at Manchester United. The fans wanted Edwards gone, and Fergie, too. There were regular chants from home crowds for the board to sack the manager, and there were serious doubts among the powers that be at Old Trafford that Ferguson was the right man to bring back the glory years. In fact, in early 1990, just a few months later, Alex Ferguson was just one defeat from dismissal.

At the turn of the year the team were languishing in fifteenth place in spite of the heady opening-day optimism in the sunshine in the preceding August, when Knighton showed off his ball-juggling skills on the Old Trafford pitch, when United beat the champions, Arsenal, 4-1, all this after the costly recruitment of Gary Pallister, Paul Ince, Neil Webb and Mike Phelan.

They had suffered nine league defeats including a 5-1 whipping at Maine Road, the home of Manchester City.

That leathering occurred on 23 September 1989, when Knighton was still smiling, still signing autographs, still sitting in directors' boxes and still carrying his trademark portable phone in case good news arrived from elsewhere. It was Knighton who had authorised the record-breaking signing of Gary Pallister, but this new player, together with other new signings, was still not adjusting to life at Old Trafford.

If the players were disappointed – Pallister said the 5-1 debacle was the lowest point of his career – the manager was devastated.

Pallister described Alex Ferguson as being 'in shock and practically speechless'. Observers were waiting for the inevitable axe to fall on Ferguson's neck and waiting to watch his head roll out of the gates at Old Trafford and down the Warwick Road. By January, 1990, there was frenzy amongst fans and in the red top press to see Ferguson sacked from his post.

Ferguson's last chance was in the FA Cup in which United had been drawn to face Brian Clough's Nottingham Forest, on 7 January, a formidable task at their rival's City Ground. The pitch was a midwinter devil of a mud beach at low tide. Floodlights were peering through the blear and grime as Mark Hughes received the ball on the left wing and curled it with the outside of his right boot around two defenders and into the flight path of Mark Robins, a young product of the United youth system. Robins headed the ball into the Forest net for a desperate but critical victory. Knighton turned and hugged fellow directors, and said to all who would listen, 'The FA Cup is ours this year, I feel it in my bones. Lady Destiny is with us.'

Robins' goal was the one reputed to have saved Fergie's bacon, though it would be just as accurate to highlight the serial missed chances of the Forest attackers in the second half, or the disallowed Forest goal three minutes from the end of the match. United goalkeeper Jim Leighton had flapped at the ball like a wounded albatross with the ball ending up in the net. Ferguson, momentarily, must have felt the fear of failure flail about his heart just as Leighton had flailed and failed to gather in the ball.

Fergie's job at Old Trafford had been saved, not only by Robins' goal, but also by a referee's whistle for a dubious foul on the United goalkeeper.

Manchester United progressed by beating Hereford United 1-0, Newcastle United 3-2 and Sheffield United 1-0, all away from home, and in the semi-final beat Oldham Athletic 2-1 after a replay. At Wembley they defeated Crystal Palace 1-0, also in the replay after an initial 3-3 draw. This made irrelevant any doubts about Ferguson as manager.

With the issue of the manager's position settled for the foreseeable future, an unspoken, unacknowledged axis between Knighton and Ferguson, the newcomer and the manager, began to blossom. The relationship between the two men remained enigmatic and indeterminate, and always completely unacknowledged by the parties concerned, but produced results. Knighton and Ferguson worked in separate worlds, moved along parallel lines that were distances apart, and yet they had a symbiotic relationship, each feeding from the other's success in their individual spheres of influence.

Every penny brought into the club's coffers as a result of Knighton's commercial reforms was made available for the strengthening of Ferguson's team, and each new trophy Ferguson's players won for the club strengthened the commercial potential of Manchester United and improved the ability to win new and profitable commercial contracts, as recommended in Knighton's financial *Blueprint*.

Not that Edwards would probably ever acknowledge that obvious fact.

The relationship between Knighton and Ferguson, however, did not begin so harmoniously.

According to Ferguson's autobiography, *Managing My Life*, Knighton's showboating on the pitch on the first day of the new season annoyed the manager, who felt it was detrimental to his team's preparation for the match. At the time, however, Ferguson said nothing about it to Knighton, and the fact that the display of ball juggling by the chairman elect preceded United's best display of the 1989/90 season might suggest the manager should have requested a repeat show prior to every home match. If Ferguson was at all displeased by Knighton's admittedly extraordinary antics on the Old Trafford pitch, he soon cheered up when the new man solidly supported the manager's desire for fresh blood, for bringing in new players.

Early in the morning of Saturday, 26 August, prior to a depressing 2-0 defeat at Derby County after which Manchester United fell to an unacceptable ninth in the First Division, Knighton, in his role as chairman elect and seen by the manager as the effective new owner of Manchester United, was asked by Ferguson and Edwards to come to a meeting at Old Trafford. The confirmation of Knighton's takeover awaited only the results of due diligence reports, with the option agreement for the sale and purchase contract between Knighton and Edwards having been signed and exchanged weeks before. When Knighton arrived in a side room adjacent to the main boardroom, Ferguson came straight to the point.

'Michael,' he said, 'how much money can I spend?'

The manager's eyes were as wide as a boy's in a sweetshop. 'I'd like to buy Gary Pallister from Middlesbrough, but his club won't budge unless I go higher than the £1.8m I've already put on the table, and the chairman, Martin, says that's it, no more cash is available.'

Knighton was in no mood for hesitation.

'Go ahead, Alex, go and get him, whatever it costs. You have my full backing and support; we must buy this player today.'

Ferguson's smile widened, his eyes widened, whether in relief or in disbelief it was hard to tell.

'We more than need him right now,' Knighton said. 'In fact, break the bank, and go and break the British transfer record to get him.' Knighton spoke with an assurance drawn from his satisfaction with the deal he had done with Edwards. 'This club's going nowhere without Pallister,' he added.

Ferguson could hardly believe his ears.

Neither could Edwards for that matter.

Previously, Edwards had stalled the deal at £1.8m, baulking at Middlesbrough's asking price of more than £2m. Ferguson still looked in need of reassurance, so Knighton said, 'Alex, go back to Middlesbrough Football Club. Manchester United will pay whatever we have to, and that is a personal guarantee from me, Alex; that's what we must do.'

Ferguson stared at the chairman elect, still incredulous. The last the manager had heard from Edwards on this point – and also often in the past – was a lecture on the necessity for financial probity. Indeed, Edwards had been fond of saying, 'If we carry on buying players, Alex, we'll be forever in the financial mire.'

Knighton was already initiating a financial revolution within the club.

'Alex,' he said, 'we've no choice, just go and do the deal, today, now, I'm insisting. Phone Middlesbrough now and tell them the deal is sanctioned at board level.'

'Oh,' said Ferguson, then nodded an agreement and made for the door.

The manager's hand was on the door but Knighton was not quite finished yet.

'You know better than I do, Alex, the team needs fresh blood.'

Knighton smiled at the witticism to come.

'Indeed, in my view we need a transfusion if we're ever going to turn around the current situation. And make sure the deals for Paul Ince and Danny Wallace are home and dry, too,' Knighton added, referring to the talented, young West Ham United midfielder and the speedy, tricky Southampton winger.

Ferguson was backed by Knighton 100 per cent and an embryonic partnership was up and running. Edwards, meanwhile, shrugged his shoulders, appearing reluctant in his agreement, but deferring to this new alliance, and perhaps thinking, *It's not my money anymore, it's Knighton's money they're spending now.*

What was indisputable, however, was that Gary Pallister was now on his way to Old Trafford, and the Manchester United money tree had been shaken like it never had been before. Knighton had made his points. He had demonstrated his solid support for his team manager and outlined the new direction the club would take under his leadership.

'I had to show everyone concerned that the man heading up this new regime was prepared to put his own and the club's money where his mouth was in a thoroughgoing drive towards success,' Knighton said later. 'That stance was essential to the whole project.'

During the sixty-two days when Knighton was chairman elect, he initiated a revolution at Old Trafford.

'It had to be done, and it had to be done this way, to bring the only people that really matter at football clubs onside – the supporters and the team manager.'

Without this period of clear leadership, without Knighton's authorisation of player purchases, it is probably fair to assume that nothing fundamental would have changed at Old Trafford in the immediate and foreseeable future; mediocrity would have continued under Edwards as officially enshrined club policy.

The eventual signing of Pallister, on 29 August 1989, less than two weeks after Knighton's debut on the Old Trafford pitch, marked the end of an era of austerity at Manchester United. It had been a decade of Edwardian penny-pinching, during which time the club had missed out on numerous transfer targets, including, in the previous summer, England's finest young talent, Paul Gascoigne, who signed for Spurs because of the London club's superior offer.

To add insult to Ferguson's ire and injury over the lost deal, Gazza signed for Tottenham while Edwards was supposedly sunning himself at Midani's Marbella Club in Spain. Now, with the promised money in his back pocket, Ferguson had to be glad to see the back of Edwards. After all, it was only two years since the new manager had gone public with his complaints about the chairman's parsimony.

'I came here thinking I would have the luxury of buying players,' he had said in 1987. 'I have done a lot of hard work at youth level but to win the league we have to buy. The chairman is now facing two very tough choices between having a very good team or balancing the books. It is impossible to have both at present.' Ferguson's analysis was spot on, and remained true until 1989. With Edwards as chairman and chief executive it was impossible to have cake and eat it, but with Michael Knighton, Ferguson saw that it might well be very different. His analysis was correct.

Knighton did not plan to develop and exploit the commercial revenue streams of the club in order to finance and finesse his own bank overdraft, and stated quite clearly at the press conference on 18 August that he would take no salary from the club. Instead, he wanted to overhaul the financial side of the club so that Ferguson could rebuild the team, so that Manchester United could be restored to its former glory and so that Fergie could emulate Matt Busby in winning league championships and the European Cup. Ferguson could see all this the moment

Knighton effectively said to him, *We need Pallister, go back and spend what it takes.*

Knighton also had a broader vision, encompassing the football industry in general.

'I feel passionately about this game,' he told the assembled hacks and blinking cameras at his initial press conference. 'My ancestors were involved in football at the inception of professional sport in this country. My roots in the game are there for all to see. And now,' he breathed deeply, 'it is my turn to contribute.'

Knighton wanted to overturn the class thing about football – all the stuff about it being a working class sport.

'This is everyone's game,' he pleaded, 'and it belongs equally to the directors in the boardroom and businessmen in the executive boxes as well as to the people on the terraces.'

This was radical, though not necessarily populist stuff.

'We are all supporters now.' He paused for effect. 'Even prime ministers are in on the act. It has become a fundamental prerequisite for every politician, and certainly the PM of the day, to declare their colours, to nail them to the mast of one club or another.'

In this, as in other matters, Knighton was prescient.

Tony Blair was always keen to declare his undying devotion to Newcastle United and David Cameron – in spite of his inability to tell Aston Villa from West Ham – was also keen to cash in on the football phenomenon.

Knighton, though, was frustrated with the mismanagement of the industry at the highest levels, the people who had allowed these class divisions to fester, allowed the beautiful game to fall into ugly disrepute, facilitated the equation of football with yobs, louts and hooligans, and the violence that was the inevitable bedfellow of inequality. His face clouded as he spoke.

He was proud of his working class origins – and proud of rising above them – but he could not recognise his father's values of hard work and thrift, of community and solidarity, in any of the mindless, nihilistic, ongoing orgy of destructive energy that was blackening the name of the sport he had loved since childhood.

He did not say this but he thought it: *these hooligans, they are not working class because they have descended far beneath any class of civilisation I can conceive of.*

In Knighton's eyes, football's hooligans were simply uncivilised, pathetic yobs who rode on the back of sport simply to attract attention to themselves and their warped and evil views of the world.

What he did say, however, was that he wanted to make a difference.

'Yes,' he admitted, 'the disaster at Hillsborough, more than ninety dead at the stadium where my great-grandfather used to ply his trade, was a tipping point. And yes again, I am sufficiently arrogant to believe what I am saying is worth saying. This game simply has to change, and the way we treat our supporters is crucial to that change.'

Part of Knighton's deal with Edwards was the funding of a £10m redevelopment of the Stretford End, the old banked concrete terracing, spiritual home of generations of United fans but also the breeding ground of violence and vitriol, of a fanaticism that had replaced both class and community.

'I believe,' he told the journalists, 'in encouraging whole family attendance at sport and in the provision of spectator comfort and security. I want to create an environment in which people feel they almost have to wipe their feet before entering a football stadium.'

In 1989, the year of Hillsborough and of cages to contain the animal behaviour of football hoodlums, and of race riots in Dewsbury, IRA bombs in Shropshire, book burnings in Bradford and the introduction of electronic tagging of criminals, Knighton's vision was not just revolutionary but also seemed ridiculously idealistic and naïve.

'The supporters,' he said, 'are the real owners of Manchester United. The supporters should own the entire industry wherever that is possible.'

This was visionary stuff.

'Of course we can all still shout and rant and rage and cheer, but we will all of us, those on the terraces and those in the executive boxes, all share in the same culture. I see football as a great social leveller.'

This was sport as social engineering, and social engineering at its best, not worst.

This was also the year, however, when the gutter press had already descended to the cesspits and the sewers, with *The Sun* running its fabricated stories of Liverpool fans stealing from the pockets of the dead and dying at Hillsborough, pissing on the police and beating up constables who were giving dying fans the kiss of life.

Press coverage of Knighton's entrance on to the public stage, of his initial press conference, however, was mostly positive and occasionally flattering. Peter Fitton in *The Sun* reported factually and accurately on the bones of the deal with Edwards and his back-page headline writer opted for a relatively sober screamer: *£40M. That's what the new boss will spend to make United great again.*

The report deconstructed the shocking total as £10m for Fergie to spend on new players, £10.8m for Edwards, £10m for other shareholders if they wished to sell and £10m for the Stretford End.

Edwards was reported as saying, 'This is a pressure job and I've been in it for ten years. It's right for me to go because I believe the club can now go in a new direction with more financial backing.' This was somewhat disingenuous of Edwards. The deal with Knighton specified that Edwards would continue as the salaried chief executive of Manchester United for at least the next three years.

There was only one sour note to the press proceedings. Tommy Docherty, the former United manager sacked for sexual impropriety, stuck his dizzy head above the parapet and said, '£20m is peanuts for Manchester United. I wouldn't sell it for £500m and nor would Matt Busby.'

Aside from the doubling of the price agreed with Edwards, accounted for by the new man's commitment to rebuild the Stretford End, Knighton would have agreed with the Doc's every word. He knew the Old Trafford empire would in time be worth even more than half a billion pounds.

While Knighton had described himself at the press conference as 'a very emotional and shy person', he would soon find that his enemies would not be shy in coming forward. He would discover, over the next few weeks and months, emotions he never suspected existed, and would come to understand his supposed shyness would be no defence. Shyness, though, does take many forms.

The day after the press conference, Knighton paraded his showmanship on the pitch at Old Trafford. He has always maintained that such an act needed to be done, simply to show the fans that he was not just one more businessman come to exploit a football club.

'I was a football fan first and a businessman second. At the time, in 1989, there was a massive disconnection between the boardroom and the terraces. I had to bring the two sides of the club together if we were to see the club prosper going forward. And just look at the faces of the fans on that opening day of the season when I appeared on the pitch. They were smiling, they were happy, and they were excited, just as all fans should be at a football match.'

At this stage, Knighton was still reading the papers but perhaps should have taken more note of the Docherty intervention, especially its affecting and baggage-ridden reference to one of his predecessors as manager, the Munich survivor and European Cup-winning legend, Matt Busby.

There was more to come, much, much more like this, and worse, from pundits and reporters in the British gutter press.

* * *

Perhaps Knighton thought he was consolidating his position within the club when he asked Edwards if he could meet Busby before any formal announcements were made. Perhaps he imagined the elder statesman would be an important ally in any battles that might ensue. Perhaps, though, he failed to understand that the old man no longer had any semblance of power within the club and there were some who believed that Edwards had seen to that. For now, however, Edwards arranged for Knighton to meet Busby in his first floor office at eleven in the morning.

The old man, having celebrated his eightieth birthday earlier in the year, was shuffling papers on his desk and sifting fading memories in his head as the younger men appeared at his door. Edwards had not warned Busby of their arrival. This was the man, remember, who made Manchester United from the late-1940s through the 1950s and the 1960s. It is easy to forget the state and status of the club when Busby was appointed manager in 1945.

Before the Second World War, United were a club yo-yoing between the first and second divisions of the Football League. Having narrowly survived bankruptcy in 1932, they finished twentieth in the Second Division in the 1933/34 season, avoiding relegation only by winning the final match against Millwall. In the season before league football was abandoned for the duration of the hostilities, Manchester United finished fourteenth in the former First Division.

In addition, during the war, Old Trafford was destroyed by German bombs. By sheer force of will and genius, Busby overcame events and overthrew mediocrity, creating a dynasty of success and dragging the club kicking and screaming into a brave new world.

Manchester United finished runners-up in the First Division in 1947, 1948, 1949 and 1951, won the FA Cup in 1948 and the championship in 1952. Much of this was achieved while playing home matches at Maine Road while Old Trafford was rebuilt. This is to say nothing of the Busby Babes and Munich, and of winning the European Cup, at last, in 1968.

As they entered Busby's office, Edwards provided the introduction and the explanation. Knighton was apologetic for the intrusion. Knighton thought the great man dapper, but that undervalued him. He was smart then, in a grey suit. His hair was thin but immaculately white and his face, Knighton thought, was a picture of triumph and disaster met with equanimity and suffering. Hands were shaken, warm hands, welcoming hands, encouraging hands; Busby greeted Knighton with a wide and genuine smile, with a twinkle in his eyes.

Who knows, Knighton pondered, what this great man really thinks of it all? There had to be some remembrance, surely, of times past, when his office was the origin, the hub, from which all decisions, all action, proceeded. Knighton smiled broadly. He was here to celebrate, to reassure the old man of his place in the new scheme of things. But it was sad, nevertheless, to see Busby so reduced, so cheapened to the role of figurehead, ambassador.

Just one day later he would become the pawn in Docherty's game with the press.

The new man felt a natural warmth emanating from Busby. It was a privilege to meet one of the genuine greats of British football and it turned out that they had much in common. There was Scotland, the chairman elect's castle at Killochan, not so far from Busby's birthplace in Lanarkshire. There was Scottish football too: Knighton's father-in-law's involvement with Hibernian and his wife's godfather's position at Celtic, related to one of the founding fathers of the Irish Catholic club. Celtic had been set up in the late-nineteenth century to raise funds to help poverty-stricken children in the surrounding East End of Glasgow. There was less common ground on religion, although both Knighton's wife and Busby were Romans.

Best of all, though, most important of all, was that Busby's father and Knighton's father had been tough, hard-working coalminers, salt of the earth people from communities in which each soul depended on the support of others and where a togetherness unknown outside mining communities thrived despite the hardship. Busby had been born in a two-room pitman's cottage in a mining village. Knighton could relate to that class thing. Edwards, with his easy and early privilege, was excluded from all of this and assumed the position of the outsider of the three. Later, Knighton got on famously with Busby's son, Sandy, but, by then, both of them were out with the rags and the dirty washing at Manchester United.

Edwards indicated it might be time for the audience in Busby's office to conclude and Knighton rose to his feet, glad in the heart of his heart to have met the great man, to have felt his warmth and humility, to have understood that his ability to make others feel special was what marked him, just as much as his achievements as manager of Manchester United.

'No delusions,' Knighton muttered to himself. Busby had no delusions of grandeur.

* * *

Back at the press conference, Knighton was in his pomp. He had already begun to articulate his vision for Manchester United and beyond and his own role as a new model chairman.

'I am a winner,' he said. 'I have a plan, and I know I can make this plan work for this club of all clubs.' It was heady stuff. 'United will be great again, perhaps even greater than before.'

Edwards concurred. 'It was a sad decision for me.'

He did not look too sad, though, with the option contract signed and sealed five days earlier entitling him to a happy and fat profit on his dealings in United shares and enough to spare to buy his wife that house in the Lakes.

Still, Knighton thought, as the two men left, *It's not been easy for him, Edwards, chairman at only thirty-four, and now ten years of relative failure to live with, and the memories of how the fans baited him and hated him. He must know how he is truly loathed by sections of the United fans. It must hurt.*

They shook hands once more, as if to confirm their pact. Knighton prided himself on both his attention to detail and on being as fair as possible to all and sundry. There were things about Edwards which most fans simply didn't know. In spite of his cuts from the transfer deals, in spite of his salary and his suspect dividends, in spite of his flirtation with basketball when it looked to all the world as if he had lost all interest in football, Knighton began to know him as a friend, understood his difficulties, knew him to have been a fan of Manchester United since his father first took him to Old Trafford, knew that Edwards had once correctly answered 876 questions out of 1,000 in a mammoth quiz on Manchester United, knew somehow that his football club would always be his specialist subject. He respected Edwards for that, at least.

Knighton was certain, however, that his own chairmanship would be utterly different. Of course it was about money, but what really mattered was the direction in which the cash flowed. Knighton would ensure that income earned by the club would be retained by the club, spent on its infrastructure, its players, and not go into the personal bank accounts of those privileged enough to be sitting in the seats of power; by the summer of 1989, Edwards had taken from the club over £750,000 in salary, bonus payments and shareholder dividends. By way of stark contrast, in the three years Knighton was a director of Manchester United, he took not a penny in payment, and not even a penny in expenses.

That was to come, though, and in August of 1989 it looked like it was a whole new ball game that had just kicked off.

**Knighton 1989**
*He came into the dressing room with a blazer on and had his hand tucked into the inside pocket, like Napoleon*

**Willie Layton of the Wednesday**
*Knighton's great-grandfather, a superstar of the first generation of northern professional footballers*

**The Wednesday won the Football League championship in 1902/03 and in 1903/04 and the FA Cup in 1907. Willie Layton is the fourth player from the left in the middle row**
*All the Sheffield Wednesday people are in heaven*

**Harry Storer and his dog, Billy**
*Storer was a legend in Derby, still expected to be allowed immediate access to any talented footballer he wished to talk to*

**Knighton's Ayrshire home, Killochan Castle, where the deal to buy Manchester United was sealed**
*This castle must keep as many secrets as there are stones in its walls*

**Knighton and Edwards**
*Edwards, oh dear: the fact is I should never have given him the contract back*

**Knighton and Edwards at a redeveloped Old Trafford**
*Edwards turns away but no one could ever tag him as a turner of the pages in history*

**Two revolutionaries: Ferguson and Knighton, 1989**
*New boys on the block, the outsiders, the bringers of new ideas, new worlds*

**Ferguson triumphant, 1996, with the Premier League, League Cup and FA Cup trophies**
*Give me a trophy every year, said Knighton*

**Knighton and Ferguson, watching together at the Palace 1989**
*An unacknowledged axis, forged in those sixty-two days, a prime mover in the transformation of United's fortunes on the field of play*

**Thumbs up! Wearing a United kit, Knighton is warmly greeted by the fans, and makes the national news**
*He would do the same again given half the chance*

**Knighton on the Old Trafford pitch, August 1989**
*Get that football off your head, Michael*

**When United were the best team in the world**
*Alex Ferguson was to blame for needing a bigger trophy cabinet*

**Gary Pallister with the Charity Shield**
*Break the bank, break the British transfer record. This club's going nowhere without Pallister*

**Charlton at Old Trafford**
*That pitch there, that's not for the likes of you, Michael*

## Chapter Eleven

# Hat-trick

### *The First Game of the Season, Old Trafford, Saturday 19 August 1989*

KNIGHTON SAYS his decision to appear in Manchester United kit, playing keepie-uppie before smashing the ball into the back of the net at the Stretford End, was completely spontaneous. In retrospect, he believes it was damaging to his cause yet is also convinced it was an utterly necessary act.

'Look, there was a crucial point to the apparent egocentric showmanship and buffoonery. I needed to show the fans that I was not just another in a long line of rapacious businessmen coming after their football club. I wanted to show the fans I was one of them, of their blood and of their emotion, a man of the terraces, a supporter who was just as passionate about the game as them.'

He has absolutely no regrets.

'How else was I to make my point?'

Even when pressed hard with contention and criticism, even when he knew it set men with power against him, even when he knew the outcome, still he says he would do the same again today given half the chance.

'In 1989, there was an undeniable, bitter gulf between the terraces and the boardroom, a gargantuan disconnect. I had huge ambitions for the club which were impossible to achieve without the most important people being on my side. I didn't care one jot what Edwards, Charlton, the press, the players, or even Ferguson thought about my unorthodox introduction. I understood this showmanship, this show of confidence, was necessary for the whole project to succeed. The fans had to see that I was different and would really make a difference.

'Manchester United was in desperate need of change and I was determined to be the one to initiate that revolution. A massive shake-up, a massive wake-up was needed, and I knew I was the man to provide both things.'

Perhaps Knighton was also saying he needed to be loved, the football club needed to be loved, and that, once that love was reciprocated, what could be achieved was limitless and that money alone could only achieve so much. And who would dare to say he was wrong? Today, the disconnect between fans and hierarchies within the higher echelons of English football has never been greater.

* * *

It was two in the afternoon, one hour before kick-off, on that first day of a new football season.

Knighton, dressed in a smart blazer and tie, was in the United dressing room introducing himself to the players, He then turned to Norman Davies, United's long-time kit man, and tasked him with finding playing gear that would fit him.

Curiously, Knighton had brought his kit bag into the dressing room, almost as if he expected a game, almost as if he intended to show the Old Trafford crowd a thing or two about wing play and how to score a goal on your debut for the Reds, almost as if he intended to show Graham Sharpe at William Hill another thing or two about the perils of bookmaking. Knighton had brought his boots.

What no one knew, though, was that he had also brought with him a copy of his renamed *Blueprint – Outline Proposals for Increasing Commercial Revenue at Manchester United Football Club plc*, the visionary document which would revolutionise not only the finances at Old Trafford but also those of the entire football industry in England, even perhaps the rest of the world. It was a master plan, destined to succeed in its entirety. When Knighton left the dressing room at half-past two that afternoon, he left the future of the beautiful game behind him in a surprisingly scruffy kit bag on a wooden dressing-room bench.

After completing the ritual of pressing the flesh with all the members of the United first team squad, and of Ferguson's coaching staff, Knighton emerged, blinking, into the sunshine, resplendent in brand new United training top and shorts. He looked sleek and slick, slim with the help of the billowing tracksuit top. His thighs were footballer's thighs, thick and muscular, primed for action. He was cradling a football as if it was the love of his life. He was remembering.

He recalled it all, in the corner of his mind's eye, his six-year-old self, running, spindly legged, unsure whether to laugh or cry, waving to his father as he crossed the white line and entered the fray, as he joined in the big-boys' match at the ground of Loscoe Miners' Welfare Football Club. For a moment, he had waited, as if assessing anew the wisdom of what he was about to do.

Then he was back at Old Trafford. Knighton walked, then jogged, released the ball, allowed the leather to caress his right foot, sensed the moment was right, may never, indeed, be right again, flicked the ball into the air, head lifting, tilting, to greet the falling ball. He knew this was his time, the momentum of the assembled multitude in the Stretford End was on his side. He juggled the ball from head to shoulder, to chest, to knee, to foot, all the while running and not once losing control. He was a master performing a well-rehearsed act.

Even before the ball rocked against the back of the net, he was standing still once more, this time arms aloft, in salutation, acknowledging the rapture of the crowd.

'Look at those smiling faces,' he says now, in defence of his impish behaviour, 'check out the photos, watch the film, see the laughter, catch the eye-to-eye contact with 10,000 fans, listen to the roars and cheers.' Knighton re-lives these moments now and again.

'You know, there's not a football fan in the whole world who would not have loved to do what I actually did on that day. I was not just fulfilling my dream, I was fulfilling every fan's dream in the whole wide world.' That, though, was not all that this showmanship was about. Knighton was making another statement about his new model chairmanship.

'It's theatre, pure entertainment, an immediate empathy.'

Through this act, he was distancing himself from the old regime. He was saying, *This is how it will be from this moment forwards.*

'I had bridged the gap between board and supporters in two minutes after a gulf of twenty-five years.' He had no idea, though, of the truly dangerous game he was playing. 'We were forged together, Knighton and the crowd, totally with me in this indecent, defiant act of solidarity.'

All this was true, of course, but surely he could not have been so callow as to think that the balance of power at Old Trafford might be found within the hearts and minds of the populace smiling at his antics from the concrete and iron terraces of the Stretford End. There would be those who would see Knighton's pre-match show as nothing short of wanton buffoonery rather than an act of building bridges with the multitude. Perhaps he thought that did not matter.

He had, after all, a watertight legal contract for the purchase of the most famous football club in the world. More likely, he was just not thinking at all. More likely, as he stood there, arms upraised as if sealed in some ecstatic prayer, basking in the adulation of his new-found friends on the banks of traditional terracing, he was remembering, dreaming, perhaps, of what might have been, recalling his own young playing career, so cruelly cut short, brought to a sudden and premature end through serious injury.

On that day, though, he delighted in, luxuriated in, that moment of ecstasy as the ball careered into the back of the Old

Trafford net, perhaps more than any other goal he had 'scored' on more legitimate occasions. Of those there had been thousands, many using plastic footballs slid between goalposts made of discarded boyhood clothes, or heavy leather balls hammered into nets in games for school and county.

He had enjoyed and endured crowds before, too – mobs of defenders surrounding him, hacking at his legs, lunging into spaces his legs had just vacated, rabbles of football club scouts following him home from school, surrounding him, camping on his doorstep, determined to catch him in their clubs' contractual nets.

From the age of twelve, no fewer than sixteen professional football clubs, including Manchester City, Liverpool, Everton, Chelsea, Derby County, Nottingham Forest, Notts County, Chesterfield and York City, had attempted to sign the boy wonder. And eventually, at the age of thirteen, he autographed schoolboy forms for Derby County, the club where his father was a season ticket holder.

It was 1964 and the age of hope and young dreams. There had been a breaking open of society, a gentle and musical tearing down of barriers, a questioning of class, an interrogation of rules and restrictions, and Radio Caroline was pulsing through the airwaves. Harold Wilson was prime minister and was making both pipe smoking and politics respectable. And, he was speaking, glory be, with not only a working man's accent but a northern working man's accent.

Knighton had queued to see the Beatles' new film, *A Hard Day's Night*, and a new programme, *Match of the Day*, on the new channel, BBC 2, had transformed Saturday night viewing on his family's black and white Bush television. England was unfolding like a springtime flower in a garden of teenage delights, but of course there were still frosts to worry about.

On the news, he saw mods and rockers clash on the beach at Clacton and heard his parents' quiet tut, tut, tut. One part of him shared the disapproval of the mother he loved and the father he adored, but another, darker, side of his brain would have loved to have been there too, smashing, breaking the old order apart. It was still the old nation of traditional crimes and eye-for-eye punishments. It was the year when the Great Train Robbers were sentenced to thirty years' incarceration and when the last hangings took place, of Peter Anthony Allen at Walton Prison in Liverpool and of Gwynne Owen Evans at Strangeways in Manchester.

Derby County finished an undistinguished thirteenth in the former Second Division that year and football, at least in Knighton's eyes, remained a world apart, a field untouched by these social changes, by the new dominions of rock and roll and Rolling Stones and street-fighting men and revolutions. Yet Knighton, the boy becoming a man, was torn apart, on the one hand drawn to this new world paradigm of pleasure and privilege, feeling it deep within his bones and within his soul, yet on the other in awe of the traditional ways, through his abiding passion for the game he loved and its unyielding traditions. The Baseball Ground, Knighton's new home, was still a shrine to time-honoured masculine values and to working class flat caps and Woodbine fags.

He did not stay long as a schoolboy footballer at Derby County, though just long enough to recall the artistry and power of the first teamer, Alan Durban.

Durban, who scored eleven goals from midfield in that dour 1963/64 season, later won both Second Division and First Division championships under the tutelage of Brian Clough, the Rams' most successful manager of all time. Knighton, too, recalled King Kevin Hector, one of the greatest players to pull on a Derby County shirt and the scorer of dozens of fabulous goals. He also remembered Roy McFarland, the best centre-half the club had ever had and thought those three greats alone worth emulating.

In the pantheon of great football clubs, Derby County was Knighton's first and last love. It was his home-town team, and one his father, grandfather and great-grandfather on the Knighton side of the family had followed for decades. In fact, there had been family connections to the Rams since the club's formation in 1884 as an offshoot of Derbyshire County Cricket Club and it was inevitable, when the big clubs came knocking at his parents' door, that Derby County would win the day.

* * *

The first attempt to lure Knighton away from the Rams, though, came one Sunday afternoon, almost three months after England's World Cup triumph in 1966. At his parents' door was former Derby manager, Harry Storer, now chief scout at Everton. Knighton had a stomach full of roast beef and roast potatoes and was watching an old black and white Hitchcock film.

There was a commotion at the front door of 17, Purchase Avenue, the house Knighton's mother and father had built in 1965, and moved into on 13 August 1966. It was a sign of their upward mobility in Harold Wilson's new classless society.

Knighton's ears pricked. Voices were raised and then struck down.

'Michael, it's Mr Storer,' his father called. 'He's come to see you.'

Storer was still a legend in Derby, still expected to be allowed immediate access to any talented footballer he wished to talk to, and still had not learned the subtle art and craft of waiting to be invited into someone else's home. He was already sitting at the Knighton kitchen table with Albert, Knighton's father, fussing around, star-struck even at his advanced age. His hand was still outstretched, still alive from Storer's hearty grip. Knighton, however, could see his mother was not so happy with this uninvited intrusion on to her territory.

'Go on, Mrs Knighton,' Storer said, 'go and get yourself busy elsewhere now.'

The man who had managed Derby County for nine years between 1955 and 1963 stared hard at the woman in his way.

'Mrs Knighton, this'll be men's talk.'

The young Knighton was agog. He knew full well no one spoke to his mother like that and lived to tell the tale. His mother was a force in her own right, a clever and outspoken woman, especially when challenged inside her own home. She made no move to move.

'I said this is men's talk, Mrs Knighton.'

Knighton saw his mother's face redden, her fingers curling and recurling around the hem of her apron.

'You just wouldn't be interested,' Storer said.

'No,' she said, 'I will not move from my own kitchen.'

His mother's voice rose to a pitch which brooked no argument. 'I don't know who you are,' she said, 'and I don't care, but you will not speak in that way to me in my own home and, if you're here to speak about my son, then you had better speak to me, or else it will be you who ups sticks and takes your leave right now.'

Knighton saw the legend that was Harry Storer take one step backwards, saw the puzzled look pass like a heavy cloud across his face, saw the former Derby County man force a wan smile, saw him gather himself to his full height, saw him stand his ground.

'I'll be busying myself nowhere but here,' his mother said, 'and I'll be staying in my kitchen to listen to every word you have to say about my son.'

Knighton wanted to run and hide, wanted to stay and watch, wanted his mother to continue her magnificent tirade, wanted her to shut up and do as she was told by Mr Storer. At least, Knighton thought, his mother was not denying the possibility of Storer's staying.

'It'll be you, sir, who are busying yourself elsewhere, not me.'

Knighton looked at his father, watched as his father's eyes pleaded with his mother's eyes. Then he saw the surrender in the old man's look, saw the shrugging of his father's shoulders in the blinking of his eyes. The young footballer was proud of his mother, Barbara, but he wished the ground would swallow her up, allow the menfolk to have their talk uninterrupted. He was desperate to discover what the legend that was Harry Storer wanted from this unexpected visit.

Knighton knew his mother loved him, at least he hoped so, but his mother had never seen her gifted son play football, never seen him score goals in almost every match he had played. He knew she was no lover of the great game that consumed her son's every waking minute, and he knew deep down that she saw no future in the game of football for her son, but he wished now with all his heart that his mother would let this visitor be. His father, in contrast, had seen all of Knighton's goals. He wished his father would speak now.

His mother sat down, planted herself, rooted herself on her kitchen chair, her bare elbows grating on the Formica tabletop, her eyes on Harry Storer. Knighton watched as the power play shifted. He saw Storer accept defeat in this opening battle, but only so that the war might later be won.

'With respect, Mrs Knighton, I am here to talk about your son, but I am not talking here about some stranger to me, about someone who means little to me, whose future I care nothing about.' Storer, Knighton saw, was not a man to be daunted by any woman, even his mother. 'I have watched your son play football, every single game he has played in the last three months.' Knighton watched as Storer paused for effect.

'Can I ask you how many times you have seen the lad play, Mrs Knighton?' Knighton's eyes swivelled to take in his mother's colouring face. She knew she had never watched her son play and never would. Before Barbara Knighton could respond, however, Storer was reeling off all the matches Knighton had played in the last few weeks, even matches he had forgotten himself, school games, district and county games, goals he had scored, positions he had played, how he had played, marks out of ten. It was an impressive performance by the Everton scout.

'Furthermore, Mrs Knighton, you just so happen to be the mother of a boy who, I firmly believe, will become one of the greatest football players this country has ever produced, perhaps even the greatest of all time.'

Knighton's head was swimming. Prompted by Storer's comments, the boy's mind overflowed with images of the recent World Cup, of Bobby Charlton's two goals in the semi-final against Portugal, of his harrying, his chasing, his tackling, his probing passes, his linking of the play between defence and attack from his deep-lying number nine role. All of that Bobby Charlton brilliance was clear in the boy's mind, there to be replayed in his head, to be learned from.

Knighton saw himself playing Charlton's role in a future World Cup.

'Yes, believe me, Mrs Knighton, your son is that good, and I've seen a fair few players in my time.' Knighton heard Storer's voice as if it came from another world.

'You know what, Mrs Knighton, if this here boy of yours does not make the grade at the very highest level, international level I mean, I'll eat my hat.' Storer was speaking now to Barbara Knighton only. It was as if she had acquired honorary male status within her own kitchen. The film, meanwhile, in Knighton's head moved on, frame by frame, to the World Cup Final.

With extra time being played, he was going to be late for his evening paper round. He saw Geoff Hurst's final goal, people on the pitch, the striker's left foot swinging to meet the ball as if destiny itself required such a climax to such a match.

*Some people are on the pitch, they think it's all over.*

Knighton heard Kenneth Wolstenholme's voice in the closing moments of the match.

*It is now,* the BBC commentator said, as Hurst smashed the ball high into the German net for his third goal and England's fourth, sealing England's World Cup destiny. Knighton saw Charlton after the final whistle, sweat-stained, exhausted, lank hair at rest at last, his bony hand sweeping the long strands of hair across his scalp, no goals but what a labour-stained performance of grace and first class, working class, pomp and power. He was third in line behind Bobby Moore and Geoff Hurst to receive his medal from the Queen.

He heard Storer, still talking to his mother, his words raucous, challenging, like waves lambasting sea walls in winter.

'We'll need new players, Mrs Knighton, if we're to ever win that World Cup again.'

'Well, Mr Storer,' his mother responded, 'I hope my son will have the good sense he's been born with to choose a more sensible career than football, one with more long-term prospects than that silly sport can offer a young boy, no matter how well he can kick a football around.'

At least, Knighton thought, she had learned the Derby County legend's name.

'Look, Mrs Knighton, I'm not here to waste my time or yours, I'm here on behalf of the richest football club in the land, and I'm here to sign this young man for Everton.'

Knighton saw a sad shake of his mother's greying head. He knew she had set her heart on her son becoming head boy at Heanor Gate School, on watching his academic progress, on seeing him maximise his full academic potential at university, because his teachers were telling her that he was a very bright, very able pupil, or, if all else failed, developing his quite extraordinary artistic talents.

'At least,' Barbara Knighton said on many occasions, 'at least the boy can paint and draw.'

She said it again now. Knighton loved his artwork throughout his time at school. He liked to hear his mother's praise, but wished she would not spoil it all by adding a damning postscript.

'Even if,' she always said, 'little else appears to interest him other than kicking a ball about for all the hours that God sends.'

Knighton turned from his mother to observe his silent father. He saw a thin, tentative smile appear on Albert Knighton's lips. His father may have been relegated to the sidelines in this battle but Knighton knew that his father knew Harry Storer and understood well enough the former Derby manager's sheer bloody-mindedness and determination to see any job through to its conclusion.

'Harry,' his father said at last, 'Derby County, look, it's Michael's local club, it's what the lad's always wanted, to sign for his home-town team, the Rams.'

It was a weak defence of the interests of the team he had supported, man and boy, and Knighton's father knew it, but he had to say something. It was immaterial, however, as Storer was continuing his relentless propositioning.

'Mr Knighton, I really cannot leave this house without insisting on securing your son's future with Everton Football Club.'

'But, Harry, the boy's with Derby, on schoolboy forms.' Albert Knighton took a deep breath, reluctant to challenge his hero, but determined to make his point, make sure what happened was really best for his son. 'They seem to rate him very highly, Harry, just like you do.'

Storer snorted with impatience. 'The lad's too good for Derby County, Mr Knighton.'

Knighton's father, perhaps stung by the insult to Storer's former club, however, was not yet for turning. 'All this talk, Harry, all this business about Everton being the richest club in the land, and being top of the First Division, it's maybe not what's best for the boy.'

No one, Knighton thought, is asking me what I want. It was as if he were a piece of meat in a market place to be haggled over, yet he knew his father loved him, wanted what was best for him, would not sell him for a new refrigerator, or a colour television, or even a new house, in the way that some boys' parents had apparently been bribed and backhanded by football clubs.

'I'll tell you what's best for the boy, Mr Knighton. If young Michael is serious about a career in this game, and about achieving a speedy route into first team professional football at the very highest level, probably within twelve to eighteen months, he must join Everton, my football club.'

Storer's voice was a sledgehammer breaking stones and breaking hearts.

'Look, Mr Knighton, Derby County, as you very well know, is still a club very close to my heart.'

Knighton glanced at his mother. She was silent, stony faced, apparently resigned to the man's world that surrounded her, enveloped her, and would defeat her.

'I played for the Rams, bless them, I managed that football club, gave it the top years of my life but, with the best will in the world, Derby County is not Everton, and never will be able to match Everton's resources or Everton's ambition.' Storer paused, glanced at the cards remaining in his hand, and played his trump. 'How many times, Mr Knighton, has your boy been training with the first team at Derby County?'

Storer still had his contacts at his previous club, still knew the time of day at the Baseball Ground, and understood that promises to fast-track the boy had been broken by the new manager, Tim Ward.

Knighton could hardly contain himself with all this unfolding of new horizons. He did not know at what point his mother had left the room. He did not know whether she had left in anger or in sadness or in resignation. He did know that he was overwhelmed by the passion of Storer and his father for his future and dispirited by the lack of interest of his mother. She stayed here with us men, he thought, just long enough to try to block my future.

'Just once,' he said, 'if she would come and watch me play, just once, that's all.'

He had not realised he had spoken out loud, but neither his father nor Harry Storer seemed to have noticed.

* * *

Barbara Knighton worked as a secretary to the company director of a building contractor and plant hire firm. She had climbed one rung higher on the ladder of social mobility than most of her peers in working class Derbyshire and she was proud of that achievement. So maybe it was a class thing, Knighton told himself, this dislike of football.

His mother had been educated at fee-paying Chesterfield College. Was that where she learned there was no future in football? She was, though, the granddaughter of one of the country's most celebrated Edwardian footballers, Willie Layton. Barbara Elizabeth Knighton was a complex character indeed. She loved her son, she knew that, she was sure of that. And yet, between the ages of five and eleven, she had subjected him to regular and horrific beatings. Her cruelty had been capricious, whimsical, and dependent on wild swings of mood.

When Knighton was a toddler, his mother would lock him in the attic of their rented top floor flat in Jessop Street, Ripley, a property that belonged to her husband's employer, Bowmers Bakery. The boy would be left for hour after hour, alone save for his beloved ragdoll, a gollywog called Jacko and a toy trolley tray full of coloured wooden bricks.

In defence of his mother's behaviour, Knighton says the young woman was barely out of her teens at the time and admits he was a handful as a small child. His aunts and uncles had told him stories that proved as much. Sometimes, they said, he would disappear for whole days from dawn to dusk into the fields and local woodlands, and this when he was barely six years old. Such was the tortuous relationship between mother and son, until her premature death from cancer, in 1990, at the unkind age of 58, that Knighton never knew whether or not she really loved him.

'I can see that dingy attic room in that little upper floor flat now, with its steep eaves, a tiny roof window beyond my reach, and a green, square-patterned linoleum floor. During those times of solitary confinement, it seemed as if my only friend in the world was Jacko.'

Forgetting is impossible, Knighton says, but forgiving is easier. For the violence at least. What he means is that he looked for reasons for his mother's behaviour. Even for the bedtime pummelling and punching, even for the night-time angry fists that stung his head like wasps, and even for the whippings with dog leads in the crazy brightness of the middle of the day.

'I guess she was suffering from a severe case of what we nowadays call post-natal depression.'

He found it harder, though, to come to terms with the constant put-downs his mother dealt him. He recalls bringing home from school a shoebox full of medals won on the school's sports day.

'You're not putting those things on the mantelpiece,' was his mother's sole response.

After the thrashings stopped, Knighton was afflicted by a sense of worthlessness throughout his teenage years that bore down on his sometimes fragile self-belief. To anyone willing to listen, Knighton's mother would say, 'Michael, he's only good at art and at kicking a football around. He's not like his brother,

Steve. *He's* as bright as a button.' It would hurt any boy to know his brother was his mother's favourite son.

Barbara Knighton was ruthless in her determination to maintain her utter lack of interest in her eldest son's sporting prowess. What Michael valued most, his mother deemed to be without value.

Knighton offers up a theory to the gods of psychology. 'So this shy and naturally introverted boy becomes the showman and the show-off.'

* * *

Back on the hallowed Old Trafford turf he had thumped the ball into the back of the net at the Stretford End three times. It was a hat-trick. He mulls over the borderlines between showmanship and showing off.

'That side of my character was always a defence mechanism, to overcome this feeling I've always had that I was someone who was utterly useless at everything I ever tried to do.'

Knighton's face is alight with the memory of his precious time on the Manchester United pitch, of those three goals scored before kick-off.

'I never feel that what I have achieved is worthy of any merit at all.'

This was unbelievable stuff. Did he truly think his attainments in the world of education, his artwork, his treasuring of period properties, his work in the football industry, were good for nothing?

'Until my twenties, I could still blush puce red, if I was in a crowded room and I thought the spotlight was on me. I can still feel that awful feeling of being insecure and full of doubts about myself and my abilities.'

Like mother, like son. Knighton, too, is a complex character.

'Yes, I suppose it's all to do with the way my mother would put me down in my younger days. But, you know, perhaps my mother was right. Maybe, I needed bringing down a peg or two.'

He recalls his mother telling him, 'Get your head out of those clouds, Michael, and know your place in life, just know your place.'

'One day,' the boy replied, 'I'm going to live in a nice, big house surrounded by lovely things.'

He knew all this was cod psychology, but he had to find reasons for his own behaviour as well as his mother's.

* * *

It took five hours of hard bargaining before a fragile agreement was reached allowing Michael Knighton and his father to ask Derby County for the boy's release from his schoolboy contract, so that he could pack his bags and head for Merseyside.

'We'll have to be seeing Sammy Crooks, then,' said Albert Knighton.

Crooks was the youth team coach and assistant manager at the Baseball Ground, the man who dealt with everything the manager did not wish to deal with, and Knighton hoped he would protest just hard enough to make the boy feel wanted and then let him go with Storer to Everton.

By the time Knighton returned to the family living room, the Hitchcock film had long since finished and the television had overheated, the screen dead and blank.

'I hope it's not the tube,' he heard his father saying.

'You should have asked him,' he heard his mother saying, 'whether his precious, his posh, Everton Football Club, have any spare televisions.'

Knighton did not care. The Beatles had just enjoyed their eleventh successive number one with the double A-side record, 'Yellow Submarine' and 'Eleanor Rigby'. In Liverpool, he thought, everything would be everything that Derbyshire was not.

* * *

Years later, as Knighton stood before the Stretford End, breathing in the applause, the affection that was pouring like sweat from the terraces, he thought of his mother.

She was not there, she had never been there.

At his mother's funeral in February 1990, no tears fell from Knighton's eyes. These did not come for a further year.

He was driving on the M62 from Manchester to Yorkshire. Tears for Barbara Knighton fell at last and washed his face. Recollections of his late mother flooded his mind and he was forced to pull over on to the hard shoulder of the motorway.

'At that moment, I would have given everything to have her back, constant beatings, chastisements and all. Even her constant harping about "that ridiculous, silly game of football".'

As Knighton sat, hunched over the steering wheel of his car, he recalled the words of that old standard, 'You Always Hurt the One You Love'. He remembered versions of the song by Fats Domino, Brenda Lee and by the Ink Spots. He prayed the hurts he endured were signs of misguided love on the part of his mother. The memories brought more tears.

'I loved and respected my mother so very much. She really was such a great influence upon my life, in spite of everything she put me through.'

He pulled off the hard shoulder and returned to the fast lane of life. It's possible, he thought, it was all for his own good. Memories fade, but Knighton clings to certain precious images.

'There's the old council house in Flamstead Avenue, off Loscoe Denby Lane.' It was where Knighton lived from the age of five to fifteen, where his parents lived and tried to love. There was the new bungalow in Purchase Avenue, their first freehold and where Harry Storer persuaded his parents to permit Knighton to join Everton on an extended trial basis. There were later memories, too, of Liverpool, the Cavern Club where the Beatles were born, the docks, the slums, the famous Liver Bird building, the new Catholic cathedral known as Paddy's Wigwam, and the senior players at Goodison Park, Ray Wilson and Alan Ball, both World Cup winners.

These remembrances, these echoes, were all now drowned beneath the waves of sound roaring from the throats of the Old Trafford faithful. Yes, Knighton thought, I've scored goals before, but never a hat-trick in front of the Stretford End, and, yes, I have played in front of large crowds before, but never one as vast, as deep, as wonderful as this one, God bless them all, every one of them.

* * *

He did not score goals in front of the Gwladys Street End at Everton.

It should have been a paradise on earth for a boy of fifteen, but he had never left home before, and soon found Storer's promises to be straws in the wind. It soon became clear that he was no nearer a first team place at Everton than he had been at Derby, and after a few short weeks of homesickness, Knighton headed home.

* * *

At Old Trafford twenty-three years later, as kick-off approached, Knighton was back in regulation blazer and tie and in the directors' box, exchanging pleasantries and nothings with Edwards.

Still his mind wandered, headed back home, back to the safety of the past. In Derbyshire, in late 1966, Knighton, now a former Everton trialist, saw that the football scouts had returned and were once more camping out in the front garden.

The boy knew he had run away once and must not do so a second time, yet he also understood he was turning on the carousel that was this football game and that he would not be allowed to get off this madly turning world, even if he wanted to. He continued to play for fun, and for his future. The scouts were like bees about nectar.

Most persistent, most persuasive, was Peter Hill, chief scout and youth team coach at Coventry City. When Hill talked, he spoke Knighton's father's language, down-to-earth Derbyshire language. He had played 285 games for Coventry but was a Heanor lad.

There was nothing flash about Hill, who, like so many former professionals, had nothing to fall back on when he finished as a player and was desperate to avoid the dole or the dingy pub where so many footballers ended up pulling pints and reliving glory days; he was aware of his good fortune in having found a way to remain in the game.

He knew his place in the scheme of things at Coventry City – fourth place if he was lucky in the management team led by Jimmy Hill, fifth place on a bad day behind physiotherapist Norman Pilgrim and his mad scientist's long white coat of a uniform, and out of the door altogether if he failed to find and develop young talent like Knighton.

'It's such an exciting place to be, Coventry,' he told Knighton's mother and father, unsure as yet where the real power lay within this household.

'There's Jimmy Hill, for a start, the manager, he's already won the Sky Blues the Third Division and Second Division championships.' The scout paused for effect. 'This last season the team went twenty-five games unbeaten and now we've reached the promised land of the First Division.'

It was the early summer of 1967. The young Knighton was stronger now and thought this might be my club.

'Yes,' said Peter Hill, 'with Jimmy Hill in charge, Coventry City's in with the big boys now.'

Knighton watched his mother's eyes as they lit up with laughter. 'What did you say your name was?' she said, unable to restrain her amusement.

'Hill, Mrs Knighton. Oh, I see what ...'

It was a rare and precious moment, his mother's smile, his mother's sparkle in her eyes.

'No, no, Mrs Knighton, Jimmy Hill, he's no relation to me, but he is my boss and he's told me to go and get your son for Coventry.'

Knighton's father, however, wore a more serious face. He was listening intently, all too well aware of the Coventry City manager's achievements: 276 games for Fulham, former chairman of the Professional Footballers' Association and successful campaigner for the abolition of the football industry's maximum wage of a meagre £20 a week.

What no one knew at this moment, however, was that Jimmy Hill would shortly be leaving the Sky Blues and joining the BBC as technical adviser for the football based drama, *United!* He would be replaced as team manager for the forthcoming 1967/68 season by Noel Cantwell, ex-Eire international and Manchester United stalwart. In the event, the change of management mattered not one jot, not to Knighton anyway.

His father, though, was weighing matters with care and precision, only too aware that his son's dreams were in the balance, depended now on paternal wisdom. He knew all about the wizardry of Jimmy Hill in transforming Coventry City from unheralded never-has-beens into top-flight hopefuls, but he was also well aware of the pecking order of management within football clubs, understood the almost total control Jimmy Hill had at Coventry City and wondered whether Peter Hill, this Derbyshire man with a sense of humour, wielded any influence at all at his football club.

He had seen Jimmy Hill on television, and thought the sharp suits and sharp ties and the sharp beard covering that famously elongated chin all told their tales. Knighton's father had done his homework and comprehended the secondary role of Alan Dicks, the assistant manager at Coventry who had played one game for Chelsea in their championship-winning team of 1955 and who was also allowed to sport a smart suit, though a less expensive one. In third place in the Sky Blues' hierarchy was coach Pat Saward, an Irish international and stalwart of Aston Villa defences but relegated to the tracksuit position within the club's pecking order.

Albert Knighton was no fool and thought his son might have a chance under the care of Peter Hill, an honest, hard-working, journeyman-professional. He reckoned he might just keep Michael's head out of the clouds and understood how hard the coach would push – for his own sake, for his own survival – any prodigy he recommended to the club. As things turned out, however, none of these thoughts mattered much either.

The young Michael Knighton was better prepared this time and understood what was to come – that sharp pain of separation from his home roots. In Coventry, at least, he would not be taken by the surprise of it all. On his first day at his new club's

Highfield Road Stadium, Knighton was given club training kit and taken by Peter Hill to the training ground at Ryton. Here the senior and junior pros were already about their work. An eleven v eleven game was about to begin and Hill asked Knighton if he fancied a game.

It was a youth team versus first teamers and reserves setup, kids against gnarled old pros, and Knighton loved it. He scored a hat-trick in less than twenty-five minutes and made fools and possibly enemies of seasoned footballers. These were the kind of players who had scraped livings out of the game year after year, struggled with mortgages or rents or alimonies, played that little bit harder whenever contracts had been up for renewal, moved on, moved around, just one step ahead, if possible, of smart young brats like Knighton.

At half-time, Knighton was removed from the fray and offered an immediate place as a ground staff boy – an apprentice professional – to be paid five guineas per week for himself, and five guineas per week for lodgings. The latter would be paid direct to Mrs Quinn at 84 Swan Lane, a small terraced house directly opposite the City stadium. This time, Knighton thought, there would be no turning back, no homesickness. The deal was agreed in less than five minutes, with the boy also promised a signing-on fee on his seventeenth birthday together with a club car.

'There was not an agent in sight,' Knighton recalls. Like his fellow revolutionary at Old Trafford, Alex Ferguson, he has maintained a lifelong antipathy towards the leeches that are football agents.

Peter Hill was smiling, too, his future at Coventry City secured, he thought, with just this one signing. Everyone at Highfield Road understood the scout had done well. The boy Knighton was a coveted catch, a coup for the newcomers to the First Division. It was a tragedy that it did not work out as planned.

* * *

Knighton's digs were convenient, and Mrs Quinn's two up, two down, terraced cottage was from the beginning a home from home. His landlady appeared to be a brick and made efforts to get to know her young lodger. She hoped he would soon make friends with his team-mates.

Knighton, though, was something of a loner, always had been, always would be, in spite of his occasional penchant for public performance, understanding from an early age that his interests in poetry, art, architecture were not those readily acceptable within his peer group of fellow footballers. In Knighton's childhood neck of the woods, there was Eastwood, home of D H Lawrence, whose work the young footballer devoured, and not just *Lady Chatterley's Lover* either. The novelist and poet was a working class hero.

Eastwood was a small coalmining community a few miles from Heanor. The two towns might have been twins separated at birth, such were the similarities. Nearby was Lord Byron's family seat at Newstead Abbey. The contrast between poverty and privilege, between Lawrence's and Byron's upbringing, was not lost on Knighton and stayed with him. He became passionate not just for the poetry but also for social change and, when angry, for revolution.

In summer holidays from school, Knighton walked, with his dreams of poetry and fame, in Lawrence's and Byron's footsteps. He could not help but love and absorb the charged, romantic atmosphere of the magnificent abbey's ruins and gardens. Knighton shared these adventures with neither parents nor peers, and certainly not with his fellow apprentices at Coventry City.

Or with Mrs Quinn.

Knighton's landlady was becoming miserly with her warmth and empathy and was quick to nag and nurdle at the young man's freedoms. Knighton began to feel trapped, bullied and persecuted, and began to take solitary evening walks into the heart of the city. He spent most evenings in Coventry Cathedral, listening to the sweet sounds of the choristers and admiring the way the light shifted through the colours of the stained glass windows, showing off its fractured beauty as it shone on motes of dust, transformed them into stars, into fractal universes he could only begin to understand. It also shone on sinners like Knighton and on saints at prayer in the pews, making no differences between them at all. He revelled in, marvelled at, Sir Basil Spence's masterpiece of architecture.

'When there was no music, I would stroll around the cathedral for hours, studying the astonishing and innovative genius of Spence's design, Sutherland's iconic tapestry of Christ, Bridgeman's *Mater Dolorosa*, Piper's modernist miracles of windows, and I would take out my sketchbook after evensong on Sundays and try to capture the essence of Jacob Epstein's bronze sculpture of St Michael's Victory over the devil.' He sighed as he remembered.

Knighton was learning another trade through his visits to Spence's cathedral and in later life produced magnificent artworks of his own. At fifty-six, Knighton's masterpiece, a Corpus Christi triptych, produced under the pseudonym of Kongthin Pearlmich, was exhibited in King's College Chapel, Cambridge. Even his revolutionary impact on the commercialisation of English and world football would pale into insignificance beside the grandeur of this fifteen-feet-high, three-ton triptych, *Hand of God, Foot of Man, Heart of Eternal Life*, which would match anything on display in Spence's cathedral. It may prove to be Knighton's enduring legacy to the world. His artwork was born, in part at least, from his time spent musing and sketching in Coventry Cathedral.

* * *

Knighton's preference for solitude is part of the eternal enigma of the man. One of Knighton's contemporaries at Coventry was the young goalkeeper David Icke, who would soon be a BBC presenter and later became as notorious as Knighton in his role as New Age conspiracist and propagandist for the view that world leaders including George Bush and Queen Elizabeth II were really reptilian humanoids.

Icke held none of these views while struggling to come to terms with the beginnings of rheumatoid arthritis and while attempting to keep clean sheets for the Coventry youth team.

He was a dedicated trainer, determined in the face of adversity. Knighton liked Icke and thought him to be a keeper with a great future in the game, even a future England number one, like his hero, Peter Shilton, both of them Leicester boys.

Icke also recognised a sublime football talent when he saw one.

'Knighton?' he said. 'Boy, was he quick, was he slick as a young player! His body swerve, his dribbling skills, his balance, phenomenal, you know, he was skipping past seasoned, first team pros, like a knife through melting butter, so quick, so skilful.

'Look,' he said, and when Icke says look, his piercing eyes repeat the command, 'Michael was seriously talented, his running, his dribbling ability, very much like George Best, and he had a shot that Bobby Charlton would have been proud of, that's for sure. And I should know – he put many a thundering shot past me in training.'

Knighton remembers Icke, especially from times of voluntary additional training at Highfield Road. He recalls his team-mate snatching at muddy footballs, smothering them against his stained net-minder's jumper, his hair falling across his brow as if trying to escape its fashionable Beatles mop-top style.

'We all called him Elvis,' Icke said. 'That's who Knighton looked like in those days, not to mention the way he could swivel those hips as he waltzed past players, leaving them stranded in his wake.'

Typical Knighton, when the whole world wanted to be John or Paul, or maybe George or sometimes even Ringo, he slicked back his hair like Elvis Presley.

Some seven months into this Coventry idyll, mixing football and contemplation in the cathedral, more football, more goals and even more football, disaster struck. It was just another sunny day, training time in heaven, when Knighton stretched, floated and hung in the air, his body horizontal to the ground, his right boot making sweet contact with the ball, leather on leather, timing as honeyed as a kiss. He no longer cared, though, whether the ball had hit the back of the net because he fell awkwardly and pain took control of Knighton's world.

Later, he was told the thigh muscles in his right leg had been ruptured – torn to buggery may have been the rough-house phrase used at the time – and on top of that, cruciate ligaments in his knee had also been severely damaged. In 1966, these were injuries all players feared. No one returned from cruciate damage to former glories, and most never returned at all. Knighton's times as a professional footballer were over before his career had time to begin – forgotten, he says, before he was remembered.

* * *

He was devastated at this denial of his talent and his future.

The disappointment was heaviest when he understood he would never emulate the feats of his great-grandfather, Willie Layton.

Knighton, though, was never one to dwell, to stand in a place where the ground had shifted beneath his feet. He told himself that Lady Destiny must have something better planned, and perhaps she had. He set his sights on returning to full-time education, was welcomed and nurtured at South East Derbyshire College and then gained a place at Durham, where he would train as a schoolteacher.

He pondered sometimes on the fickleness of fate. But at least, he thought, his friend David Icke had been able to play thirty-seven times for Hereford United in the old Fourth Division before the arthritis spread from his left to right knee, to ankles, elbows, wrists and hands, making goalkeeping impossible. He was pleased Icke enjoyed somewhat better fortune than himself and was astounded at the goalkeeper's ability to play through the pain for so long.

* * *

By the late summer of 1989, Knighton had long since lost touch with his Coventry City colleague, but he still knew enough about quantum physics to understand that what Icke was saying about parallel universes made more sense than the drivel most journalists wrote about both these former footballers.

All these thoughts passed through Knighton's head in immeasurable fractions of moments, like photons through matter. There was space and time to spare, Knighton understood, within these worlds that interacted, overlapped to form his story.

* * *

In the directors' box at Old Trafford, Knighton was talking to Martin Edwards a few moments prior to kick-off in the First Division game between Manchester United and Arsenal. The chairman elect was still a tad breathless after his ball-juggling performance, his heart beating maybe ten pumps per minute faster than normal, fast twitch muscles still struggling to decelerate, adrenaline still buzzing and blurting its way around his system.

'What were you saying, Martin?'

But Knighton was not really listening, too consumed by a confluence of times, too overheated, too damn lucky to be alive at this magnificent moment.

He was in a daze of delirium, temporarily inhabiting one of the alternative universes that David Icke had written about in his controversial books, tuned in to the frequency that enfolds football supporters on Saturday afternoons on terraces and in grandstand seating. He had no real idea what he had done by communing with enraptured fans at the Stretford End, by slumming it with the club's supporters. He could have no inkling of the beast he had awakened and had no idea, even, that the game had kicked off.

When Edwards nudged his elbow, asked him if he was alright, Knighton was taken back to the first professional football game he attended with his father. He was only six years old and he had asked, perhaps ten minutes into the match, 'Daddy, has it started yet?'

At Old Trafford, Knighton had missed only the first few moments of the game, but he had let slip much more in the moments of indulgence and genius spent on the Old Trafford grass. The net result was that the chairman elect, with his on-field antics, had offended almost everyone who really mattered in these matters, those with the power to persuade, those with the power to frown and disapprove, those whose power might be slipping, sliding away, those who were watching from the boardroom and from the press box.

* * *

Ferguson was not one of those with real power at this juncture. He was a man living on borrowed time, on death row, hoping for a stay of execution, dreaming that this new man, Knighton, would live up to his promises of money to rebuild his team, to rebuild his confidence.

Ferguson was watching the new owner cavorting on the Old Trafford turf on a television monitor in his office, alongside the Arsenal manager George Graham and two senior pros, all leaning together like bookends without books. Later, Fergie was quoted saying, 'I was starting to have a terrible gut feeling about my new chairman.'

What Alex Ferguson said, though, and what he truly thought were rarely in strict accord during his long tenure at Old Trafford. He was too clever in the latter years of his career not to align himself with whoever wielded power. It was not always so and in his firebrand early years at Old Trafford, Ferguson would give best to no one, employers and all. In 1957 Ferguson had the makings of a raw-boned and bludgeoning, goalscoring centre-forward. He debuted at sixteen with the Glasgow amateurs Queen's Park, and scored twenty goals in his thirty-one appearances for the club. If he had never scored goals, however, if he had never made it as a footballer, Ferguson might have been a consummate politician. At nineteen, he was already a trade union shop steward, working as an apprentice in the Clyde shipyards as well as playing football part-time for Queen's Park at Hampden Park and later in Perth for St Johnstone, where he regularly used negotiating skills and sheer front and bluff to demand transfers whenever he did not make the first team.

This, though, was juvenile politics and it was only when he became manager of Aberdeen and briefly Scotland and, most importantly, of Manchester United, that his artfulness as a politician reached maturity. At Old Trafford, contrary to popular opinion, Ferguson always toed the party line. He was a football manager and understood only too well the paramount importance of having sufficient boardroom support to facilitate transformations of football teams.

While Edwards was in charge, there would be only muted and careful criticism of the old regime. So when Ferguson possibly thought to himself that Knighton might just have screwed up by prancing and preening in front of the Old Trafford faithful, he may already have been hedging his bets, maybe swimming with the new tide that suggested today's new man might not be tomorrow's man after all.

In later years, Ferguson was notorious for his unflinching support of the Glazer family, who completed their takeover of Manchester United in 2005.

The structuring of the Americans' purchase of the football club through loans secured against the club's assets has, so far, cost United approaching one billion pounds, with interest payments alone costing £60m every year.

Even after inevitable retrenchment on the playing budget, Ferguson was still saying, in July 2012, 'they have been great, the Glazers. They have always backed me whenever I have asked them. I have never found any opposition.' The necessity for this bond with the boardroom was learned early and often in the school of hard knocks that was Scottish football – in 1978, Ferguson was sacked from his managerial position at St Mirren.

There was, too, the story that his playing career was never allowed to flourish at Protestant Glasgow Rangers after he married a Catholic girl. Ferguson later said his split from Rangers was down to his disobedience of orders, or dereliction of duty, in failing to mark the Celtic captain, Billy McNeill, at a corner in the Scottish Cup Final of 1969, a final Rangers lost to their bitter sectarian rivals from the other side of the Glasgow tracks. For that error of judgement, Ferguson was subsequently forced to play in the Rangers junior teams. It seemed a remarkably harsh punishment for a young man who, twelve months previously, had been the club's leading goalscorer.

By the summer of 1989, not only was Ferguson facing the likelihood of dismissal as manager of Manchester United, he was also having to make calculations as to where power at his football club would eventually lie. If Knighton really had offended Fergie by his pre-match antics, it would not have mattered because at that mad moment, Ferguson wielded no power whatsoever. He was an almost busted flush.

Neither did the opinions of any of the players count. In 1989, professional footballers were still the bits and pieces of any football club, the rags and the bones, and they were bought and sold like expensive chattels. So when Neil Webb, after his debut for United in their 4-1 demolition of Arsenal following his transfer from Nottingham Forest for £1.5m, said to the press, 'We had heard about the takeover, but this chap came into the dressing room before the game, introduced himself as the new owner and then asked for a kit,' it didn't matter a great deal either.

'We thought he just wanted to join in with the warm-up,' Webb continued, 'but I couldn't believe what I was seeing when he ran on to the pitch and whacked the ball into the net at the Stretford End.'

Footballers were – and still are – a conservative lot, really, and they like their routines, their security in the regularity of the patterns set for them by their superiors.

'It was hilarious, unbelievable. He just decided that he wanted to go out there and have his own little cameo role.'

Webb paused, before adding, 'It was the kind of thing that football chairmen just don't do.'

And there was the rub.

Football chairmen were fusty from their time spent in dark and alcohol-soaked boardrooms, from staring at monochrome photographs of past glories. Their pockets were deep, and the hands that filled them were veined with age, grimed with money, and shaking with the cubes of ice in glasses brimmed with gin and tonic. They did not interfere with the playing side of things, they did not intrude, because their job was to mind their own business, even if their business was the business of the football club. They did not borrow football strips and enter the gladiatorial arena to entertain the crowd.

Ever, full stop, amen.

Clayton Blackmore had more to lose than most from Knighton's arrival. He was 'a squad player', 'a utility player', phrases applied to footballers to damn them with faint praise. He was twenty-four and making his 100th first team appearance for United, but his place in the team was no more secure than a hanging man's on a gibbet. His memory of Knighton on that day was as sharp as his tackling from left-back.

'He came,' says Blackmore, 'into the dressing room with a blazer on and had his hand tucked into the inside pocket, like Napoleon. I didn't want to make a snap judgement but going out on to the pitch like that wasn't the cleverest thing to do.'

However, if the players really did not matter, had no say in the scheme of things, and if the manager was a mere plaything of boardroom politics however hard he tried to trim his sails to the prevailing winds, there were people out there who did have power. In the Old Trafford boardroom, Midani and Burrows were spitting bile. Charlton, too, was upset, as he believed in the concept of the hallowed turf, on which only great players and great former players were permitted to tread.

It was bad enough watching footballers like Blackmore, Donaghy and Phelan, journeymen-professionals who most thought were not fit to tie the laces of the legends who died at Munich or of players like Best and Law, who had teased and tormented both Charlton and opposition defences, without now being forced to witness the man who had destroyed his dreams of becoming Manchester United chairman playing keepie-uppie on his watch, on his turf, on his manor.

Knighton was watching the match now with enthusiasm and mounting excitement as the new era for United unfolded with a

Steve Bruce goal against the champions in the second minute. He believed in destiny and in his own crucial role in forging that new future for Manchester United. He also believed in the untouchable option agreement contract he had agreed to purchase Edwards' shares. Knighton did not care right now what the other directors were thinking, what they might or might not be already plotting.

Later, Edwards claimed he was scandalised by Knighton's behaviour on that momentous first day of the new season.

'I was horrified,' he said, with the convenience of hindsight, 'absolutely horrified. I was sat in the stand thinking, *What the hell have I done?* I couldn't believe what I was seeing. I kept saying to myself, *What the hell have I done?* I realised that I had made a big mistake. The other directors felt the same. They cringed and began to turn on Knighton.'

In fact, according to Edwards' autobiography, *Red Glory*, he never actually witnessed Knighton's performance on the Old Trafford pitch. He was apparently entertaining guests in the directors' room at the time.

Edwards, though, may be rewriting history, a privilege granted to him as he stayed on at Old Trafford beyond the summer of 1989 to reap the harvest of his uplifted shares.

In fact, he was in a splendidly good mood that afternoon. His team won 4-1 and he was about to become debt-free and a millionaire several times over.

So what if Knighton had over-indulged himself in a touch of showmanship; so what if the new owner of Manchester United had an ego the size of his bank balance; so what if the Stretford Enders had fallen in love with him; so what if Charlton felt anxious because of this young whizz-kid's antics?

By the looks on his flushed face, the chairman elect certainly didn't and he was the only one with the right to terminate the option agreement.

* * *

If only everything, Knighton said later, was as simple as hands shaken and option contracts signed, as simple as scoring goals at the Stretford End, and as easy as leaning back in his favourite armchair and reading the press reports in the Sunday papers.

There was one in the *Mirror* he especially liked. He showed it to Rosemary and laughed out loud.

*Knighton showed he can juggle a football as successfully as he can financial figures and had the fans and the photographers eating out of his hands.*

Knighton's attempt to build bridges between the terraces and the boardroom appeared to have worked a treat but his amusement at the press coverage was probably his last laugh for a very long time. Certainly, these were the last words in a newspaper owned by Robert Maxwell that Knighton ever relished.

## Chapter Twelve

# Own Goals

*The Derek Jameson Show*
*Thursday 24 August 1989*

THERE ARE a few things Knighton now knows: that there are a few days of calm before all storms; that there is a cliché to fit all situations; that when the proverbial hits a fan it's better to be on holiday in Majorca, as Edwards was, than to be in London waiting to appear on the Derek Jameson television show.

It started the following Thursday with a headline in the *Daily Express*.

*Don't Juggle with United, Mister Chairman.*

Inside the paper James Lawton suggested that Knighton 'may have self-glorification on his mind'.

Knighton could ignore headlines for a while but not the sheer, bloody spleen of men whose ambitions to own Manchester United had been thwarted. They were like lovers spurned, these men, Midani, and Burrows, in particular. And Robert Maxwell, too.

All of them in their different ways capable of metaphorical crimes of passion.

* * *

On the same Thursday that the *Express* article appeared, Knighton was preparing for the Jameson show. The host, with his star-spangled toothy grin as wide, as fixed, and as empty as the space between football goalposts, was an amiable chat show man. His bearing, Knighton thought, was full of creases born of midlife crises that have ended with smiles. When he talked, this former editor of the *Express*, the *Daily Star* and the *News of the World*, his face rippled like the back of the net when a goal had just been scored.

Knighton's fellow guests on the programme were George Best and Samesh Kumar, the recently installed chairman of newcomers to the Third Division, Birmingham City. Inspired by Knighton's recent performance on the Old Trafford pitch, there were rumours that the guests would indulge in a £5m keepie-uppie charity challenge bet as part of the show. Knighton, though, was more excited by the prospect of meeting Best than of appearing and performing on live television. He says he never had heroes but that he made an exception for the Northern Ireland internationalist.

He and Best shook hands and Knighton detected a half-camouflaged shyness in the Irishman's sparkling eyes and words. They say, Knighton thought, you should never meet your heroes. Best, however, was warm, complimentary.

'People like Michael,' he said, 'young, extrovert, new chairmen, first class, excellent for the game.'

Best's beard was full and black but, studied closely, there were flecks of white to be seen, hints of mortality amid the vigorous profusion of hair. His eyes were still a piercing blue, the same eyes that held Miss Worlds and opposing footballers in equal thrall. His body remained trim but had advanced a fair way from the skinny Belfast bag of bones he was when he first played football for more than fun. Knighton could smell that Best had been drinking but he was not yet drunk. Kumar was fresh and pleasant. His family were in the rag trade in Manchester. Despite being nervous and in awe of Best he at least had had the bottle to turn up.

A reporter had come up with the bright idea of a ball-skills challenge for chairmen and had invited all the First Division bosses to participate alongside Knighton. Kumar might have been Third Division but was still keen to take part. Lights were flashing in the studios and someone said 'Five minutes' as Jameson appeared with photocopied papers tucked under his right arm. His grin, this time, Knighton thought, was more like a coffin about to be laid in the ground.

'Michael,' he said, 'here, come here, and take a look at this.'

The TV man's voice grated, his East End accent ground.

'Well, Michael, wot do you fink of this?'

His voice was both a foghorn warning of the rocks ahead and the siren sounds of the stones themselves. Jameson was thrusting a sheaf of crumpled papers into Knighton's face. Someone had faxed the chat show host copies of the front page of the *Manchester Evening News*.

Knighton read and he knew immediately that his world was turning upside down.

'Wot do you fink, then, Michael, wot have you got to say about this?'

Assistants were hurrying people, lights and cameras into position and Knighton could hear an audience some way in the distance being warmed and primed for the show. The fax had been removed but the headline was scorched on his brain.

*THE MEN WHO REALLY BOUGHT UNITED*

The article provided the names of two big-time businessmen, Bob Thornton and Stanley Cohen, only one of which Knighton had ever met in his life.

A production assistant was anxiously encouraging him to take the stage.

'Come along now, please, Mr Knighton, we're live in two minutes.'

Another auxiliary ushered him forwards and Knighton walked, without knowing he was walking, along a corridor with walls that seemed to be closing in. Then, bright lights and raucous applause enfolded him. Somewhere, Jameson was still jabbing with his question, as insistent as a boxer with his opponent on the ropes.

'Completely untrue,' Knighton said, as he sank into his seat, 'this is all utterly untrue.'

* * *

Indeed, the story could not have been further from the truth.

It was, however, a wake-up call. It was Knighton's first stinging taste of the criminal behaviour of news editors and their journalists, and their lack of professionalism in running with completely ungenuine headlines and unconfirmed stories when lies would sell more papers than truths.

'It's their standard and corrupt stock-in-trade,' Thornton later said to Knighton.

Thornton was a respected figure in City business circles. He was the former chairman of Debenhams and was once hyped as the world's greatest retailer. He had recently fought and lost his battle against a hostile £550m takeover by Burtons and, as a result, was cash rich from the sale of his shares. The recent sale of Schreiber Kitchens to the MFI furniture group had also boosted his bank account, this time by untold millions.

Knighton first met Thornton soon after buying the Killochan Castle Estate in 1988. Thornton was a neighbour and over Sunday lunch, having sworn Thornton to secrecy, Knighton revealed his bid to buy Manchester United.

'I'd love to be involved with that deal Michael,' Thornton said. 'I'll take a small share in it if you like Is there any equity available?'

Thornton paused, smiled, waited for the ripple effect of the pebble he had tossed into Knighton's waters.

'If I can be of any help, you know, with my contacts in the City, you know that you only have to ask, and I'll be there for you.'

Knighton liked Thornton and thought it possible he might come to like the sound of his offer.

'I really do think I might be able to help, you know. All my life has been about deals, and big ones, too,' Thornton proffered.

The agreement with Edwards to buy Manchester United had been Knighton's deal and his deal alone and until this moment it had never crossed his mind to permit anyone else to join the party, to share in this project.

It was not as if Knighton could not do the deal himself. He had more than sufficient personal assets to raise every penny of the required funds.

Thornton, though, might just prove useful down the line, especially when it came to his plan of floating the club on the London Stock Exchange. He knew so many people in the City. Who knew when Knighton might need a few allies in that austere place?

Thornton said, 'You can never have too many friends, Michael, especially in business.' He would introduce Knighton to some tried and tested contacts. 'I know all the right people, Michael, especially if you're planning to float the club.'

At this moment, Knighton began to see all of the advantages and none of the disadvantages. Besides, he really did like Thornton, and the lunch had been relaxed and convivial. He saw Thornton's name could only add gravitas to his deal.

At first, Thornton suggested twenty per cent as his share, but soon it rose to forty per cent. Still Knighton was agreeable and happy, too. The project remained clearly Knighton's show, his controlling interest unambiguous. Glasses chinked together in summation of the deal.

'Just one more thing, Michael, I don't want my name mentioned at this stage. I hope that's okay?'

They were standing now, Thornton ready to depart. Knighton nodded, offered his hand, could see no reason why his friend's anonymity might be a problem. So when Knighton was asked later, at the press conference, if this was his deal alone, he said, 'In business, I'm a one-man band, and there are no major consortiums or even small ones in this with me, although I may be asking a few close friends to join me eventually.'

* * *

Knighton always said, he would have been only too happy to announce a business association with Bob Thornton if he had not given his word that the private arrangement would remain secret until Bob himself was ready to disclose his participation. Knighton had no reason to keep secrets other than his promise, and a gentleman's word was his bond.

He wished now, of course, that he had done the whole damned deal by himself, as he had always intended.

'I always work better on my own.'

Knighton understood he should have known better. A further regret was his agreement to Thornton's second request at the conclusion of their lunch at Killochan.

Beware when one more thing becomes two more things.

At Killochan, Thornton had said, 'I have a friend, someone I always do business with.'

Knighton nodded, waiting.

'Stanley Cohen, he's a great mate of mine.'

Still Knighton waited, perhaps suspicious.

'Would you have any objection if I offered him a piece of my pie?'

Knighton had never heard of Cohen, but what difference did it make to him if Thornton sold some of his stake?

'He is a brilliant businessman, Stanley.'

Thornton was a good salesman on behalf of his friend.

What Knighton knew now was that too many fingers in the same pie can be very messy indeed. He had never before been in business except on his own.

* * *

Cohen, it turns out, was a vintage car and football enthusiast, the founder of the Betterware Group. Like Thornton, he was the possessor of a pocketful of liquid cash following the recent sale of one of his many companies.

One of the things that Thornton and Cohen had always done together was buy up failing companies, turn them around and sell them on. The bankrupt Schreiber furniture empire was one example.

If Knighton had known that at the time, might he have been more wary, might he have considered the possibility that the dynamic duo were thinking they could do something similar with Manchester United, in the nicest possible way, of course? Cohen, at this time, had several businesses to his name, including Parker Pens, but still had spare time as well as spare cash. Thornton offered Cohen twenty per cent of his own forty per cent in the United deal.

According to the *Manchester Evening News*, it had been a friend of a relative of Cohen's that was the source of the leaked news.

If all this were true, Cohen's indiscretion was not personal or malicious but it was careless all the same. It seemed that a young relative of Cohen, a student at Birmingham University, had boasted about the deal.

Something like, my friend's uncle, he's buying Manchester United. That is what always happen when too many tongues begin to wag and the news, like all news, ended up in a newspaper.

The *Manchester Evening News* claimed it had been attempting to contact Knighton all afternoon but Knighton was beginning to understand the ethics of the British press: print first, ask questions later.

To be fair, Jameson did not push too hard once the show went live.

'Yes,' Knighton said, 'it's true I know Bob Thornton, and it's true he will be participating in this deal, but it is not true that it is his deal.'

The chat show host nodded sagely, encouraging his guest to say more.

'I have always said I was going to ask a few friends to join me in this enterprise and Bob Thornton is definitely one of those friends.'

Knighton smiled but was sick at heart. He was not stupid. He knew that his credibility in the eyes of the ever-cynical British press had been severely damaged and that there were people out there waiting for him to fall flat on his handsome face. He was relieved when the football appeared, when the charity challenge bet began.

Knighton went first, twenty nods of his head, twenty times the ball was propelled into the air, easy-peasy, more straightforward, certainly, than juggling with questions from the press.

Though Knighton had a way with words, it was different from his way with a football.

George Best followed, and was more flashy than the chairman elect, but equally effective. Kumar played with his feet, stumbled and fumbled at eighteen or nineteen.

'Where's my five million quid?' Knighton says, whenever he sees Kumar.

After the programme, he knew he really should be attending to business, readying himself to deal with the fallout from that afternoon's headline, but he could not resist a drink with Best. They were buddies for a while, arms around each other, in agreement with each other and with the whole world. They enjoyed a truly brilliant night out. That was why it hurt Knighton so much, a few days later, when Best joined in with the press onslaught on the chairman elect's purchase of Manchester United.

'A Fiasco', Best screamed from the back pages.

The chairman elect's hero had put his name to a scurrilous piece penned by some hack and pocketed a fat fee in the process, no doubt to fuel his thirst for booze.

*What a mess, what an embarrassment, what a stink! Knighton must go! I will never set foot inside Old Trafford while Knighton is in charge there!*

It was just the press doing what the press did, selling rags to punters with whatever storyline they thought would shift their papers off the shelves. It was just what happened when young relatives of businessmen couldn't hold their tongues after a few drinks. And what happened when businessmen couldn't keep secrets from young relatives at university.

It was as if Knighton had committed unconscionable crimes, having had the temerity to appear from nowhere and apparently purchase Manchester United from beneath the noses of supposedly more credible characters already at Old Trafford. He almost succeeded, too, where Maxwell, where Midani and Burrows had failed.

## Chapter Thirteen

# What Is Going On at United?

*Reports in the Press*
*Friday 25 August 1989*

THE PRESS in the morning after the Jameson show was less forgiving than the chat show host. Eddie Shah's *Today* newspaper was one of the fastest out of the blocks.

*WHAT IS GOING ON AT UNITED?*

*Chaos and confusion reigned at Old Trafford last night amid claim and counterclaim over who is providing the money to buy Manchester United.*

Knighton was described as 'angered' by the takeover rumours. In fact, he was incandescent. Publicly, he admitted to being 'very disturbed and rather irritated' by the initial report in the *Manchester Evening News.*

'I've had to spend the day walking around, not just with egg on my face, but with poached egg, and a fried egg, too.' He was never one for understatement, never would be. 'Someone has put two and two together and come up with fifteen.'

Part of the chairman elect was enjoying this skirmishing with the press.

Playing the wounded innocent was a role he took to rather well.

'The facts,' he said, 'are there for all to see.' His eyebrows were arched, his smile polished. 'Bob Thornton is a close friend and neighbour of mine in Scotland and has been an adviser throughout. He does have an interest in my company, MK Trafford Holdings, and he is a minority shareholder.'

He was learning to play journalists like an old man of the sea played big fish.

'About two and a half months ago, we had lunch and I told him I was about to buy a very famous football club. Something very exciting was about to happen and I wanted to share this with him and to seek out the wisdom of his experience.'

*Wanted his money more like.*

Knighton ignored the catcall from the back row of the assembled multitude of hacks.

'When I told Bob the total cost of purchasing Manchester United was £30m, he said it was mere pocket money to him as he had just sold Debenhams for £600m. He is now a participant in this business, but in no way does he have any say in the running of either my company, MK Trafford Holdings, or Manchester United. He is not even going to be a director of the club.'

When questioned about the involvement of Thornton's partner, Knighton was more guarded and there was a hint of exasperation in his voice.

'I have never met Stanley Cohen. He is a friend of Bob's, and Bob informed me that Mr Cohen would like a minor degree of participation. I have not agreed to this, or anything else at this stage.'

Cohen, by now, had been tracked down in his hiding place.

'I cannot talk about this,' he said, 'but, yes, we are behind the takeover, but you place me in an embarrassing position.'

If Cohen had been paid good money to sabotage the deal he claimed he was behind, his choice of words could not have been more effective.

* * *

Meanwhile, Maxwell was sharpening knives, polishing his own vocabulary. According to insiders at the *Daily Mirror*, Captain Bob was furious that Knighton had succeeded in pursuit of Edwards' shares where he had failed.

'Fucking stitch him up.'

One *Mirror* journalist claimed Maxwell was screaming across the newsroom full of hacks that the paper's owner had assigned to the case. 'I want that fucking Knighton fucked.'

Maxwell's face was purple with rage.

'How dare he? How dare he fucking do this to me?'

The newsroom was spared a moment's calm before the storm really broke.

'Who is he anyway? Who the fuck is this Knighton?'

* * *

Journalistic sources more friendly to Knighton had informed the chairman elect that Maxwell had been allegedly briefing his senior sportswriter, Harry Harris.

Certainly, Harris was quick off the mark.

'Destroy him,' Maxwell is said to have said.

Of course, only Harris knows the truth of the matter, but it is undeniable that there followed a string of articles highly critical of Knighton, and one radio discussion in which Maxwell's senior writer was hostile in the extreme to the chairman elect's cause.

It was a severe reaction on the part of the newspaper magnate. He neither knew nor cared about Knighton. He could not know that Martin Edwards and the man to whom he had sold United had mocked his table manners.

Maxwell, though, knew a good story when he saw one, and knew how to invent a good story when there was no story to see. He knew how to sell newspapers, but this appeared to be personal. He wanted to down the deal and wanted that so badly it hurt. He wanted to bring Knighton crashing down, and Edwards with him if he could, and he wanted that even more than he had wanted to buy United. Maxwell knew that if anyone could get this job done it was Harris. He knew that his best hack had the inside track on events at Old Trafford, knew that Midani and Burrows would be eager to talk.

* * *

Knighton, though, was not without his own contacts.

In October 1989, David Walker, a young journalist on the staff of the *Daily Mail*, told the chairman elect, 'Some of them, they make it up, Michael, that's how it works. These *Mirror* journos will write anything. They're tailing you, they're trying to tap your phones.'

Knighton knew this already, but it was so interesting, so important, to have all this confirmed.

'These bastards are out to get you, Michael, and you need to be very careful.'

Knighton thanked Walker and was glad to know that the whole world was not against him.

'They'll stop at nothing to destroy you and your reputation.'

Walker told Knighton that Maxwell was so obsessed that the owner of the *Daily Mirror* was either writing some of the articles himself or changing Harris's copy, writing his own headlines, dictating the tone of the entire attack.

'It's revenge, Michael, that's what it is, for being rebuffed by Edwards and for being beaten to the post by someone no one's ever heard of.'

According to Walker, Maxwell had between twenty-five and thirty-five journalists digging for dirt. Knighton already knew that all his family and friends had been contacted.

One university room-mate, Stephen Atkinson, later to play minor counties cricket for Durham, and for Hong Kong, was offered a small fortune for smut around and about Knighton's time at college.

'Is he queer? Does he do drugs? Is he a piss head? There must be something?'

Atkinson joked that he wished Knighton had been less straight and then he could have made himself a fortune. His buddy remained utterly loyal to his college friend, however. He remained unmoved by the press baron's attempts at bribery, not in the least tempted to invent stories in order to turn a dishonest penny or two, and according to Atkinson, Knighton's only vice at college was his obsession with physical fitness.

The problem for Maxwell was that there was no dirt to dig, but still he and Harris continued to ask the destructive questions.

*He's the son of a bloody coalminer and he lives in a castle.*

*How does he do it?*

*Keep digging, Harry, keep on fucking digging.*

*He's only a fucking schoolteacher.*

*How does he do it? How does he do it?*

Maxwell was obsessed with the destruction of Knighton's credibility and the problem for Knighton was that every red top rag followed Maxwell's lead. There was nowhere for him to run, nowhere to hide.

On Friday 25 August, the words about Knighton under Harris's name were both challenging and damaging.

*No one in the City had heard of him, no one in Scotland had heard of him, no one in the Isle of Man where his company, MK Trafford Holdings is based, had heard of him.*

If there was no scandal to be found, the news had to be the mystery.

*Yesterday, the* Manchester Evening News *were confident enough to splash across their front page the names of the men they believe are behind the so-called Mr Big.*

Mr Big had become code for an unnamed, and as yet unknown, someone for whom Knighton was merely a pawn. It was the best that Maxwell could come up with as he and his paper strove to destroy Knighton, his reputation, and his bid for Manchester United.

Harris, though, had been doing his own research on Thornton and Cohen and revealed that together they owned Queensway Guarantee Corporation, 'the company they use to make investments in businesses they want to run'. The two men, Harris wrote, were credited with turning around Betterware, a doorstep company bought in 1985 with a turnover of around £1m and sold on in 1988 when sales topped £16m. The inference was clear: Thornton and Cohen were using Knighton as a front in order to gain control of a treasured national institution which they intended to turn over for some fast bucks as if it were some downmarket company selling brushes door to door.

*The fact is Martin Edwards does not have a penny piece in advance of the deal he has signed with Knighton.*

*If Knighton wanted to sell his controlling percentage of MU shares he could do so without ever having to seek anyone's permission and without ever putting down any money.*

It was probably fair to say that, just two weeks after the deal was announced, Knighton was no longer enjoying reading the papers. It was also true that, from then on, Knighton was on the defensive, in retreat, entering some dark and dreaded zone of damage limitation.

'I can assure all Manchester United fans that I have enough personal cash to complete the deal.' This was true. 'I have more than sufficient finance, with the support of my personal bankers, to finalise the purchase, and I don't need the involvement of anyone else.'

The fact was that Knighton undoubtedly did possess the means to buy the club. No one else had ever been needed. It had been the most calamitous mistake to involve Thornton, and to permit his Scottish neighbour to involve his partner Cohen. If the disastrous duo now had to be edged aside, Knighton would make his own banking arrangements.

In response to the unmerited attacks from the gutter press, Knighton hastily cobbled together a strategy of response. First, he needed to put some distance between himself and an apparently loose cannon called Stanley Cohen.

'I have never met him,' said Knighton's press release, 'and I want to make that point most forcibly.'

Knighton had never before inhabited this kind of dangerous terrain. Cohen was also on the defensive, and, to be fair, this was a new ball game for him, too.

'Bob and I,' he said, 'have been partners for three years. I returned from holiday recently and he asked me how I fancied being part-owner of Manchester United. Of course, I said, yes, more for reasons of prestige than cash. I have many interests, from chocolates to textiles, and I love football. This is a very exciting deal but I am leaving Bob to sort it all out.'

* * *

Back in Manchester, Edwards was apoplectic and Knighton was apologetic, but they still had the agreed contract for the option to purchase the club.

However, it wasn't only the chairman elect's reputation that was on the line here; Edwards was damaged by his association with Knighton, damned for selling his soul to an unknown businessman. Not only that but some were talking of Edwards' foolishness in selling the club so cheaply.

From this moment, the fortunes of both men were locked in an embrace that was both symbiotic and perilous. Until one man released his grip on the other it seemed that both might drown in a sea of vitriol and verbal violence. To be fair, and Knighton always liked to be fair, Edwards seemed genuinely concerned, not merely for his own good name but for the standing of the football club of which he was still nominally chairman and chief executive.

And as the days shortened and the plot darkened, Knighton, too, was concerned, not only for his own emotional and reputational well-being but also that Edwards might be on the verge of a nervous breakdown. Such was the scale of the stress that both men had to endure, brought on by the daily onslaught of negativity in the national media.

It had been both a front and back page barrage for weeks and weeks.

* * *

Burrows seemed ever-available to his new-found friends in the press and reports duly followed suggesting Knighton hadn't got the money.

Nobody, it seemed, knew where the new man might get the £30m or even £40m needed to complete the takeover.

The intentions of whoever was planting stories in the press were clear: to create a mystery that would envelop Knighton, doubts and suspicions concerning his financial wherewithal.

Those inside Old Trafford still wanting Knighton's bid to come to fruition were convinced it was Burrows feeding the frenzy in the press.

Knighton could hear echoes of the lies exploding in his head.

*He can't complete the deal, he hasn't got the money, he hasn't got the money, he hasn't got the fucking money.*

Some people, it seemed, would stop at nothing to discredit Knighton.

* * *

Bobby Charlton, as befitted a legend of propriety, was more circumspect in his dealings with the press, but no less forceful in his own way.

He made it clear that he, together with his fellow directors, would be looking to Knighton to provide a clearer picture of what was going on at the match at Derby on Saturday.

To be honest, given Charlton's lack of knowledge at the time of Knighton's finances, it was easy to understand, and to empathise with the great man's concerns.

So far, Charlton's words were neatly orchestrated passes to better-placed colleagues, but next came the trademark thunderbolt shot from the blue, from outside the penalty area, his aim true and firm, and brooking no argument with either team-mates or opposition.

'We don't care,' he continued, 'where the money has come from as long as it is for the good of United and causes no embarrassment to the club.'

The heavy leather ball slammed into the back of the goal and the net rippled in warm response. Knighton pictured the great man leaping into the air, one hand raised to the skies in triumph, his rebellious strands of hair catching the winds of fate and flying with his words. The chairman elect had overwhelming respect for Charlton as one of the world's greatest ever football players. Knighton was less sure, however, based on everything he had heard and seen from the legend behind the scenes, what to make of Charlton the man.

## Chapter Fourteen

# Goals Against

*The Baseball Ground, Derby*
*Saturday 26 August 1989*

ON THIS day, there was no more ball juggling by the chairman elect on an emotional return to the Baseball Ground. He was not exactly contrite when he met with the directors, but he was more conservative. At half-time, however, he noted the gaggles and the cliques, the gathering of Burrows and Charlton and Midani and Edelson.

'What more could we have done,' he said to Edwards, 'other than tell them the truth?'

Before the game, Ferguson was cock-a-hoop and lifted the prevailing mood. He had just returned from a shopping trip, spending what he assumed to be Knighton's money on Pallister, whose imminent arrival he assured all those prepared to listen, would be the signing that transformed the fortunes of Manchester United.

Less than two hours later, the manager was less sanguine. The team had lost 2-0 to Derby County and Ferguson was hair-dryer angry. Even football results were deserting Knighton now. He did not know whether to laugh or cry.

Ever since the new season's fixture list had come out, and ever since he had shaken hands with Edwards, he had been looking forward to returning to the first love of his football life, the club of his heroes Steve Bloomer, Harry Storer, Tim Ward, Alan Durban, Kevin Hector, Roy McFarland and now of the peerless Brian Clough.

The day, of course, had been long since ruined by Maxwell and by those inside and outside of the club, by Burrows and his ambitious associates and cohorts in the press, all wanting to see Knighton's deal fail.

## Chapter Fifteen

# Holding Firm, Sticking Together

*Old Trafford*
*Tuesday 12 September 1989*

IN ONE sense, results of football matches paled into insignificance when placed in the context of the background shenanigans, the plottings and the politics. And yet. The problem was that United's disastrous results on the football pitch had now become part of the problem. Knighton pondered what might have happened had his Lady Destiny not turned her back on him at the moment he needed her most, had Manchester United not slumped from top to sixteenth in a disastrous run that began with the defeat at Derby County.

Shit was hitting fans and most of it was sticking to Knighton.

After the defeat at Derby, Manchester United lost 2-0 at home to Norwich City and 3-2 away at Everton and then, unforgivably, 5-1 to rivals Manchester City in an utterly humiliating defeat. While Knighton's control at Old Trafford was slipping away, the sense of chaos in the boardroom was echoed and amplified by goals scored and not scored on the playing field.

Three days after the damaging defeat at Everton, Knighton lunched at Old Trafford with Edwards and Thornton. There was still a sliver of hope and Knighton was still fighting, even if firefighting was not quite what he had in mind when Edwards handed him the keys to Old Trafford.

'It is of the utmost importance,' he said, 'that we hold firm, that we stick together on this.'

The lunch, on 12 September, had been arranged so that Edwards could meet Thornton. In a world in which the barrage of press abuse continued unabated, the meeting had something of the air of rearranging deck chairs on the sinking *Titanic*. Knighton, though, was still trying hard to build bridges. Thornton was silver haired and silver tongued. Bob's best business buddy might have let the side down badly with his irresponsibility and his incontinence, but Knighton was still trying to make things work. Was the chairman elect just too nice? Or was he thinking how indispensable Thornton might prove to be when the time came for the flotation of Manchester United shares, a plan that he had not yet revealed to Edwards?

Knighton could see that Edwards liked Thornton, could imagine the chairman wishing he had met the former boss of Debenhams before he had met Knighton or, at the very least, that Knighton had made sure that Edwards had met his junior partner in the takeover before the troubles began. If only Edwards could have introduced the two men together at the press conference, it might have allayed all fears of the unknown or that Knighton was a fly-by-nighter.

Was Edwards thinking now just how Thornton might be hoping to count pennies and pocket prestige through participation in this deal? Was he wondering how long it might be before Knighton's Ayrshire neighbour asked for a larger share in the equity in return for seeing the deal through to its conclusion? Edwards, Thornton and Knighton all agreed that now was not the best of times to lose collective nerve. Knighton, however, had to hurry away to a meeting with *Financial Times* journalist Paul Cheeseright and had no time to worry about what Edwards and Thornton might get up to behind his back.

It was typical Knighton, this courting of the broadsheet press when any publicist worth his salt would have been pressing the harassed chairman elect to find friends among the tabloids. Knighton, though, did not employ advisers. Cheeseright gave him a good write-up in an article entitled, *Keeping Red Devils Out Of The Red*. It was all about his ideas and predictions contained within the pages of his *Football Blueprint*, the document Knighton would give to Edwards just before he joined the Old Trafford board of directors in October 1989. It would be the instrument through which the financial revolution at Manchester United would be facilitated.

'Here you are, Martin, read this,' Knighton said. 'I think you'll find it very, very interesting. It's what I want to do to develop the commercial side of the club.'

He was a trusting soul, Knighton.

'It's something I've been researching for a long time, Martin, football finances in general, and the mismanagement of the game, lost opportunities for profit, those sorts of things, but it all applies to Manchester United, most of all, in fact, to our club.

'Apply these ideas, Martin, these principles, and the league championships and the FA Cups, even the European Cups, they'll all be returning to Old Trafford sooner rather than later because, with the profits that will come rolling in, we will be able to buy any footballer in the world.'

Edwards looked stunned, disbelieving, but took the document.

'I'm going to revolutionise the finances at Old Trafford, Martin, believe me, I'm going to do just that, and then build a team that will win everything, all from the profits from these new commercial initiatives.'

Knighton can recall a suspicion of jealousy on Edwards' face. It passed like a summer's cloud and was replaced with a smile of something akin to forbearance.

'I mean it, Martin.'

The expression on Edwards' face shifted to disbelief with a hint of condescension, pity even for Knighton's foolishness.

'It will happen, Martin, trust me.'

Knighton watched as Edwards began to read, the chairman's face revealing he comprehended the pertinence of the *Blueprint*.

He commented favourably on its detail but resented, or regretted at least, the wasted years in which he had failed to arrive at similar conclusions. It crossed Knighton's mind that his gift of the *Blueprint* might be premature, even rash or foolish, but he had Edwards' handshake to rely on, his sense of the Manchester United chairman's inherent goodness, his public-school understanding that a gentleman's word was his bond, that Edwards would help Knighton's plan come to full fruition, in good time.

'Read it, Martin, that's all I ask.'

* * *

Now, as Knighton sat opposite the man from the *FT*, he reminded himself that he had Edwards' signature on the option to purchase contract.

It reassured him.

'Let me tell you,' Knighton told Cheeseright, 'I will turn this club, Manchester United, into a £150m leisure vehicle.' The chairman elect's smile, more forced perhaps in these testing times, was insufficient to convince the seasoned *FT* journalist.

'The last time I looked, United's turnover was a mere £7m.'

'I am buying potential,' Knighton replied. 'It is all about brand building, and I will make Manchester United the greatest sporting brand in the world.'

The *FT* man smiled a further, tolerant smile, perhaps trying to be less cynical than his tabloid colleagues.

'Look, I will create a football club that will be in a position to buy any player in the world via the profits that my business model will create and foster, and Alex Ferguson will deliver at least one major trophy every single year.'

The journalist's eyebrows shifted quizzically and it was clear he remained unconvinced.

'Football,' Knighton said, 'is a product that has such worldwide appeal it is a global brand in its own right.' Knighton paused, waited for an encouraging nod that never came. 'Just wait until satellite TV truly arrives, and this product will then be sold around the world for billions.'

The journalist had done his homework.

'According to the last available figures, Manchester United made a year-end loss of some £1.3m. They've hardly ever made it into the black in the last twenty years.'

Knighton knew all this. He was more interested in the future than the past and could see the journalist thought him charming but bonkers.

'Just like everyone else,' he said.

'Pardon?'

'Only by making profits can Manchester United begin to dominate football at home and internationally.' Knighton was only too aware that profit was a dirty word among most football fans, but he had to make his point. 'How else can you possibly produce a successful sports team with United's current losses?'

He was speaking now to the Stretford Enders as much as to the readers of the *Financial Times*.

Not that too many of those denizens of those steep, concrete terraces were likely to be consumers of that particular newspaper.

'We must have profit at Manchester United if we are going to be in a position to attract the best footballers, both domestically and internationally. Best finances, best footballers, best success. It's not rocket science.'

Knighton paused for breath and to allow all this to sink into the journalist's mind.

'In order to achieve that profit, we must sell everything we can to our loyal supporters via merchandising and via every possible peripheral profit stream. It's essential for the ultimate success of the team on the field of play and that's what my business model is all about.

'Manchester United will become a financial and sporting powerhouse the like of which the football world has never before seen.'

Knighton even talked of Manchester United holidays and credit cards, cosmetics, tee shirts and swimming trunks.

'We will sell everything, every conceivable product line of merchandise to our captive market fan base.' He knew the fans would not like being talked about like that but it was for their own good.

'We will even have our own club TV channel that we will sell to our fans.' Knighton's voice attacked and defended at the same time.

* * *

Although he had absolute faith in the inevitability of his financial predictions, he was only too aware that fortune-telling of such a gold rush made him sound both rapacious and unrealistic.

'Let's kick off with television revenue.'

'Forty-four million pounds,' said the journalist, 'shared between the ninety-two professional football clubs.'

'I tell you, though,' Knighton answered, 'soon broadcasting rights for live football games in this country will be worth half a billion pounds a year.' He paused to allow this forecast to sink in. Knighton knew the journalist thought him mad but did not care. 'This will come about once the new satellite broadcasting facilities are commonplace and readily available to TV owners around the globe instead of being the rare novelty they are today.'

He saw his interviewer stifle either a yawn or a giggle.

'It's all there, in the *Blueprint* that I have researched and written.'

'Well, it seems a tall order to me,' the experienced journalist said.

Knighton knew the times of day and understood the journalist's incomprehension.

'Look, I am buying potential, and I will turn this club into a £150m leisure vehicle,' he repeated.

Knighton grinned. He was enjoying the disbelief on the journalist's face. It was knowing with total certainty that he was right that widened his smile even further.

'It is possible to turn this club around, you know.'

The journalist was halfway to the door.

'Manchester United will become so profitable there will not be a player in the world the club will be unable to afford to buy.'

The journalist took copious notes as Knighton talked and some of his points were faithfully reproduced in the following day's paper, although only a small number of Knighton's predictions were used. The overall tone was sceptical but Knighton still considered his time to have been well spent. He knew the fans wouldn't like his plans but also that they wouldn't object once the trophies and titles started arriving at Old Trafford. Perhaps, Knighton mused afterwards, the journalist was trying to protect his own reputation by omitting what he clearly believed to be Knighton's wildest forecasts. Or maybe it was kindness and Cheeseright was attempting to save him from himself.

Whichever it was, Knighton was eventually proved right.

In 2014 the club's chief executive, Ed Woodward, announced that 'United have the funds to buy anyone.' Knighton's vision, Knighton's promises, had come true.

By the second decade of the second millennium, it was undeniable that Manchester United were able to outbid any other football club in the world for any player on planet football.

In August 2014, the British transfer record was broken when the Old Trafford club purchased Angel di Maria from Real Madrid for £59.6m. The following year, the Manchester United board, in conjunction with new manager Louis van Gaal, announced a revised transfer policy for the summer window: from then on, only *galacticos*, superstar footballers, would be purchased by United. In August 2016, the French international Paul Pogba was signed by new manager Jose Mourinho for a staggering world record fee of £89m.

The worth of the club itself also soared. Knighton predicted a company turnover of £150m, which was laughed to hell and back in 1989. But in the 2010–11 financial year that figure was more than double Knighton's forecast, at £331m.

In the 2012 valuation coincident with flotation on the New York Stock Exchange, Manchester United was assessed as being worth a staggering £1.49bn, even after a relatively disappointing sale in which shares expected to trade between $16 and $20 eventually sold for just $14 apiece.

Four years later, in 2016, turnover was £590m, the second successive year the club had broken the half a billion pound mark. That same year, Manchester United was described by *Forbes*, the American business journal, as the world's most valuable football club and worth $3.69bn. And that figure had risen to $4.9bn by the summer of 2019.

Martin Edwards also benefited. Within fifteen years of agreeing the share deal with Knighton for a mere £10m, Edwards was inside the top 300 richest people in Britain, with, according to the well-respected, annual *Sunday Times Rich List*, a personal worth of £108m.

It was Knighton's *Blueprint* that had made this possible, both Manchester United's unfeasible wealth and Edwards' personal fortune.

* * *

Back in 1989, however, Knighton knew he was casting pearls before swine. Predictably, the *Financial Times* article failed to stem the tide of doubt, distrust and downright abuse that continued to flow in Knighton's direction. He was sliding fast on a slippery slope, heading for an abyss whose depth he could not yet conceive.

The vultures were circling around Knighton, whose names might well have included Burrows, Harris, Maxwell and Midani. The press were continuously in Knighton's face. The fans were also turning, soured by all this agitation.

Thornton and Cohen were no more enjoying the heat than Knighton and Edwards. And neither were their friends in the City. Knighton knew this. He had to keep reminding himself he was a winner, always had been, always would be, and that he could do this deal himself, although that would now take time, of which he had much less since allowing Thornton to participate.

## Chapter Sixteen

# On the Brink

*Citicorp Offices, Hayes Wharf, London*
*September 1989*

WITH THE wastage of valuable time taken up by the Thornton and Cohen debacle, Knighton needed to act quickly in order to ensure that more of his personal assets could be utilised in funding the agreement to buy United.

Knighton always had the financial wherewithal to complete the deal himself.

It was just that nobody, however wealthy, kept the kind of money needed to complete the Old Trafford option to purchase in liquid cash or loose change.

Rather than sell assets in property or operational businesses, liquid cash would be raised by borrowings against Knighton's assets.

Misunderstanding this fundamental business principle may have led some to repeat the Maxwell mantra that Knighton was a man of straw.

Knighton flew to London, his heart heavy with misgivings. He knew what he had to do and was not looking forward to it. Thornton's City associates had met several times that week and Knighton was becoming suspicious of the procrastination, the innumerable discussions as to how the deal would be put together, how the money would be pampered and packaged.

He was not a patient man and was unimpressed by Thornton's dealings with the merchant bank Citicorp Scrimgeour Vickers, which would provide the funds. The final straw was an interminable discussion over a compulsory purchase order for one of the Old Trafford car parks. What Knighton did not yet understand, though, was that these City people were cautious people and were nervous about the publicity surrounding his deal.

*These City types,* Knighton thought, *they do their business in the dark. That's how they like it, that's how they've always done things, not in this blaze of ballyhoo and spite.*

He was also slow to realise that they were Bob Thornton's people and would not bend to Knighton's bidding, even if it was his money paying for all this wasted time. These Citicorp people wanted to show Knighton how it was done around here, and juggling balls of any kind, not least footballs, was not how it was done in the secretive world of London's skyscraper banks.

Knighton never regretted his appearance on the Old Trafford pitch, but he began to suspect that this one action might be the prime cause of all this delay in the delivery of the money being raised against his assets – it had been just too much for the stuffed shirts, the hollow, pinstripe-suited men with their red braces and red socks and heads smoothed and shined with Brylcreem. He found out later that Citicorp Scrimgeour Vickers had its own internal fiscal challenges to worry about.

In the midst of all this stalling, Thornton stunned Knighton by asking, like Oliver in the Dickens novel, for more.

'I wonder,' he said in that silver fox way he had with those less fortunate than himself, 'I wonder, Michael, whether it might not be a good idea if Stanley and I took a rather larger stake in this business.'

Knighton could not make up his mind whether it was a question or a statement or some kind of bizarre directive.

'It might,' Thornton continued, 'smooth a few wrinkles, soothe a few furrowed brows.'

Knighton could see immediately how it might be more acceptable to the world at large were Manchester United to be taken over by a respected City figure with a solid track record in serious retailing, a man who had lost a battle in a very British and dignified manner against the might of Burtons in a recent shops-for-sale skirmish, a man who would not dream of donning a Manchester United tracksuit and investing in charisma and charm on the Old Trafford pitch.

He could see, too, how it might benefit Thornton and Cohen, and how it might always have been building to this moment. He could see how he might have been misled, let down, led astray, if not downright betrayed.

'No, Bob, no thank you.'

After all, he had given his word to Edwards that, even if he should offer some equity to friends, this deal was still Knighton's show and his show alone, that he would always be the majority shareholder and the key driver of the deal. This was Knighton's purchase and had been from day one.

'We've been upset,' said Thornton, 'both of us, me and Stanley, by the negative press.'

'And my credibility is also on the line because of it, Bob. My reputation is suffering more than anyone else's here.'

'That's why I thought it might help, Michael.'

Knighton had been calm until now, a model of a public schoolmaster, a man who had looked on triumph and disaster with equanimity, a man who might have built the British Empire years ago.

But now the anger came.

'Why did someone from Stanley's quarter have to tell anyone about our deal, Bob?'

Thornton was all innocence and hurt.

'I swore everyone to silence, Bob. We agreed that. Even your name was never to be mentioned. You have both let me down in that respect.'

The silence was deafening.

'He's your bloody friend, Bob.'

Knighton spat out the words. He was finished now, his anger spilled and spent. He had made up his mind. This was the end game for Thornton and Cohen. Knighton no longer wanted them on his team, no longer wanted anything to do with them.

He knew he had made a huge mistake, the greatest and gravest error of his commercial career. He had been seduced by Thornton and his array of City contacts, and by the pair's experience of the wider business world.

Knighton ended it.

'I am on my own now, Bob.'

'What are you going to do now, Michael?'

Simple, Knighton thought, I'm going to do this the way I always planned it. He looked about the room and saw nothing of value.

'I'll complete this deal without your help, gentlemen.'

I have several million pounds liquid cash, he thought, and that's not a bad start, along with property assets aplenty.

Knighton shook hands with Thornton.

'No hard feelings,' they both agreed.

Knighton's generosity of spirit in this amicable parting was breathtaking.

He says there was never a cross word between them. Later, he said the same about Edwards and it was almost possible to believe him. Knighton and Thornton never met again except as neighbours, and Cohen never met Knighton at all.

* * *

Knighton now had less than six weeks to complete due diligence and come up with at least £20m so that the legal requirement to offer all Manchester United shareholders the same price for their shares as he had offered Edwards could be fulfilled.

He was not daunted.

He was not quite back where he started at the end of those summer negotiations with Edwards but he was buoyed rather than disheartened by his split with Thornton and Cohen. He was not quite Mr Micawber, but knew something would turn up.

And it did.

* * *

It was the hullabaloo from the press, and it got worse before it got better.

On the morning after the meeting at Citicorp, *The Sun* ran with the banner headline

*KNIGHTON PARTS COMPANY WITH COHEN AND THORNTON – KNIGHTON REALISES THEY WERE THE WRONG PEOPLE FROM THE START*

This time it was Thornton and Cohen who were really quite upset.

Being pushed aside before being allowed to jump always hurts.

**Legends: Law, Charlton, Best, 1995**
*They say you should never meet your heroes*

**Amer Al Midani, United director**
*He's not one of us*

**Michael Edelson, United director**
*We basically followed Knighton's plan*

**Knighton and Sir Matt Busby 1989**
*Hands were shaken, warm hands, welcoming hands, encouraging hands*

**Barry Chaytow, Nat Lofthouse, and Knighton**
*I have a football club you might be interested in*

**Robert Maxwell in happy, Derby days**
*I could never sell Manchester United to a man with such appalling table manners*

**Graham Sharpe of William Hill**
*What odds would you give me about me being picked to play for Manchester United?*

**David Murray, chairman, Rangers 1988–2009**
*Together, Michael, we can rule the football world*

**Sir Angus Grossart (left), Scottish businessman supreme, with Gordon Brown, Chancellor of the Exchequer, Dr Alan Greenspan, former Chair of the US Federal Reserve, and Mervyn King, Governor of the Bank of England, all receiving honorary degrees**

*I still don't know to this day why Michael walked away and left the money on the table*

**Knighton's masterpiece**

*Hand of God, Foot of Man, Heart of Eternal Life*

**Michael and Rosemary, August 1989, the grand salon, Killochan Castle**
*You are the girl that I will marry. Three children, that's what we'll have, two boys and a beautiful daughter, lovely as her mother*

**Crowds on the pitch at Bradford City's Valley Parade, 1985**
*A ghastly commentary on the capitalism prevalent in the final quarter of the twentieth century*

**Juventus v Liverpool, prior to the European Cup Final, 1985**
*The choice of the Heysel Stadium, built in 1930 and unaltered since, an accident waiting to happen*

**The Battle of Orgreave, 1984, a key moment in Thatcher's destruction of mineworking communities**
*The power of the state: South Yorkshire policemen charge and beat picketing miners*

**Demands forjustice after the Grenfell Tower fire 2017**
*Peterloo, the Blackwell Colliery disaster, Hillsborough, the Grenfell Tower fire, establishment cover-up games that always shame the truth*

**Hillsborough: An injured man on the pitch**
*Something must be done, surely, something must be done*

**A prayer meeting of Covenanters in seventeenth-century Scotland**
*Men and women who refused to yield to the brutal power of the state or to bend their knees before anyone but their God*

**Knighton, 2019**
*FOOTBALL'S GREATEST VISIONARY?*

*Book Three*

# The Second Half

## Chapter Seventeen

# Come Back

*Ibrox Park, Glasgow*
*13 September 1989*

ONE OF Knighton's problems is that he gets on with everyone.

Another is that he does not always have the patience to wait for the right person to come along. He liked Thornton, he might have liked Cohen, and soon after Knighton dropped them as business partners, he met David Murray, the chairman and owner of Murray International Metals and Glasgow Rangers Football Club.

Murray was almost certainly the right person, but was it now the right time?

Murray had lost both legs after a car crash and was known affectionately by friends and business associates as Metal Mickey. He was a former Young Scottish Businessman of the Year and shared several characteristics with Knighton, including drive, ambition and intelligence. Both were workaholics.

At the time of their meeting, Knighton was distraught over the way matters had been handled by Thornton and his advisers but he was not downcast. Soon after, he accepted an invitation from Steve Samson, a Manchester-based editor of *The Sun,* to watch the European Cup match between Rangers and Bayern Munich on 13 September 1989.

Bayern were three-time European champions while Rangers under Graeme Souness were becoming a team of big money, big name signings, having taken advantage of the ban on English clubs playing in UEFA competitions imposed after the violence at the Heysel Stadium in May 1985.

Souness, a three-time European Cup winner himself while playing for Liverpool, had signed a bevy of English players including England number two goalkeeper Chris Woods from Norwich City, Gary Stevens and Trevor Steven from Everton, Mark Walters from Aston Villa and Ray Wilkins, formerly of Chelsea, Manchester United and Milan, from Paris St Germain. All of them were past, present or future England internationals. Terry Butcher was another recruit and was pictured on the cover of the matchday programme. He was an England stalwart, a blood-and-thunder hard man signed from Ipswich Town. It was a serious group of footballers that turned out for Rangers that night.

A towering Butcher header in the first half created havoc in the Bayern box and led to a penalty that young Mark Walters coolly scored. All went wrong for the Ibrox men after half-time, however, and they lost 3-1.

It all went right for Knighton, though, when he met Murray after the match.

They might have been twins, these two. Both were born in the same ripe, rich and sometimes rotten autumn of 1951 when England gloried in the Festival of Britain, when the nation deceived itself that it remained a Great Power, when the dying embers of Empire still flickered, when the Cold War was elbowing its way into prominence as a ready-made replacement for the Second World War, when China captured the Tibetan capital city Lhasa, when Winston Churchill returned as prime minister, as if a reminder of the recent war, when JD Salinger's novel, *The Catcher in the Rye* was published, when *I Love Lucy* debuted on CBS television and when Judy Garland was still singing 'Somewhere over the Rainbow' at the Palace Theatre in New York.

1951 was also a year when Rangers and Manchester United were runners-up in their football leagues, to Hibernian and Tottenham Hotspur respectively.

In the boardroom after the Rangers match, Knighton commiserated with Murray and reminded him there was a second leg to come in Germany. The Scotsman was realistic, however.

'No, Michael, the chance was here, and now it's gone.'

Knighton smiled and shrugged his shoulders in what he hoped was a sympathetic gesture. Of course, he did not really care, but there was an immediate empathy between the two men, electricity almost, a recognition and appreciation of similarities. Most telling was their passion for the game, and not just the game of football but also the game of life; they both knew that the winner was the one who rolled the dice, who took one more card from the dealer's hand, the one who dared to place the bet. Both had also agreed famous deals to purchase two of the most iconic football clubs in the world. The similitude was uncanny, shocking.

One year previously, Souness has told his friend, Murray, that the Rangers owner, Lawrence Marlborough, was looking to sell and that £6m should turn the trick.

'Twenty pounds a share, Michael,' Murray said, 'what a bargain that was for all this history, all this potential here at Rangers.'

Knighton had agreed exactly the same share price with Edwards for the purchase of Manchester United. Both men were genuine entrepreneurs, men who had made their own fortunes without the let and sometimes hindrance of inherited money, and both had endured moments of despair that had driven them on to creativity.

Knighton is quick to admit that almost losing a son is not the same as losing both legs at twenty-two years old, though the resulting motivating effect was similar. When they met, he already knew about Murray's tragic accident – the rugby game, the drive home, the nightmare, the wire fence that had sheared straight through his thighs, his luck in still being alive.

No one could fail to be impressed by David Murray's recovery from such a setback at such a tender age. And just as Murray's trauma was probably the greater, so his wealth was too in 1989: £90m in cash and assets.

The Scot suggested they retire to the Blue Room where they could be alone to talk. Murray knew all about the Knighton deal, about the loss of Knighton's would-be partners. It was as if he had been expecting him, waiting for him to arrive in Glasgow.

The Rangers chairman undoubtedly had his contacts in the English press.

The Blue Room at Ibrox was ornate and elaborate. It had a fireplace sculpted in Italian marble, murals of football men painted by Murray's first wife who had died of cancer, and a carpet in Rangers blue. The chairman of Rangers put down his crutches and hugged Knighton close.

'How can I help?' Murray said.

The next day, the two men met in Murray's office.

'It's the most wonderful deal you have there, Michael, you should be very proud of yourself.'

*He seems genuinely pleased for me,* Knighton thought, and nodded his appreciation of the compliment.

They enjoyed lunch and agreed to work together in the future. Murray suggested a joint merchandising venture between Rangers and United.

'Together, Michael,' Murray said, 'we can rule the football world.'

They discovered Murray knew Rosemary's family, knew them as the Croan fish people. They also agreed that Murray would introduce Knighton to the merchant banker, Angus Grossart, the best and most respected fixer in Scottish business circles, and the founder, chairman and owner of the merchant bank Nobel Grossart.

'We must not talk to the press, Michael, must not let them know we are talking.' Murray had not become so successful without being forceful.

*It is as if life is happening all around me,* Knighton thought, *through me sometimes, but not right here, with me, inside me.*

* * *

The Rangers man wasted no time in arranging the meeting with Grossart, at Murray's offices in Edinburgh.

'Is he a friend of yours, David?' The banker's voice betrayed his understandable caution.

Murray nodded, indicating that Knighton should be cut some slack, should be a friend of Grossart's, too. Murray's piercing eyes, his good looks, his neatly parted hair all said the same.

When Knighton arrived he explained his deal and the contents of his *Blueprint* for the development of Manchester United.

'He's right,' Murray said, 'this man's deal with Manchester United is worth £50m, £60m, maybe even £70m, not just the £20m he is paying.' He paused for emphasis. 'In fact, it's the best deal I've ever seen in my life.'

Grossart nodded in apparent agreement.

'We should make sure,' Murray said to Knighton, 'that we work together in the future on as many football matters as we can.'

## Chapter Eighteen
# A Loan Deal

### *Edinburgh*
### *September 1989 and Onwards*

A FEW days later, Murray and Knighton met in the swanky Edinburgh offices of Bird Semple Fyfe Ireland, the Scottish legal firm that acted for Murray. There, too, were Knighton's legal team and accountants from England. It was clear that Angus Grossart had thrown his significant influence behind the deal. The merchant banker and the Rangers chairman were old friends.

Grossart, Murray and Knighton were three entrepreneurs together.

*These are the people I should have had on board from day one,* Knighton thought.

Overnight he had done some homework.

Grossart had founded his own bank in 1969 at just thirty-two and had previously honed his business skills selling reject toffee from a Barrowlands stall. Like Knighton and Murray, this silver haired and silver tongued man had paid his dues and was now possibly the most respected man in the Scottish business community.

'The Bank of Scotland will do it,' Murray said. 'Consider it done, and we'll have the paperwork ready over the weekend.'

Murray was on Knighton's side throughout the discussions with the Bank of Scotland and with Grossart.

'I'll put my own neck on the line, if you like.'

Murray was a force of nature.

'The man is right,' Murray told the bankers, 'the man Knighton's right, and the deal is right.

'Frankly,' he said, 'you should be pleased he's giving you the opportunity to be part of the funding package. Frankly, you should do as you're fucking told on this one.'

Grossart, whose business manner was quieter, more conservative and reflective than the Rangers chairman, was also very much onside with the entire package Knighton had presented to him and to Murray.

'We'll get it done,' Murray said to Knighton. 'Angus says so. And what Angus says gets done, and stays done.'

It was clear to Knighton that the chairman of Glasgow Rangers and of Murray International Metals enjoyed considerable influence at the Bank of Scotland.

'Gavin Masterton, the CEO at the Bank of Scotland, he will drive this deal through on your behalf, Michael,' Murray confirmed.

Knighton, however, knew in his heart and his head that his business plan would have carried the day with any banker, although he was grateful for the support of two of the most significant Scottish entrepreneurs of their generation.

* * *

Soon afterwards, however, it turned out that the sole insuperable barrier to the provision of funds from the Bank of Scotland turned out to be Knighton's own thought processes.

He doubted he wanted the Bank of Scotland's money after all.

His reluctance became a turning point, a watershed moment in his life, and his hesitation was entirely uncharacteristic. Without doubt, timing was tight in terms of how quickly Knighton could put together the finances to complete on his option to buy

Manchester United. But it was also true that Knighton had the wealth and assets – estimated at the time to be well over £13m – to complete the purchase: his multi-million pound castle in Ayrshire, his highly respected private school in Huddersfield and his portfolio of Georgian town houses in Edinburgh. In addition, he had the backing of a major bank offering him a facility to draw down £24m. That deal was done – and in the shortest possible time – and merely required Knighton's signature to access the money.

Public confidence in Knighton's financial status was not advanced, however, when Maxwell's *Mirror* published a picture of Knighton outside a terraced house he owned in Yorkshire which the article implied was his sole residence.

*This is where the man who claims to be buying Manchester United lives.*

It was not a caption conducive to belief in Knighton's wealth.

The problem, of course, was not a problem at all.

No one in their right mind would expect Knighton to buy Manchester United by selling all his property assets.

Everyone lucky enough to be in his shoes, or his castle, would borrow the balance of money needed to pay Edwards and the other United shareholders by using some of his property as collateral.

The problem only became a real problem after Knighton had invested faith in former partners who had failed, for whatever reasons, to come up with the assistance they had originally promised, and he was left with no corporate infrastructure, and with only a relatively short period of time to raise the money to complete on the deal.

The delay caused by the debacle with Thornton had left too little time to turn the extensive properties Knighton owned into liquid cash, but Murray's intervention in the middle of September 1989 appeared to be heaven sent, coming almost immediately after the Thornton and Cohen agreement fell through, and as Manchester United suffered three consecutive defeats and slid down the First Division table.

The alleged plotters within the Old Trafford boardroom still gathered strength and encouragement from Maxwell's press campaign.

In less than a week after the split with Thornton and Cohen, Knighton was ready to sign an agreement with the Bank of Scotland for an overdraft facility of £24m. All he had to do was put pen to paper to solve most of his problems. His worries would have been placed in a black bin bag and dumped, with his enemies back in England trumped, and years later it might have been Michael Knighton rather than Martin Edwards on the *Sunday Times Rich List*.

Instead, he turned his back and walked away.

No one, least of all the jilted pair of Murray and Grossart could possibly comprehend why Knighton had elected to simply walk away from the bank's £24m loan facility.

* * *

Years later, on 7 May 2007, at a celebratory dinner at an Italian restaurant in the heart of Edinburgh attended by around twenty-five luminaries from the art world including international dealers from the Tomasso family, Knighton was a guest of honour of fine art auctioneers Lyon & Turnbull which was chaired by the recently knighted Sir Angus Grossart. The company had just sold some of Knighton's art and antiques for a handsome sum of around £400,000.

At this dinner, it was clear that Grossart was delighted to meet up with Knighton once more. Holding court, the celebrated Scots businessman said, 'This is the man whom I, together with the Bank of Scotland, gave £24m to some eighteen years ago. The cash was to buy Manchester United. The paperwork was complete and all Michael had to do was to sign it and pick up the cheque. I still don't know to this day why Michael walked away and left the money on the table. Perhaps, I'll find out tonight.'

All eyes turned to an older, perhaps wiser, certainly fleshier, Knighton. He did not respond except to order another magnum of bubbly so that he could replenish the glass of his old banking chum. Too much water, he thought, too many bridges, too much champagne to bother with all of that just now.

Grossart's eyes betrayed a suspicion of disappointment at a lack of response from Knighton, but he was determined not to press the point on a reluctant guest. The banker looked away and continued with his story.

'When Michael approached us via our mutual friend, Sir David Murray, owner of Glasgow Rangers FC, to help Michael fund the deal to buy Manchester United, we put the whole financial package together in just three days. We did the deal right here in Edinburgh, just down the road at Bird Semple Fyfe Ireland lawyers' office.

'It was such an attractive proposal, and Michael had prepared a brilliant business plan. We couldn't believe that he had managed to pull off the deal to buy Manchester United for just ten million quid. We gave him an overdraft facility there and then for £24m and he could have come back for more if he'd wanted to.

'It's all a mystery to me why Michael never took the money. One day we were doing the deal, the next day he had left town, and that was it, the end of our involvement.'

Grossart's expression suggested that Knighton's rejection of the finances he had put together with such enthusiasm was an affront both to his person and his intelligence. He had come to know Knighton pretty well through his involvement with the art world, particularly as Sir Angus was by then also chairman of the trustees at the National Galleries of Scotland. He knew Knighton sufficiently to understand that the man was a conundrum whose mysteries he would never unravel. 'Bloody fool' might have been a description used by Grossart in 1989, but now he understood Knighton better, Grossart knew that only a fool himself would deem Knighton to be of that same ilk.

Perhaps what most matters to Michael Knighton thirty years on, in 2019, is that people understand that he really did have the money to complete the Manchester United deal.

Sir Angus Grossart's testimony in this matter is unimpeachable, his standing and authority unquestionable.

Even Edwards nowadays – much too late – concedes that Knighton did have the financial wherewithal to complete the purchase of the club in 1989, something he denied for two decades, until suddenly changing his tune recently. Perhaps time really was a healer in Edwards' case, or perhaps he had had enough of untruths in this respect and no longer felt the need to hide behind his claim that Knighton was the scoundrel in the aborted bid of 1989.

Knighton had been Edwards' fall guy for a long time.

These days, Knighton finds it impossible to believe that some fools still believe he was a penniless charlatan.

'Does anyone seriously think that I would have been appointed to the Old Trafford board had Edwards thought I lacked the wherewithal to buy the club in the first place?

'Look, this corroboration of the truth of the matter comes from the mouth of the most unimpeachable source. This is Sir Angus Grossart, the most respected Scottish businessman of his generation, we're talking about here.'

Another onlooker at that same celebration dinner in Edinburgh's heartland was Paul Roberts, deputy chairman of Lyon & Turnbull.

'It doesn't surprise me that he turned the money down,' Roberts said. 'In fact, nothing about Michael surprises me. Twenty-four years ago I was introduced to him by my next-door neighbour, a prominent dealer in antiques, as a man who wanted to buy my city-centre Georgian terrace house. I was in the pub at the time and in walked my neighbour with Michael and said, "This guy will buy your house, he's a good client of mine."

'I told Michael I wanted a quarter of a million pounds, and he shot out his hand and said, "Deal done." I found it difficult to believe him as he'd never even seen the inside of my house and, after all, I didn't know him from Adam. A few weeks later, though, he bought my house together with half the bloody furniture, but then he never moved into the property. He kept it for a couple of years, then sold it on.

'I lost contact with Michael for a number of years, then I got a call out of the blue in late 2006. I want you to sell a few things for me, he says, art, antiques, the stuff you deal in, Paul, before this world experiences the greatest financial crash of all time. "Whoa," I said, but Michael carried on. It will be, he says, bigger, more disastrous even than the crash of 1929 and the Great Depression. It's coming, trust me, Paul.

'Well, that's a good two years before anyone else has a sniff of any great crash. At the time, we all laughed, of course, we just thought Michael was being a bit eccentric and a bit dramatic. He was bloody well spot on, though, as we all now know what happened with the great financial crash of 2008, though how the hell he knew this a full year or more in advance I haven't a clue.'

It seemed that sometimes, Knighton was a dab hand at predictions.

In the *Blueprint* he researched and wrote between 1986 and 1989 he not only set out the path to financial expansion that Manchester United has followed ever since, but also foresaw the football industry's Big Bang of the 1990s, the creation of an ever-expanding universe of money and yet more money from sponsorship, marketing contracts, television and beyond.

In one uncanny section, Knighton even told of the arrival of multinational corporations, billionaires from overseas, specifically mentioning the possibility of the arrival of Russian oligarchs. He even suggested that English football clubs might be purchased by sovereign funds of foreign governments. No wonder he is known in some circles as the Nostradamus of the football world.

In 2019, a majority of Premier League football clubs are foreign owned, and all are controlled by millionaires and billionaires. Manchester City, the current champions, are owned by the Abu Dhabi royal family. Previously they were owned by the alleged human rights abuser and former prime minister of Thailand, Thaksin Shinawatra.

Even more interesting, from the point of view of the future development of club football, is the ownership of the French club Paris St Germain by the petrodollars of Qatar. Claims have been made that the Qatari state may have not only bought into French football but also purchased through bribes the right to host the World Cup in 2022. Concrete proof of the latter allegation, though, has yet to be produced.

In the summer of 2017, PSG paid Barcelona an astonishing £200m for the Brazilian international, Neymar. Soon afterwards, a loan deal was arranged with Monaco for the eighteen-year-old French starlet, Kylian Mbappe. His £160m transfer was completed in 2018. Six years earlier, Knighton had smiled wryly when English Premier League TV rights were sold to BT and BSkyB for £3.018bn, an increase of £1.25bn on the previous deal. Three years later, those same rights were sold for a whopping £5.136bn. Knighton says he always knew the day would arrive when such mind-boggling sums were paid for the TV rights of the people's sport.

'I saw it all coming. All these developments were predicted in the *Blueprint* that I gave to Manchester United.'

* * *

If, however, Knighton had really believed in this exponential growth in the value of the football industry in general and in Manchester United's profitability in particular, why did he walk away from the Bank of Scotland overdraft offer?

To understand that, it is necessary to better understand Knighton, his fears and insecurities, his brash and bravado, the generosity of spirit of an essentially private, family man, and his relationship with money.

Knighton is a man who has never coveted money for money's sake.

That has never been his style. He has given most of his money to those who have really needed it, to family and to charitable causes.

As Knighton left Scotland with the promised cash still on the table, as the plots thickened around him, as the game he was playing reached injury time, he continued to reveal himself through his actions and inactions, and his words.

Only you can decide whether to believe in them.

## Chapter Nineteen

# Injury Time

*Manchester, Mostly*
*September, October and Ever After, 1989*

WHAT KNIGHTON says about his sudden return to Manchester, about his leaving the overdraft deal unsigned, is perhaps more prosaic than storytellers might wish for.

He claimed rejection of the deal with the Bank of Scotland enabled him to keep his options open. His accountants, Robson Rhodes, had advised Knighton not to sign the agreement until he had, at the very least, attempted to contact some of the people and parties queuing up to take the places of Thornton and Cohen.

Among them was Andrew Sykes, a former student at Knighton's school in Huddersfield, whose father was so rich in oil there would have been no need to involve any bank at all. There was also a rumour that Frank Warren was interested in joining forces at Old Trafford. Warren was the son of a bookmaker and had trained as a solicitor's clerk, but was making his way in the mazy, punch drunk world of boxing after managing Terry Marsh to the light-welterweight championship of the world.

Knighton, though, never talked to Warren personally, and doubts this rumour's veracity.

Next in the queue was Lancashire media mogul Owen Oyston, who had £35m in the bank, and who also offered to partner Knighton in his Old Trafford venture. There was an Arab consortium somewhere too.

He was also approached by Eddie Shah, proprietor of the *Today* newspaper who wrote to Knighton to congratulate him on his business coup.

The letter ran something like this:

*Dear Michael*

*I am a great admirer of yours! What a coup! Congratulations!*

*I would like you to know that my financial acumen and my full business resources are at your disposal.*

*I'm interested in this deal from an investment point of view.*

*Please contact me ...*

Someone, probably from Knighton's professional team, said let's ring Eddie Shah. Someone else, probably his accountants, said yes, Shah sold his Messenger Group of northern newspapers for £40m so he's definitely good for a bob or two. Shah had once described himself as a maverick, someone who liked doing things people said couldn't be done, so he really should have got on with Knighton.

All of this took place with neither Knighton's knowledge nor permission. Afterwards, Shah claimed in the press that the chairman elect was trying to sell the club on for a profit.

Nothing could have been further from the truth.

* * *

Meanwhile, Manchester had become an unwelcoming place for Knighton.

Everywhere he went, he was told he was the man bringing Manchester United into disrepute, the man who had no money, but who still wanted to buy the greatest football club in the world. There were so many lies, there was so much garbage in the gutter press.

On 14 October 1989, *The Sun* decided that Knighton had cancelled a holiday in order to *face the hate mob.*

*The property magnate,* wrote Michael Morgan, *is set to face the fans who despise him. The punters are fuming over the humiliation and ridicule heaped on their club.*

In fact, Knighton said, most fans were charming, full of good humour and welcoming most of the time and it was Edwards, not Knighton, who was still the focus of fans' vitriol during that autumn of discontent.

That same October day brought United's home game against Sheffield Wednesday. Knighton would not miss it for the world, for his great-grandfather's memory's sake, but he decided not to take Rosemary to any more games if the flak continued, as he suspected it might. The match was a drear and drab 0-0 draw and United sank to a new low of seventeenth in the league. Even Knighton understood it could not go on like this forever. He suspected that the media circus was impacting on the team's performance. One newspaper article even claimed Knighton was so poor he was receiving food parcels from Scotland from his mother-in-law. Many articles seemed to have no purpose other than to discredit Knighton, to bring him to his knees and, just as he had tried to beat back the incoming tide of journalistic flotsam and jetsam by talking to the *Financial Times*, he now talked to another financial scribbler, Lawrence Lever of the *Mail on Sunday*.

He spent some time and some considerable effort in trying to explain that in order to buy Manchester United it was not necessary to have £20m asleep in a bank vault. He was wasting his time. The article concluded that Knighton clearly could not afford to buy Manchester United. Lever said he had made a thorough search of Companies House records and could only find St David's School in Knighton's name.

Knighton could have saved this particular journalist a lot of trouble by telling him that the school was his sole business registered in his name at Companies House. Lever, however, ignored what Knighton told him, did not bother to research Knighton's other assets.

Knighton even thought of taking legal action against some of the newspapers, but didn't want to put himself and his family through all of that just to increase the circulation of the libellous tabloids and the notoriety of the man from the *Mail on Sunday*.

Knighton, for a man so pilloried in the press, was remarkably unlitigious, only once in his life choosing to take legal action, against Reed Publishing International, at that time the largest publisher in the world, for gross inaccuracies in their book, *The Sunday Times Illustrated History of Football*. Appropriate compensation was settled out of court and the company were required to read out a humbling apology inside the courtroom. Interestingly, not one newspaper reported this climbdown, not one interested in the facts of Knighton's matter.

Even so, he had been on the front and back pages of many newspapers for so long and he was tired now.

Where the *Manchester Evening News* had led the way, with a classic journalistic scoop, Maxwell's *Mirror* followed with attempts to drag Knighton into the same gutter from which most of its stories emerged. The rest of the press pack tagged along for the ride, for the thrill of the chase. These were the days of total press freedom, of unrestrained muckraking journalism, and before Lord Justice Leveson's inquiry into the abuse of phone hacking and the ethics and culture of the UK media.

Knighton was beginning to fear for everyone involved, particularly his family, but was also, like Edwards, genuinely concerned about the damage to the well-being and reputation of Manchester United caused by the incessant and unremitting negativity of the press coverage. He understood that all this ordure may have been the root cause of all these bad results, and of United's freefall down the league table.

Of course, Knighton told himself, if he headed north to Edinburgh, he had a cheque for £24m waiting for him to cash. At least, he hoped it was still there waiting for him. He thought of Davies, the tramp in Pinter's play, *The Caretaker*, who only had to get himself down to Sidcup to find his papers and all would be well.

*I could have done this all by myself*, he thought. *I could have gone to my own bank and they would have jumped at the chance to loan me the necessary money to complete the deal.*

*That's what I should have done.*

But it was all too late now.

* * *

If it was less than good for Knighton, it might have been worse for Edwards.

The chairman had returned from his holiday to find Old Trafford in a state of ferment and fury, much of it directed at Knighton and, therefore, by damaging association, Edwards. This was not what Edwards had expected when he shook hands at Killochan Castle with the man he thought he knew and trusted. This was not the dignified retreat from antagonistic crowds, from the stench of half-recognised failure that Edwards craved. This was frenzy and this was hatred, and it was dragging Manchester United into disrepute and Edwards into an ever deepening mire.

It is easy to imagine Midani and Burrows saying to Edwards, *We told you so, we told you Knighton never had the money. This debacle, this disgrace, this ignominy would never have happened if you had sold the club to us.*

*What should I do?* Edwards may have said in response.

There was nothing anyone could do unless Knighton capitulated and handed back the option contract.

Or produced the money.

* * *

Edwards telephoned Knighton.

'What are we going to do?'

'There's a mole in the camp, Martin.'

Knighton was so angry his voice was barely intelligible.

'Is it Burrows?' he asked.

'Who knows, Michael?' Edwards replied. 'But it's true enough someone's fuelling the fire and fanning the flames.'

* * *

It was also true that it really was not about the money with Knighton.

He talks a good game of money, he likes to feel the value of a deal, likes to be on the winning side, but, in the final analysis, it's only money and it comes and it goes. There are things he cares more about, and these are not the things that money can necessarily buy.

At that moment, he might have felt himself to be a man more sinned against than sinning, but he is no saint, so let's say that first, he was worried about himself.

He had been depressed before, in the months when he and Rosemary did not know whether Mark would have a future after the horrors of his birth. Then, Knighton did not know how he continued to get up in the mornings, buy flowers for the shop and sometimes just for his wife, to get her through it, plan lessons for the school and mark books while he wondered just what a lack of oxygen could do to a boy just born.

He recognised the symptoms again now, the twin feelings of hopelessness and helplessness, the loss of interest in outcomes, in the performance of duties.

It was as if it was someone else, someone unrecognisable as himself, who was doing all these things, phoning Edwards, meeting with Edwards, meeting with Midani, reluctantly, doing press calls, not answering phone calls from Scotland, from Murray. He recognised the guilt, the irritability, the intolerance.

Ah, yes, the guilt. Knighton was beginning to reproach himself for bringing about this turmoil, not just for himself and his family, but for Manchester United, too. He was beginning to believe what he read in the papers, the crap he believed Burrows and Midani were feeding to an insatiable gutter press. He was beginning to think he might want out, to be rid of all these falsehoods and all this mud- and shit-slinging.

In retrospect, Knighton says he had the good name of Manchester United primarily at heart, and this is probably the best explanation for what happened next.

After all, the tarnished reputation of this famous football club, as a result of all this hype and hullabaloo, was being smeared with every splash across the tabloid pages and Knighton could not remain untouched by and innocent of this forever.

There was enough going on to make anyone think about changing their mind about the purchase of a famous football club.

* * *

What Knighton needed to understand, in the latter days of October 1989, was that when shit happens, it happens in spades, in shovelfuls, and that there was always a ready supply of willing press room shovellers of all that stinking stuff.

Even Knighton seems unclear about what happened next.

Maybe there were discussions between Knighton's people and Shah's people, maybe there was sufficient talk to generate paperwork, and maybe that nonsense ended up in the *Manchester Evening News*.

Others who may have talked to Knighton's people included Owen Oyston, chairman of Blackpool FC, sometime socialist millionaire and later a jailbird rapist, probably, and Dave Whelan, former Blackburn Rovers footballer and later owner of Wigan Athletic, possibly.

The only one of these Knighton spoke to in person was Oyston, and that was a waste of time.

It is possible, probable even, Knighton's team were trying to help, talking to all and sundry, trying to keep their boss's show on the road.

Knighton, by this stage, no longer knew, no longer cared.

He told himself he had never asked anyone for help.

Whatever the truth of it, the result was more and even harsher shellacking of Knighton in the press. He was being gutted like a landed fish. The usual suspects were claiming he was an utter charlatan, a dreamer of the first order. He did not have the money, he did not have the backers, and now he was trying to sell the contract on for personal profit. He never intended to do anything with Manchester United except turn a deal, as if the most famous football club in the world was just another property in his portfolio, to be sold on when it suited, without ever being lived in or loved.

There was an intricate web being spun here and there were many spiders in the house.

Knighton knew that Shah played at the Mere Golf Club in Cheshire where many of the Manchester United hierarchy were also members. Who knows whether Shah might have been talking to some of Knighton's professionals involved in the buyout? If he was thinking about all this at all, he guessed Shah might have mentioned something to his friends on the United board.

Knighton knew he should have done more to stop all of this nonsense.

But he no longer cared about what was being said or who was doing what in whose name. He could not deal with any of that right now as his sole concern was for the welfare of his nearest and dearest.

He was thinking more and more about his family and what his arrogance, his ambition, was putting them through.

He was thinking, too, of the damage being done to the football club.

He was more than tired now, he was exhausted.

Someone told him that Edelson and Charlton were signing an affidavit to get an injunction to stop the disclosure by Knighton of confidential information about the club. Edelson claimed the directors were all 'totally humiliated and embarrassed'. Burrows, too, blathered about his football club having become 'the laughing stock of the world'.

And, at that moment of maximum damage to Knighton, Charlton admitted to the press that yes, in these difficult times, with all these disturbing and hurtful events going on, he would be prepared to take on the burden of the position of chairman of Manchester United. Charlton was still a man with clean hands in the eye of the dirt of the storm.

But Knighton could not deal with any of that right now.

He could, though, phone Edwards.

'Martin,' he said, 'we have to put a stop to all of this.'

'I agree,' said Edwards.

'We have to bring to a halt all this negative press coverage that my bid for the club has triggered.'

'I agree,' said Edwards.

'I'm concerned for everyone, but especially the reputation of the football club, but there is just one other matter.'

'Yes?'

'We'll talk more, Martin, when we meet.'

The two men agreed on a meeting place and a time: the Novotel, Manchester, shortly after Knighton's thirty-eighth birthday.

The arrangements completed, Knighton took himself north, to Scotland, not to sign any loan documents that might or might not have still been waiting for him there in Edinburgh, but to breathe the autumn air in an attempt to rebuild something from the wreckage of his rational world.

Still, though, he could not avoid the newspapers.

He saw a report in *The Times* that suggested Midani and Burrows were preparing to join in Knighton's bid for United.

Where did they get this stuff from?

And yet, less than a month later, Knighton did meet Midani.

At the latter's suggestion.

Knighton was curious to meet him if only to find out what was happening inside the Old Trafford boardroom.

In his own mind, however, Knighton was firm and clear that he was set on aborting the deal to buy Manchester United.

Even so, might it have crossed his mind that an unholy marriage of convenience between himself and Midani might just have worked? Edwards might rail in private against Manchester United being sold to a foreigner but Edwards was no longer in a position to have the slightest say in this unless Knighton tore up the contract between them.

And, all the while, the media circus continued, unabated in its fury, swirling about Knighton and all the characters in the play, dizzying them all, attempting to destroy them all.

* * *

Midani was dapper, moustached like Knighton. They had nothing in common except for Manchester United.

Midani's father was a jet-setting billionaire, Knighton's a retired, honest and hard-working miner.

The talk was civil, polite.

It was clear, however, that Midani would have been prepared to stitch up his former allies in the boardroom, should Knighton have given him any encouragement to join him in the bid for the football club.

In fact, Midani offered Knighton £4.5m to become his partner in the deal.

Knighton remained determined, however, knowing he was best out of all of this madness, all this nonsense. He never had the slightest intention of being seduced by Midani's millions.

His withdrawal from the agreement with Edwards would be best for him, for Rosemary and the kids, and best for the club, too.

* * *

Shah, though, was still dancing, apparently still considering the possibility of moving in on the deal, but tiring of the whole damn thing. Knighton guessed the newspaper magnate believed he might now be implicated in a Dutch auction designed to flush out bidders for the benefit of Knighton's pockets. It was not true, but beliefs, in those dark days, had more currency than realities.

Knighton and Edwards resumed their conversation about end games. Knighton had clarity of purpose almost within his grasp, but all the while there were new players in the game, new possibilities to explore. It was difficult to settle with Edwards. Knighton knew the deal would have to be aborted, though, and also knew that he was the only person who could make that happen.

## Chapter Twenty

# Extra Time

### *London, Late On, October 1989*

KNIGHTON WAS in London on the day before his thirty-eighth birthday for an interview with Harry Harris, Maxwell's go-to reporter. God only knows why he had agreed to this – some idea, perhaps, of hugging his enemy close.

Apparently, it had been arranged by Roger Levitt, financial adviser to the stars. Levitt was on the phone to Knighton now.

'Michael,' he said, 'all your problems are over.'

Knighton hoped that organising meetings with the enemy was not the finance man's only trick.

At this time, Levitt was the owner of the UK's largest independent firm of financial advisers, whose unlucky clients included Frederick Forsyth, the novelist and author of *The Day of the Jackal;* Michael Winner, the film director whose most recent film, *Firepower,* featured Sophia Loren, James Cockburn and OJ Simpson; and former pop idol Adam Faith. All three of them lost the shirts from their backs when Levitt's empire crashed and burned in 1990 with accumulated debts of £34m.

Curiously, Faith, a man who once described himself as a collector of contemporary banknotes, was responsible for Winner's introduction to Levitt and, after Levitt's downfall, the film director was overheard saying, 'Adam Faith is to financial advice what Frank Bruno is to English literature.' Knighton thought Winner may have been unkind to Bruno, Britain's former favourite heavyweight boxer and pantomime dame.

In October 1989, however, Levitt also headed up a stable of sporting stars that included Sebastian Coe, former Olympic gold medallist, Lennox Lewis, rising star in the world boxing firmament, and John Hollins, the Arsenal midfield enforcer.

'I am going to protect you, Michael,' he said. 'Let the Levitt Group envelop you now and keep you from all this flak.'

Knighton had seen his photographs in the press, had assessed his sharp suits and sharp face, all angles and power points, seen that his eyes were like caves that never saw the sun. He was not entirely sure he wished to be saved by this man with the voice of a snake charmer and the slipperiness of a snake.

A year later, Levitt's business was shown to be rotten to the core.

'Sorry, Roger,' Knighton said, 'but I'm rather busy right now.'

This was true. He had Harry Harris to deal with, a prospect and three quarters even if the *Mirror* back-page hit man and Maxwell hack had promised to be kind.

As it turned out, Harris and Levitt were acquainted.

'Don't worry, Michael,' the adviser said. 'Harry will write you a good piece, I promise you, and the next day we'll meet up.'

Levitt was persistent, too, and asked his secretary to make an appointment for Knighton to have breakfast with him the following day.

The meeting with Harris passed in the same fog of unreality as everything else in this time of persecution and pressure. Afterwards, Knighton could not remember what he had said and knew he would never read the results. He was now far and fast beyond caring.

At 8.45 sharp the following day, the time of the planned breakfast with Levitt, Knighton phoned the financial adviser and instructed his secretary, 'Please, convey my apologies to Mr Levitt, but I will not be there to meet him.'

A few minutes later, she called him back to say her employer was upset. 'What about lunch? Or dinner?'

Knighton declined. He knew his gut feeling to have nothing to do with the man was the correct one.

Levitt had not only offered him protection, but had told him he could put money down to do the Manchester United deal on Knighton's behalf, if that was what the chairman elect wished him to do. Knighton, however, knew he would be seeing no one, except maybe his family on his birthday.

If he had the time or energy.

Except maybe Edwards. He knew he had to see the Manchester United man again soon, to try to sort out this godawful mess.

## Chapter Twenty-One

# End Game

### *Manchester Hotels, October 1989*

KNIGHTON DROVE north, fast, above the speed limit. Motorways passed in quick succession, all the same, all grey and bleak, and as full of traffic as his head was full of demon thoughts.

He did not celebrate his birthday but he had remembered he had agreed to meet Edwards a few days later, on 9 October, at the Novotel, on the periphery of Manchester.

Finally, he had utter clarity of purpose.

Watkins, club solicitor and Edwards' loyal shadow, was at the meeting, too. Knighton did not mind. He had always got on well with these two principal characters at Old Trafford. He recalled that this was how the negotiations had begun, and now this was how they would end, as would this crazy world of claim and counter claim, of chasing paparazzi, and of the world's media spying on and lying about every move he made.

The hotel was dark and modern at the same time, though Knighton conceded he may have been mistaken about the darkness as everything seemed black to him. This was a good place, he thought, for a secret meeting. The conspirators had hired a small conference room, all plush and lush, cheap and tawdry, but it would do.

Knighton was shocked by the way Edwards looked, sunken, graveyard bones beneath the skin of his taut face, eyes grey as ash, cold, after the fire had died out. His hair looked unwashed, his clothes appeared to have been slept and overslept in.

'Yes,' Edwards said, 'it's bad, isn't it?'

Knighton wondered whether Edwards' disarray was solely down to the fact that he now understood he had massively undersold his football club. He knew Edwards' unkempt appearance was so unlike the man. Watkins was the one who spoke next.

'What is your view of it all, Michael?' His voice was small and calm but somehow broken, too. 'How can we bring this situation to an end, put a stop to all this uncertainty and trouble? I am concerned about the effect all of this is having on our club.'

Knighton said, 'I suppose there are several options.' He looked at the faces before him, both furrowed and worn. Watkins also looked defeated by the horrors of the past months.

'I could carry on,' Knighton said, 'and complete the deal, I could prove to the world just how wrong everyone is.' Edwards' and Watkins' mouths both opened, but no words fell from their lips. 'I could show you – and Nigel Burrows and the rest of them – that I can complete this deal.'

'How can we bring all this to an end, Michael?' Watkins said.

Knighton waited, turned from Watkins to Edwards.

'We have a proposal, Michael,' Edwards said.

Knighton nodded, assented to consideration at least.

'The media circus, Michael, it's got to end,' Watkins said, 'for the sake of the club, for the sake of us all.'

Knighton looked closely at Watkins, a man he had great respect for, a highly successful Manchester lawyer, a man who had been at Edwards' right hand through all the machinations, all the twists and turns of this deal. He was the voice of reason, of common sense. He was not well, though, Knighton thought, his face grey, a mask of worry and torment.

My God, Knighton thought, this thing will kill us all.

'We want to offer you a place on the board, Michael, together with a gifted shareholding,' Watkins said. 'Let's take this club forward together.'

'We think you have a real contribution to make at our club,' Edwards added, having recovered his composure.

There was a silence so deep as to be unfathomable.

'Well,' Knighton said, at last, 'maybe I don't have to own the club.'

He saw the stress drain from the faces of Edwards and Watkins. 'It's never been just about that.'

'By working together,' Edwards said, 'we can make your hopes and your plans for the club's future really work, put all this uncertainty, this negativity, behind us.'

The silence that followed was deep but temporary.

It was Knighton's move.

'There is one more thing,' he said, 'and it's not an ego thing, but what I really must do, gentlemen, is demonstrate to everyone that I could have completed on the deal, prove to the press and all the critics that I always had the wherewithal to finalise the purchase, show that the rest of the world has been entirely wrong on that score.'

Knighton relaxed back into his seat.

'This is absolutely essential to me,' he said, 'and totally non-negotiable.'

He watched comprehension dawn across Edwards' face.

'You will understand this point, Martin?'

Edwards signified his assent with a thin smile.

'I have to be allowed some dignity and respect here.'

'I agree.'

'I have to prove to the world and his wife that I could have done this deal, that I possess the requisite cash, otherwise this entire episode will be viewed by history as little more than a charade, and that cannot be permitted to happen.'

Edwards smiled again, more widely this time.

Watkins, too, was beaming, exuding relief and sweat in equal measure.

'Clearly, if I am refusing cash from my bankers, if I am bowing out, it is solely for honourable and legitimate reasons, and I want everyone to know that is indeed the case.'

Edwards put away his smile, perhaps out of respect for Knighton's position, perhaps because he was relieved, or maybe because he felt an inkling of triumph, but knew it was bad form to show this.

'An honourable exit, Michael? You know, that's all I ever wanted too.'

Knighton either failed to note the irony, or chose to ignore it.

'My main concerns at this time,' Knighton said, 'are the welfares of both the football club and my precious family.'

'Mine, too,' said Edwards, and his voice was soft as gratitude for an answered prayer.

There was a handshake of sorts, part embarrassed, but one, at any rate, that was far less fervent than those exchanged between the two men at Killochan, no clasping of shoulders in brotherly love this time around.

Watkins stood, too, and offered his hand.

Knighton saw a frown pass across Edwards' brow.

He understood the chairman of Manchester United knew now that, in this game of Monopoly, he would not be passing Go, would not be collecting his £10m.

Watkins, too, was passing up a fortune, but Knighton knew him well enough to understand money had never been his driving force in all of this.

At this moment, all three men were putting money in its rightful, secondary place. 'Credit where it's due,' Knighton said, 'both Edwards and Watkins put their love of their football club before their love of money.'

There are other possible interpretations of their actions, Edwards' and Watkins', but Knighton's generosity is worth preserving.

He was almost there now, Knighton thought, wherever there was, wherever there might be.

There was one more thing to confirm.

'The ideas,' he said, 'the ones I've set out in my *Blueprint*, they must be implemented.'

The two men opposite nodded in agreement.

'I have your word on that?'

More sweaty hands were shaken.

'If I become a director,' Knighton concluded, 'I must be permitted to make a proper, significant contribution.'

* * *

Somewhere across town, in the Midland Hotel in the centre of Manchester, Knighton's team of advisers had been working on a document which would offer shareholders other than Edwards the same price for their shares. It was already overdue but, while the lawyers were still talking, there remained the possibility of completing the takeover. All that was needed now was to tie the shoelaces of the deal.

Those minions still shuffling papers to and fro in the Midland Hotel had no idea that afternoon of what had transpired across town.

* * *

Inside the Novotel, the meeting between Knighton and Edwards and Watkins was not yet set to finish.

'All you have to do, Michael, is tear up the contract,' Edwards said. 'And that's it, over for all of us, and we can all move on, get back to work, and focus on the club.'

Edwards' voice was soft now, hypnotic.

The choice was stark but not that simple, even though Knighton had already made up his mind. At some point he had been granted this clarity of vision he had prayed for, although he had no idea when or how it had arrived.

* * *

One problem, though, was that some people would just not leave him alone.

It wasn't the press this time, or Edwards and Watkins.

It wasn't even the bouncers and the flouncers supposedly working on his behalf in the Midland Hotel.

Instead it was all those people still wanting to offer him money, millions and millions of pounds, if only Knighton would let them share a piece of his cake.

In fact, he could have sold on the deal to a third party, tripled his personal wealth overnight, and been hailed in the City as the cleverest and coolest dude the financial world had ever known.

If Knighton had been motivated by money and money alone, he could have sold out to the highest bidder and been heralded in the business world, in the capitalist world, as one of its brightest stars, one of its heroes of wealth creation, simply by understanding the true value, the hidden value of an asset and realising that value, and all without spending one single penny of his own money.

None of that appealed very much to Knighton, though.

Out of the wide and blue, the biggest offer came from someone Knighton both admired for his business acumen and respected for his decisiveness, bluntness even, straightforwardness at least.

This was an innocent time, before Philip Green had been knighted for his services to the rag trade, before his castigation in the national press for his part in the British Home Stores debacle, and prior to his alleged sexual and racial harassment and bullying of employees, which the billionaire, by the way, still vehemently denies.

By 2019, however, Green, according to some members of the third estate, had been labelled Sir Greedy and Sir Shifty, and to some politicians had become the unacceptable face of capitalism.

It was just the system, though, just an unregulated capitalist market, that's all it was, that's all it ever was, that's all it will probably always be, world without end, amen.

* * *

It was astonishing to Knighton that all those in his story were almost the same age as him, including Green who was just six months younger.

Many of them, though, enjoyed a helping hand or two along the way. Green, for example, had the promise of his father's successful property and retail business at twelve years old.

In October 1989, Green was living in St John's Wood in London. He was a friend of everything Tottenham Hotspur, especially its chairman, Irving Scholar, who was a man who knew a thing or two about the value of money, and of football clubs. Green was hard-nosed and direct, a deal maker, some would say, without scruples, and immediately saw the value in Knighton's deal with Edwards.

Knighton had met Green previously, in boardrooms at Tottenham Hotspur and at Old Trafford. They had exchanged small talk and banter only. Now, out of the blue, he telephoned Knighton.

'Michael, listen to me, for fuck's sake listen to me.'

Knighton was listening. The telephone was switched to loudspeaker mode and so Rosemary Knighton and one of Knighton's lawyers were listening, too. In fact, they were agog.

'Don't give him the fucking contract back, Michael, do not give this back to Edwards.'

The telephone line could hardly cope with the volume of Green's rant.

'It's worth a fucking fortune, Michael, and I know that and you know that, so what the hell are you fucking about at? I can't believe that you're thinking of handing that contract back to Edwards. Get some sense into that brain of yours, Michael.'

Knighton could not get a word in edgeways.

'People will give anything to own fucking, gold fucking Trafford, and you've got the bleeding contract in your back pocket.'

Knighton wondered whether this was a wake-up call from God or temptation from the devil.

'Don't be a fucking schmuck, Michael. Just sell the fucking contract to me, now.'

Green's voice, across the miles of telephone wires, was manic, desperate to be heard, and absolutely certain that shouting, screaming even, was the way to do it.

'I've got a fucking seven million fucking pounds banker's draft for you here and now – it's in my fucking hand – it's a banker's draft, Michael, and it's yours, it's all yours. Just think what you could do with seven million fucking quid in your pocket. And the deal's cost you fuck all at the moment, so that's seven million clear fucking profit.

'It's here waiting for you, come down to London now, just jump in a fucking taxi and I'll pay for you to get here tonight, St Johns Wood, that's where I am, I'm here, Michael, fucking waiting for you to come and take this money from me now.'

Knighton imagined Green waving the piece of paper above his head as he shrieked and shrilled.

'Get that fucking football off your head, Michael, and come and take the money.'

Knighton could not help laughing out loud. He could not remember the last time he had done that, maybe not since the euphoria of the first day of the football season at Old Trafford, when the football was indeed dancing with delight on his head, on his thigh, on his feet, on its way into the back of the Stretford End goal.

He began to listen hard.

It was an unbelievable deal that Green was offering. All it required was his assent and his signature on a piece of paper.

*I have been here before,* Knighton thought, recalling a contract still unsigned with the Bank of Scotland, which was maybe still on a table somewhere in Edinburgh, or locked away in some dark filing cabinet.

*Once upon a time,* Knighton told himself, *I pulled off the deal of the century to buy Manchester United for a bargain-basement £10m.*

Green's offer was close to being the second best deal of all time. The retailer's voice was frenzied. Knighton needed some time for reflection but understood, too, the urgency, the opportunity, of the present moment.

'You've no role for me at Old Trafford, then, Philip?' Knighton's voice was sweet, cajoling. 'What do you say, Philip?'

After all, this was what mattered to Knighton, his ideas, more than the money.

At first, Green said, 'No, no role for you, Michael, you've had so much shit in the press,' but then he relented. He offered Knighton even more incentives than a fat £7m cheque. 'Go on, then, you twat, you can be the fucking CEO of the club if you want, Michael, and you can have a twenty-two per cent share in any uplift in the value of the shares. Come on, Michael, that is a fucking deal I've done right there for you.'

It was true, Knighton thought, that was a deal alright, and a half, and three quarters too, an amazing offer, dazzling in its daring strategy of entrapment. It was just that it never really was about the money.

'Take the fucking money, Michael and don't be a fucking schmuck.'

A twenty-two per cent profit share on the uplift of Manchester United stock at today's values would have been worth over £770m.

'Listen, you twat, Michael, don't you dare give fucking Edwards that fucking contract back.'

Knighton was thinking as well as listening. 'Just get your fucking arse down here, Michael, and you can stay at mine tonight, and it'll be done and dusted in the morning.'

It would take fifteen years of property dealing to make the kind of money Green was offering with none of the guarantees of a banker's draft. Such a bargain was equivalent to half of Knighton's wealth again and would take his worth past the £20m mark in the blink of an eye. It would also give him the power within the club to implement his *Blueprint*.

Knighton knew, too, Green was known as a man of his word.

The fans at Old Trafford might not mind Green. For them, in autumn 1989, it was anybody but Edwards. Green, too, might not be the worst ever chairman of Manchester United. After all, the rag trade man had watched Scholar at Spurs at close quarters and the Tottenham chairman was no mug. The

Spurs man had floated his company on the Stock Exchange, a first for a sports club.

Later, in 2001, Scholar was a leading player in a BBC documentary, *The Men Who Changed Football.* Knighton was invited to appear as the programme's keynote speaker but declined on the grounds that his Manchester United years were over. Still, he thought at the time, it might have been me as the headline act, as the revolutionary chief of Old Trafford.

Green, meanwhile, had stopped shouting down the telephone, and the sudden silence was curiously frightening. Knighton had time to ponder the madness and the originality, the sheer evil genius of capitalism, its ability to create profit out of thin air, out of nothing, in this obscene yet beautiful way.

'I'll think about it, Philip,' he said.

He did, and he talked to Rosemary, too. For the first and only time in their married life, Knighton's wife offered her clear and carefully considered advice to her husband.

'Take the money, Michael,' she said in her softly lilting Edinburgh accent. 'You have to take the money, darling.' Knighton's eyes were wide with something that might have been surprise. 'Look,' she added, 'it's ridiculous, it's preposterous if you don't.' Knighton held his wife close. 'After all everyone has said and done to you through this whole business. Please, Michael, just take the money.'

The next day, Knighton returned Green's call.

'It's a more than generous offer, Philip, more than fair, but I'm not here for the money.'

'What?' Green's voice was incredulous as well as loud.

'I'm sorry, Philip, but it's no deal.'

There was a momentary silence, an emptiness of disbelief.

'Look,' Knighton said, 'I am very grateful for what you have offered me, and thank you for that, but I'm really not in it for the money.'

'Everybody's in it for the fucking money, Michael.'

Now there was silence on Knighton's side. 'Michael, what the fuck is the matter with you?'

Knighton smiled and thanked Green once more for his interest, and replaced the telephone receiver in its cradle. It was the end of negotiations with Philip Green. A few weeks later, Knighton and Green enjoyed dinner at the retailer's London home. The pair discussed what might have been, and there were no hard feelings.

In 2019, Knighton admitted, 'I don't know enough about the recent media scandals, the BHS debacle, the alleged abuse of non-disclosure agreements.'

Perhaps Knighton was thinking about his own mistreatment by the press.

'Green was one of the very few businessmen who immediately grasped the value of that deal and its amazing potential. It took him about twenty seconds to comprehend its magnitude. All those other so-called clever accountants and commercial lawyers I employed at the time, they never really understood or believed in the value of the club. What they all really liked were the fat fees they were earning at my expense.

'Apart from David Murray and Sir Angus Grossart, Green was the only one who understood the true magnitude of the deal.

'I liked Philip.'

Knighton, though, almost always likes almost everyone.

'Green was brilliant in his assessment of the value of Manchester United, his bravado was typical of the man, and his offer of help and cash was generous indeed.'

* * *

The end game for the most publicised takeover bid in football history came at the Midland Hotel, smack in the happy heart of Manchester.

Outside, the hotel was all redbrick and terracotta, polished marble and polished glass. Inside, it was all elegance with a hint of arsenic and old lace, bitterness and conflict. It was a product of the dying glory of the Edwardian age, a watering and alleged whoring hole for the clients of the Midland Railway.

Knighton appreciated the hotel's specious splendour, its worldly grandiosity. Here, he had taken two suites of rooms for his teams of lawyers and accountants who had been drafting documents and performing due diligence on the finances of Manchester United.

For one moment, he pondered the injustice of the English class system. This hotel had been built by labourers and skilled craftsmen, not for the usage of their peers, the railway workers, engine drivers, footplate men, stokers, guards, porters and ticket collectors, the men who made the money for the railway bosses. Instead it was for those bosses to waste on whiskey and young girls, cheap talk and wagers on the price of corn, the price of women and the value of nothing.

He reflected, too, on the whirlwind madness of the previous ten weeks in the unforgiving glare of the public spotlight.

According to Knighton's sources, Robert Maxwell, the Bouncing Czech, as the owner of the *Daily Mirror* later became known when financial difficulties overwhelmed him, was still writing the raging editorials and some of the basic copy against Knighton.

*Who is this man?*

*Where is the colour of his money?*

*He hasn't got the money, he hasn't got the money, he hasn't got the money.*

*He is dragging the good name of Manchester United into the gutter.*

Knighton had some sympathy, in his current state of mind, with this last view. He did worry about the effect of all this media sickness on the football club, he did feel responsible in some crazy, ill-defined way.

Edwards had also hired suites for his advisers.

It was as if Knighton's men and Edwards' men were two medieval armies lined up to do battle, to kill and to maim.

Knighton, for his part, suspected that Edwards might have realised his mistakes.

With a late summer and early autumn of hindsight it could now be said that Edwards had undersold his stake in the club.

Even perhaps, Knighton mused, Edwards might now feel he had undervalued his inheritance from his father, Champagne Louis.

Knighton, of course, had no patrimony, save his father's wisdom, his father's principles. He had made his fortune from nothing other than sheer bloody hard work, long toiling hours and calculated risk taking, from making commercial decisions for the benefit of his family, motivated originally by his boy's botched birth all those years ago.

* * *

Edwards was talking to Watkins and, Knighton thought, was as edgy as a man on death row awaiting news of his appeal.

Knighton imagined the questions roiling inside Edwards' head.

Would the man with the watertight option to purchase Manchester United return the contract? Would he take the bait? Would he bite the bullet?

He had said so, but would he do so?

Knighton was almost certain that Edwards was aware of the extraordinary offers made to him by Green and by others.

He could see Watkins smiling and apparently nodding his reassurance to his boss.

Neither of them, however, had any idea of what Knighton would do next.

The inducement, though, Knighton told himself, was a place on the board at Old Trafford, together with 30,000 shares.

More importantly, however, was the opportunity to put the ideas in his *Blueprint* into practice.

Still, though, the lying, damaging, lying headlines appeared in the gutter press. There was another fabricated story in that morning's papers.

*BLACKMAIL – KNIGHTON DEMANDS MILLIONS TO GO!*

It was a heavyweight boxer's blow to the solar plexus and Knighton knew he was on the ropes, hanging on hopelessly to a dream unwinding, unravelling into a nightmare of punches and the inevitable knockout blow. He was almost beyond anger with the gutter press. He had never demanded a penny. He had to prove at all costs that he was not motivated by money.

At this low point, Philip Green phoned Knighton once again, renewed his offers, re-branded his promises.

'Don't give him back the fucking contract, Michael.'

No, no, no, no, no, no.

'Give it to me, Michael, give it to me.'

Knighton saw Rosemary on the far side of the hotel suite, beyond the tables that were awash with the detritus of the deal.

*Take the money, Michael, take the money, Michael, please take the money.*

Knighton heard the words of his wife echoing in his head. Like a hammer on the wires of a piano.

He gazed at her as she watched all the sandwiches being scoffed and the bottle after bottle of fine wine being quaffed by the posse of lawyers, accountants and banking advisers, and he knew she would be angry, incandescent in her quiet way, at the sheer bloody waste of it all.

'Who is paying for all of this, Michael?'

Rosemary was both the least and the most of his worries right now.

Edwards was approaching, traversing no man's land, with a white flag in the one hand and Watkins alongside him. The two men greeted each other warmly and Watkins waited. It was as if Knighton and Edwards had both found an oasis of peace in the politeness of each other's company, amid the bang and crash and the haemorrhaging of money.

'We have to find a way, Michael.'

'I know,' he said.

The juiciest bait came right at the end of their conversation, a reassurance of a promise already made.

'What is it you really want, Michael?'

'It's not the money, Martin.'

'I know,' he said, although whether Edwards truly knew that, understood that, was doubtful in the extreme. He had a track record dedicated to the making and the taking of money. 'What is it, then?'

Knighton thought hard because he had long since lost sight of the man he was when all this began. He saw Watkins smiling and wondered what he had to smile about. Edwards looked really ill, and Knighton wondered if he looked the same.

'I think,' he said, 'I want to make a difference.

'Not just Manchester United, but the entire football industry. I want the fans of each club to be respected and to be able to watch their teams in the same comfort and the same safety as the directors and the executive class do. For God's sake, there must be no more disasters.'

Knighton recalled the motivation, the drive he once had, remembered Heysel, remembered Hillsborough, remembered his great-grandfather, Willie Layton, surging forward, fearless, in the FA Cup Final of 1907. He remembered the men and boys of Blackwell Colliery. He thought of his own father, Albert Knighton, wanting him, needing him, to be proud of his son.

'Come on to the board, then, Michael, and make your difference.'

Knighton turned instinctively to Edwards.

'We'll use your plan. Come on board and do what you want.'

The repetition of Edwards' promise was manna from heaven to Knighton.

Ah, he thought, the *Blueprint,* almost forgotten amid all this hurly and burly, let this plan unfold and do its work, do its best. It was this pivotal document that had underpinned Knighton's bid for Manchester United in the first place. The opportunity to see first-hand its impact, its fruition, was too good to turn down. The peace, as well, the bliss of peace, that Knighton foresaw with his decision to abort his bid made his resolution, in the end, an easy one.

He recalled the personal abuse on the streets of Manchester and the day one of his business associates arrived at an office in Eccles, parked a brand new Rolls-Royce Corniche, £100,000 worth of sleek elegance and powerful splendour, and how it was mistaken for his own car.

*Knighton, you fat, greedy bastard. Knighton, you fat, greedy bastard.*

He remembered how the car was smashed to smithereens in minutes by a group of hooligans masquerading as football fans.

He was tired of all of that.

The two sets of lawyers began to draft a joint letter to shareholders to announce that Knighton was set to hand the option contract back to Martin Edwards and terminate his bid to buy the club. This document confirmed that Knighton had turned down several financial offers that would have been financially advantageous to himself in order to preserve the good name of Manchester United.

It should also have emphasised that Knighton could have enriched himself beyond avarice and that, at any time, there had been nothing to prevent him from selling the contract on to a third party or to the highest bidder, should he have been inclined to do so.

It was Edwards' team who insisted on these omissions in order to save their client, the chairman of Manchester United, from further embarrassment.

The letter only stated some of the things that needed saying, and shouting out loud.

Remember, though, Knighton thought, the essence of any good deal is that it must make both parties equally happy.

Edwards and Knighton hoped to regain possession of their lives and bring all the press speculation and misinformation to an abrupt and clean end in the interests of the club and everyone associated with it.

Edwards would live to fight another day with his right to a controlling ownership of Manchester United returned to him. Knighton had a place on the board and the chance to put his plans into operation which was all he said he ever really wanted to do in the first place.

Most of all, Knighton hoped he would be able to reclaim his dignity, his ability to walk tall. He would hold his head high as a director of Manchester United FC, and he would watch with pride as his ideas from the *Blueprint* were implemented by his friend and colleague, Edwards, the man he had once hugged close at Killochan Castle.

He knew he would never again emerge from the players' tunnel at Old Trafford, resplendent in Red Devil red, never again thrash a football hard as a cannon shot into the goal before the Stretford End. He would exchange all that for a portion of peace, a repose of respectability.

The letter to shareholders, dated 18 October 1989, stated categorically that, contrary to rumours in the press, Knighton had never asked for compensation for surrendering his golden contract. Moreover, it underlined the fact that Knighton had turned down substantial offers for the contract to purchase Martin Edwards' shares in Manchester United, offers which were substantially to his and to his family's advantage.

For both Knighton and Edwards, the drafting, the signing, and the posting of the letter felt like cooling, refreshing rain at the end of a long, hot, and humid day.

* * *

It was not all sweetness and light, however.

Copies of the letter to shareholders were sent to local and national press. Five copies were sent to Maxwell personally on five consecutive days. No one at the *Manchester Evening News*, or at Maxwell's *Daily Mirror*, or at any red top newspaper had sufficient interest in or commitment to the truth to either reproduce the letter in their pages or to quote from it or comment on it.

Even now, three decades on, the consensus among those who still care about these things remains that Knighton never had the money to complete the deal, and this is still a great sadness to him.

His team of commercial advisers throughout these negotiations at end game were drawn from stockbrokers, Laing & Cruickshank.

'Do you really think,' he said later, 'that blue blood brokers like these, brokers to the Queen no less, would have taken me on as a client without proof of my ability to fund the purchase?'

Sometimes, Knighton is a master of understatement.

It was to set these matters straight that this book was originally conceived and why the original title was to have been *The Truth Game*.

*Book Four*

# After-match Analysis

## Chapter Twenty-Two

# After the Match

*1989–1992*

IT WAS over.

The match had not ended how Knighton once hoped it might, but there was recompense, there was peace, and there was time and space to breathe, to be, though not always, of course, to be happy all the time.

He would begin again and so would Ferguson's team.

On 21 October 1989, three days after the drafting of the letter to Manchester United shareholders, Ferguson's ailing football team took the bus to Coventry, Knighton's old stamping ground, and won 4-1.

Steve Bruce set the rampaging tone with a goal after only five minutes. This was followed by a brace from Mark Hughes and one goal from Mike Phelan.

It was as if a weight had been lifted from the players' backs, as if a sky had been cleared of clouds.

The crisis was over and United climbed to mid-table.

The restoration of Edwards, Charles II to Knighton's Cromwell, had apparently turned the trick. It was as if Lady Destiny had once more played her tricks on Knighton, just as she had led him such a merry dance during his negotiations with the board of Bolton Wanderers one short lifetime ago.

Not that Knighton saw it like that.

He was as upbeat and positive as the next United director after the win at Coventry City. For him the fresh start was crucial. Besides, he had to get along, rub along with all these people now, these fellow directors.

It was not easy, and Bobby Charlton, it was true, at least as far as Knighton was concerned, was not always the easiest.

They should have had so much in common, both having to recover from the disappointments of their respective failures to take over the leadership of the club.

At first, the Manchester United legend appeared remote to Knighton, especially in board meetings. Knighton tried to understand. Charlton may or may not have had anything to do with the alleged conspirators, Burrows and Midani. They were all disappointed men, thwarted in their pursuit of power, and had been fighting hard for high stakes. True, they had played their hands in secret, behind locked doors, whereas Knighton's game had been played out to the finish in full view. That did not mean, however, that they were hurting any less.

Before the end of the year, Knighton, at least, was in remission, much restored in optimism, in acceptance of his revised place in the Manchester United scheme of things. He was, after all, a man who preferred his own company, liked his own space, and did not need the bling and blang of polite society. His relationship with Edwards was better than cordial, even warm on occasions, and he saw the eagerness with which Edwards had greeted the ideas contained in his *Blueprint*. He detected a suspicion of gratefulness in the man who once had hugged him close in friendship. Slowly, the horrors of Knighton's monstering by the press were receding.

Sometimes, though, an event occurred to break the spell.

One of these was so bizarre it seemed as if it had emerged from the fevered imaginings of Hollywood scriptwriters. In late November, Knighton was talking to David Walker, a journalist at the *Daily Mail* and a man who had helped carry stretchers of the dead and dying at Hillsborough. He was the source of Knighton's knowledge of much of Maxwell's behaviour during the Old Trafford ownership crisis. They were friends now and Walker had further information relating to leaks from the Knighton camp during the frenzied negotiations at the Midland Hotel.

Knighton's driver and general gopher was a man called Jed Atkinson, introduced to him by the Manchester City director, Brian Turnbull. Atkinson had dirty teeth and Knighton disliked him from the off but ignored his instincts because of the recommendation that accompanied him.

Walker revealed to Knighton that Atkinson had been, and still was, hawking stories around the bargain-basement levels of the British press for as much cash as he could lay his grasping hands on. Knighton had always maintained a low opinion of treachery and left Walker with anger in his heart and went off in search of Atkinson.

When Knighton's employee saw his boss running towards him, noted his cheeks flaring and his black hair flying, Atkinson jumped into the nearest car and, with a squeal of tyres, turned and drove off.

Maybe Atkinson had his own tip-off man in the press.

Knighton smiled, commandeered another car, slammed his right foot hard on the accelerator and, when he eventually cornered Atkinson, in a busy hotel car park near Mere, just off the M56, the gopher looked petrified, broke down in tears and proffered his apologies.

'Who, Jed, who?'

Knighton was not a violent man, but he had his employee by the jacket lapels. Adrenaline was racing through his veins and, at first, Knighton was breathless and inarticulate. He understood instinctively that Atkinson was a pawn in someone else's game.

'Who's paying you, Jed?'

'You Michael, you're the one what's paying my wages.'

'Don't play games with me, Jed.'

The terrified man confessed to selling stories to a journalist in the pay of the *Daily Mirror*.

'Now, there's a surprise,' Knighton said to himself, after letting Atkinson escape.

He almost felt sorry for his former employee, who had broken down in tears that accompanied his admission of guilt and his revelation to Knighton of his serious financial difficulties.

The episode, though, was a reminder for Knighton, as if he still needed one, that certain sections of the English press would never sleep until they had brought all those high up right down into the gutter, until all lay there together.

Now, though, he could laugh.

Every good story needs a car chase, and he had survived his first audition for the part of film stuntman. That fearful pursuit, that risking of life and limb, had been a closure of sorts, a catharsis, and a cleansing of his wounds.

* * *

Knighton's attempts to buy Manchester United had cost him a small fortune – all those lawyers, accountants, brokers, bottles of champagne and packs of sandwiches, those hotel suites, that end game at the Midland Hotel.

The whole shebang had cost Knighton millions in fees and expenses of various kinds. He had stumped up the lot himself without asking Edwards or the football club for a penny of recompense.

Someone, somewhere, is probably still billing Knighton for expenses, for the use of a helicopter here and a private jet there, for drinks at the bar, for time at however many hundreds of pounds an hour these people cost, while Knighton charged no one for his time or his ideas. Still, though, he had more money left in the pot than poor Atkinson could ever dream of. His driver, moreover, was now his former driver, and without work for the foreseeable future.

* * *

One month later, Knighton and Edwards were together again at the annual general meeting of shareholders in the packed executive suite at Old Trafford.

There were lights, cameras, and no little action. There was talk among shareholders of how the football club had been brought into disrepute by both Edwards and Knighton, of the shame, the embarrassment and betrayal of the name and honourable traditions of Manchester United, all in relation to the recent events relating to the aborted takeover.

Knighton understood that it had not been easy for Edwards either.

The vilification of the United chairman and chief executive had gathered momentum as football results slid downhill once more with defeats by Arsenal, Crystal Palace and Tottenham in the first half of December. Fergie and his struggling new signings were labouring for points and returned to the bottom half of the First Division table.

There was, too, continuing embarrassment for Edwards as the extent of his foolishness in agreeing to sell his football club at a bargain-basement price to an unknown outsider was fully revealed by the press. The booing and chanting against Edwards from the Stretford End on matchdays was louder now than ever.

*Edwards out! Edwards out! Edwards out!*

The demands for Edwards to leave Old Trafford reverberated around the stadium when Spurs won 3-0 in the League Cup just one week after Knighton had abandoned his attempts to purchase the club and a few days after the restorative win at Coventry. How fickle were the fates of football, Knighton and Edwards agreed. The shouts were louder still when Tottenham Hotspur won again at Old Trafford, this time in the league championship on 16 December, and United slid to unlucky thirteenth in the table.

There was hollering against the newcomer, too, but he was now keeping a calculatedly lower profile, and his skin had thickened considerably.

At the annual general meeting someone with a small shareholding shouted from the back of the room, 'I'll say this for you, Mr Knighton, you've got some balls, to face us here in the lions' den, I will say that.'

Another gentleman, elderly, and in the highest of dudgeon, his share certificates flapping in his shaky hand, shouted his opinion that the current United side was the worst, most boring, team he had ever clapped his weary old eyes on, and that Edwards should resign immediately.

On the following Monday, the *Mirror* provided this particular dissident with a double-page spread to air his views to a broader audience. Maxwell was not done yet.

Edwards was always ill at ease in the public eye. At the meeting he shifted in his seat, his gaze unwilling to engage with onlookers. He fumbled and stumbled through his answers to questions. Edwards did not have the ability to be subtly discourteous to those who would destroy him without one jab of conscience.

The annual general meeting was the chairman's least favourite time of year. Especially this year.

Knighton, though, was keen to support and to be seen to support his colleague.

'Gentlemen,' he said, 'you should be thanking Martin and me, not blaming us.'

It was a bullring that Knighton had entered, hot and sweaty under the lights. The press were elevated to his right on a mezzanine floor and shareholders were in front and close enough to see the whites of eyes. The carpets were plush red rags to bulls.

'When I first arrived on the Old Trafford scene, your shares, gentlemen, were trading at somewhere between £6 and a generous £8 apiece.' In the preceding month or so of relative calm, Knighton had regained his poise and his charm as well as his way with words. 'Now they are worth £25 a share and you should all be delighted.'

There was no snarl in his voice. Knighton was simply stating a fact.

'If economic logic and common sense were to prevail, Martin Edwards and I should be nominated for knighthoods for realising something nearer to the true value of your club and of your shares.

'I know this football game is all about passion and all about emotion but please try to marry this fervour with commercial logic.' Knighton was determined to have his say, all the more so in the face of such opposition. 'In order to have the greatest team in the world, it is necessary to create wealth, and the revenue here through the turnstiles is simply insufficient on present or future gates. We must employ as many other ideas as we can to generate more income for the club to prosper.'

The highest attendance at Old Trafford so far in the current season was for the opening game against Arsenal, a relatively healthy 47,245. For the recent match against Spurs it had dipped to an alarming 36,230.

'In the future, gentlemen, Manchester United must learn to explore and to exploit every possible avenue of commercial revenue, and then, and only then, will your club be able to afford the very best players in the world.'

It is safe to say that Knighton's speech was not well received. Shareholders' opinions, Knighton thought, had been purchased long ago by Maxwell's *Mirror* and other fellow travellers in the journalistic gutter.

'Pearls before swine, Martin,' was Knighton's considered opinion.

The ignorance of some shareholders, some fans, was almost enough to turn anyone, even a socialist millionaire, into a Thatcherite.

But not quite, not when the prime minister was proposing rigid membership schemes for all football clubs and compulsory ID cards for all supporters, and not when she had, single-handedly, without an apparent care in the world, destroyed the mining communities of his childhood memories.

It was not easy being Knighton, and being hated and vilified for no good reason by a certain type of cheap and nasty football fan.

* * *

He recalled all this as he strolled across the extravagant Wembley turf on 12 May 1990, prior to the Cup Final against Crystal Palace. He thought back to the low point of the season, the second home defeat against Tottenham Hotspur, when a placard was unveiled in the Stretford End.

*3 YEARS OF EXCUSES*
*AND IT'S STILL CRAP …*
*TARA FERGIE*

* * *

The FA Cup win in 1990 was indisputably the start of the Ferguson glory years. The manager's legacy was now safe as the Bank of England, but Knighton's role in all of this remains largely unaccredited.

It was Knighton's unacknowledged axis with the Manchester United manager that allowed Fergie to survive and prosper. It was his permission to Ferguson to spend the club's money, back in August 1989, that provided the club with stalwart new blood in Pallister, Ince, and Wallace, and it was Knighton's ideas contained in the *Blueprint* that revolutionised the club's finances over the following years, allowing United, in 2011, to overtake Liverpool's record eighteen league championship wins.

It was Knighton's commercial revolution at Old Trafford that provided the wherewithal for Fergie's untold success.

As the United players danced on the Wembley pitch after their close-fought replay success over Palace in the 1990 FA Cup, as suited reserves ran on to the turf and hugged red-shirted warriors, as Ferguson jigged on to the pitch to join his players, as the flotsam and jetsam of years of failure floated away, Knighton looked on, and a broad smile broke on his new-boy-at-the-big-school face.

Unfortunately, the FA Cup triumph was not enough for some fans.

Outside the London station, where the chartered train was waiting at a sidings point for the directors, their guests and players to board and enjoy their victorious journey back home to Manchester Piccadilly, United supporters, from a platform across the track, spotted Knighton and Edwards and charged towards them, beer bottles and beer bellies flying.

*Edwards, you bastard! You greedy fucking, rip-off bastard! Resign you cunt!*

Spit for speech and sawdust for brains, Knighton thought.

*Knighton, you bastard! Fuck off! This is our club, not yours, you twat.*

'We've just won the FA Cup, Martin,' Knighton said.

*This is our football club, Edwards, you bastard!*

'Unbelievable.'

Knighton shifted his head just in time to avoid a half-empty bottle, drizzling beer, which hurtled past its intended target.

Edwards turned his back.

'Michael,' he said, 'it's just football fans, that's all.'

Knighton held back from boarding the train. 'Pure evil at times, Michael, just filth and slime.' Knighton, though, was reluctant to leave the scene, to leave well alone.

'Thank you,' he shouted at the gathering crowd, 'thank you so much for all your support, you are all too kind.'

Scum, he thought.

'What kind of society, what kind of politics, produces people like this, with such hatred in their hearts, such spiteful wrath?' He was addressing Edwards, but the chairman was no longer around to answer Knighton's question.

* * *

Neither did that FA Cup win paper over boardroom cracks at Old Trafford.

Knighton was the source of some discontent, without ever being its proper cause. It was not his fault, nor his problem, that Charlton did not appear always to warm to his new boardroom colleague.

It was not that Charlton was routinely rude to Knighton. In fact, he was almost always unfailingly polite, professional.

And who would not empathise with Charlton's desire to take the helm of the club where he had plied his trade with such distinction, such endeavour, and such passion?

Charlton's understandable dream of one day becoming chairman of his beloved football club had almost certainly died with the announcement of Edwards' deal with Knighton.

Now, with Edwards resuming his role as chairman and chief executive, and with Knighton aborting his takeover bid, Charlton was once more an influence behind the scenes, a power behind the throne. On football, if not on financial matters, Edwards deferred to him, perhaps had always done so, in areas in which Charlton was deemed an expert. This was in spite of the former footballer's manifest failure in management at Preston North End where, in his one full season in charge, the club was relegated to the Third Division. This was the same proud football club that had once completed the entire season of 1888/89 in the English top division undefeated, and earned themselves the nickname of Invincibles.

One well known Preston player under Charlton's charge confessed to Knighton that the England World Cup winner was one of the worst football managers imaginable, his man-management skills so bad, and his knowledge of tactics so basic, Preston players would shake their heads in disbelief.

However, at the 1990 Cup Final, Charlton's behaviour was less than its routine, impeccable politeness.

It was Knighton's first visit to Wembley as a Manchester United director and he had a coveted *All Areas Access Pass* dangling round his neck. He was in dreamland and longed to feel the lush turf beneath the soles of his shining shoes. His heart pumped with excitement. It was not quite his boyhood dream but it was the next best thing, breathing it all in, the history, the spectacle, the thrill of being at the heart of the most famous football club in the world on FA Cup Final day.

As Knighton left the VIP area and made his way towards the stairs down to the edge of the hallowed turf, he saw Charlton beckoning.

'Yes, Bobby, and what can I do for you?'

'Michael, don't you think you're going on that pitch.'

Charlton's voice was quietly hectoring, a school prefect's from the back of a classroom.

'That pitch there, that's not for the likes of you.'

Knighton was at a loss at the man's stupidity and arrogance.

'Do you understand that, Michael?'

Knighton smiled and looked straight into Charlton's eyes without saying a word.

'That's not for the likes of you down there, Michael.'

'That's a sacred pitch, that is, that's reserved, Michael, for people like me, players and ex-players.'

Knighton turned again, smiled even more widely at Charlton.

'It just wouldn't be right for you to go on to that pitch.'

Knighton's grin was now impish. Knighton turned away from Charlton and continued his walk down onto the Wembley pitch and made sure that he was the last one to leave the sacred turf during the directors' pre-match walkabout. Deep down, however, he was hurt and astonished at what he believed to be Charlton's abject arrogance and inflated sense of righteousness at that moment at Wembley.

The new boy amongst the Manchester United directors allowed for the fact that the board's elder statesman may have been soured by disappointments of thwarted ambition. That, at least, was Knighton's honest assessment of the situation. Charlton was a tried and tested failure as a football manager. Neither had he become chairman of his first and only real love among football clubs. There were reasons, Knighton concluded, for his boorish behaviour. He was protecting the one area that he could truly call his own, the one arena in which he had wonderfully excelled, and it was Knighton now trampling on his Wembley pitch as well as on his ambitions.

* * *

Charlton, though, was not merely an authority on imagined Wembley rules and regulations. In addition, he fancied himself an expert on Ferguson's perilous position back in January 1990.

'Behind the scenes,' Charlton claimed later, 'Alex was already successful. There was not a single thought, a single word about the future of Alex Ferguson at the club.'

Knighton, though, knew better.

At half-time in the match against Queens Park Rangers, on New Year's Day, 1990, Edwards sidled up to Knighton from behind, and whispered in his ear, 'If we lose today, Michael, then we'll have to be talking.'

Without turning around, without interrupting his enjoyment of a salmon and cucumber sandwich, Knighton said, 'Talking about what, Martin?'

'The manager, Michael, the manager.'

It was clear the imminent dismissal of Ferguson was on the cards.

Either Charlton was being disingenuous in his claims concerning Ferguson's job security or he was not as close to the heartbeat of Old Trafford as he liked to think.

He would have been furious had he known that Knighton's opinions on football management had been canvassed.

All in all, it seems probable Charlton was not privy to conversations regarding Ferguson's position.

* * *

As for Knighton's relationship with Edwards during this time, it was amiable rather than close.

Often, there seemed an unspoken understanding between the two men. Occasionally, it was closer than cordial. There had been no need, for example, for Edwards to include Knighton in half-time conversations.

They now had shared history as well as some shared public school values.

Mostly, though, Edwards kept some distance, whilst always politeness itself in person.

Knighton and Edwards were wounded animals, the pair of them, and they circled each other, warily, each a reminder to the other of what once went wrong. Armed camps remained armed camps, even though there was no longer anything to fight about. Knighton trod as lightly as he could in case of landmines.

Whilst participating fully in boardroom discussions, he became a happy observer, too, watching the commercial department gradually implement his ideas from the *Blueprint*, watching the cash flow.

The dawning of financial success was Knighton's gift to Edwards and to Manchester United.

He became a happy spectator, too, watching the football team win more often than the previous season, finishing a promising sixth and winning the European Cup Winners' Cup in 1991, beating Spanish champions Barcelona in Rotterdam. He rejoiced in the VIP seats at that game as Mark Hughes scored twice in a 2-1 win to secure Ferguson's second trophy.

Soon afterwards, however, Edwards made a prime fool of himself, this time in ways unconnected to selling his football club to Knighton.

The chairman of Manchester United was a difficult one to get to know.

He was easy enough in a man-to-man, smoke and drink, in a talk sport kind of way, but this was all bluff and bluster, wind and nonsense, sheer veneer. Knighton studied him closely sometimes, tried to understand, thought that if ever one man might be an island, entire of himself, that man might be the chairman of Manchester United. Certainly, Edwards sometimes behaved as if he was a law unto himself.

In October 1991 it appeared as if the entire Old Trafford club had decamped to Spain where the team was set to continue its defence of its European title, against Atlético Madrid.

Knighton had checked into the club's five-star hotel in the centre of the Spanish capital and strolled across the grand marble and gilt reception area to take the lift to his rooms on the first floor. As he left the lift and turned towards his suite – Knighton was always unapologetic when admitting that all United directors stayed in luxurious surroundings when abroad for major European football nights – he spied Edwards emerging, blinking, from his own suite.

A few steps ahead of the Manchester United chairman was a nubile Spanish beauty, who had also just left Edwards' quarters. The woman clearly made an impression on Knighton who recalled her as a 'twinkling trinket trophy' in possession of 'dazzling accoutrements, shining jet black hair, big sparkling eyes as black as anthracite, glossy red-painted pouting lips, with legs as tall as the Eiffel Tower.'

A smirk of satisfaction coloured Edwards' face as he spotted his colleague. No discomfiture at all, Knighton noted, no embarrassment. In fact, as Edwards passed, he flashed a triumphant thumbs up sign at his fellow director and Knighton was left with the ghost of the young girl's expensive perfume as she waltzed down the corridor and presumably out of the chairman's life.

Later that evening, with the football not due until the following day, Knighton was leaving the hotel restaurant after a Castilian banquet when he spotted Edwards once more, this time standing, feet shifting and shuffling, outside the female toilets on the ground floor. The Manchester United chairman's face betrayed his oblivion to all but his own thoughts. Knighton was unsure what to do.

He had observed Edwards like this on other occasions and knew what all this was about.

Time slipped in and out of focus, with hotel staff chattering, glasses making love with other glasses in the restaurant, footsteps on the stairs to his left. All this hovered around and about Knighton's consciousness until Edwards broke the spell and looked his colleague's way. The Manchester United chairman looked like a rabbit caught in the stare of a stoat.

'Fabulous fare, Martin.'

Knighton was embarrassed into speech, realising, only when it was too late, that his mutterings might be misconstrued. Edwards merely nodded in his direction and resumed his vigil, staring, trance like, at the entrance to the ladies' loo.

Shameless, Knighton thought, this preoccupation with watching women in various states of dress and undress inside public toilets, inside the restrooms of polite hotels. Not only that, but Edwards was risking so much through his behaviour – not merely his own reputation, but that of his football club, the Manchester United that was the clean-cut, wholesome, family-friendly, sporting institution.

In November 2002, Edwards, according to sources from within Old Trafford, was forced to resign from his official duties at Old Trafford, allegedly as a result of publicity following a peeping Tom incident. The chairman had been issued with an official police caution after spying on a woman in a toilet cubicle at the four-star luxury spa, Mottram Hall Hotel, near the Manchester United chairman's home in Prestbury. This followed revelations in the *Sunday Mirror* that Edwards and Newcastle United's deputy chairman, Douglas Hall, had slept with prostitutes before the Champions League draw in Geneva.

In stark contrast to Edwards' version of a voluntary and peaceful walking away from Old Trafford that was told in *Red Glory – Manchester United and Me,* Edwards' apparently ghosted hagiography published in 2017, the truth, according to trusted insiders at the club, was that Edwards was confronted by United's chief executive, Peter Kenyon, and by the club's plc chairman, Sir Roy Gardner, and told to resign from the chairmanship of the football club or be sacked as a result of the widely publicised and truly unsavoury Mottram Hall incident.

Knighton wondered whether he should have reported Edwards back in 1991, but the Manchester United chairman's behaviour in regard to women was common knowledge, common talk amongst the female staff at Old Trafford.

At the time, Knighton said he believed this talk to be mere idle gossip.

* * *

The football in Spain, when it came to pass, was as depressing as the chairman's behaviour.

United were routed 3-0, failed to produce a miracle in the return leg at Old Trafford and were out of European competition at an early stage.

At the time, Knighton could not help but like Edwards in a companions-in-distress kind of way. Sometimes – although most definitely not in the case of Edwards' sexual predation – Knighton felt his colleague was the victim of unjustified criticism by fans and by the press hacks, and they were able to rub along happily enough in the same boardroom.

Knighton knew, however, even if the idea remained unarticulated at this stage of his life, that he would not stay there forever, that he might wish to leave Old Trafford sometime, maybe sometime soon.

* * *

There were, though, things he wanted to do before he went, such as continue to watch the commercial revolution unfold, such as solve the riddle that was Bobby Charlton, though he now knows he never will.

Knighton still wanted to love Charlton, tell him how magnificent he was in 1966 and 1968, but Charlton, of course, knew all that already, and had his inalienable opinions of Knighton set in his apparent heart of stone.

Rumours circulated that one of the reasons Knighton gave up his seat on the board of directors in 1992 was because he and Bobby Charlton disliked each other so intensely that the situation became intolerable to all concerned. Reports also suggested Knighton, in fact, did not get on with any of his boardroom colleagues, that there was constant bickering over club policy.

Knighton says all of this is utter nonsense.

'That is absolutely not true.'

'Actually, I can honestly say that I enjoyed a very sound, very professional and usually friendly relationship with all my colleagues at the club across all departments while I was a director.

'It is not true that I did not get on with Bobby Charlton. We were not particularly close, that is clear, but we were always polite, very cordial to each other. We had a professional and civil relationship and there were never ever any real arguments.'

The way Knighton called it sounded perfectly possible, perfectly plausible.

He was capable of getting on with people under the most adverse of circumstances and his capacity for forgiveness was extraordinary.

Besides, by April 1992, Burrows was no longer a director at Old Trafford and Knighton, at least, felt the boardroom a better, cleaner place for the former Stretford Ender's absence.

Midani, too, by the time Knighton was contemplating leaving Old Trafford, was a fading figure after his previous failed attempts to purchase the club from Edwards.

All in all, the atmosphere in the Old Trafford boardroom was much improved.

There was one individual at the club, however, Knighton could never abide, just could not work with, and that was Professor Sir Roland Smith, who was known in unfriendly circles as 'rent a director' or 'the man of the 1,001 boardrooms' as a result of his avaricious appetite for high profile directorships and his lust for status and cash.

A Manchester Grammar boy, Smith was a long-time friend of the Edwards family and former director of their butchery business. He had since become chairman of British Aerospace and held an executive box at Old Trafford. By early 1992 Smith had been invited to chair the newly formed company, Manchester United plc, in preparation for the club's stock market flotation. Manchester United FC Ltd would be the new company's principal subsidiary. It was like a monstrous child swallowing whole its parent but it was just business, just capitalism, and Knighton was in favour of the process. After all, he would have done the same thing, had his takeover reached fulfilment in 1989. Tottenham Hotspur had shown the way as long ago as 1983.

But he would never have chosen Smith to head the operation.

'Look,' Knighton said, 'he didn't like me, and I certainly did not like him.'

He understood the club's need for City kudos, for the City respectability that Smith brought, to facilitate the flotation. After all, Knighton had made the same mistake himself, allowing himself to get involved with Thornton because of the Debenhams man's City credentials. With Smith, though, came greed as well as the need. And then there was the hint of cronyism, with the Aerospace man's links with the Edwards' butchery business.

It was so unusual for Knighton to have nothing positive to say about someone.

'Smith was a man that I just could not respect. I found it amazing that so many people saw him as a business guru. Frankly, I held a rather different view of the man. I did not rate his business acumen or even his business knowledge, at least in the real commercial world as opposed to the world of academic textbooks, where he honed his reputation. For me, Smith was the most over-rated man I met in all my life. I thought him a very poor choice as chairman of the plc board. Michael Edelson, then deputy chair of the club board, would have been much better in my view.'

Of all the United board at the time, Knighton thought Edelson perhaps the best, certainly the least ambitious. He has also outlasted them all, bar Charlton.

'At least Edelson was a self-made, successful businessman in his own right,' Knighton says, 'and a man loyally dedicated to the Manchester United cause.'

The respect seems to have been mutual.

In a *Daily Telegraph* interview in May 2004, it was Edelson who said, 'Knighton did something good for me and for United. We pretty much followed the plan that he'd laid down.'

Smith, though, got up Knighton's nose right away.

'I'll not be expensive,' Knighton heard Smith say at the club's board meeting held to decide on flotation and the new man's consultancy fees and ongoing remuneration. Smith was a gunslinger of a man, 6ft 6in, 23st. And with an XXXXL coffin booked and paid for in advance, Knighton thought. He was eating a smoked salmon and prawn sandwich and sipping fine wine at the club's expense.

'About twenty-five thou a year should do it.'

He was speaking with his mouth full.

'A modest fee by my standards.'

It was his establishment credibility that Edwards and the rest of the plc board required, much to Knighton's frustration.

'Manchester United should have been big enough to have no need, no truck with Smith, should have been choosers not beggars.'

Smith was used to claiming an exorbitant salary for a few days' work. He had made a living from doing just that over the years. Knighton felt Smith should do the job for nothing if his claims of undying devotion to everything United were even half-way true.

Smith, though, was much in demand in boardrooms up and down the country. He had even been a director of the Bank of England in his time. For Knighton, however, this said rather more about the banking industry than it did about the usefulness or otherwise of Smith.

'He would have made an excellent police sergeant, like his father,' was Knighton's summation of Smith's character and abilities. 'If he had any redeeming qualities I couldn't see one, and he was a disastrous chairman of British Aerospace.' On Smith's watch, BAe had plunged into financial crisis and his fellow directors had forced his resignation.

One Saturday matchday morning, at around 11.45, Knighton was approached by Edwards who told him Smith wanted to see him at noon sharp. Knighton watched Smith wobble down the corridor, his 23st bulk swaying from side to side. He summoned Knighton with his crooked index finger into the small video room next to the matchday boardroom. Edwards was there, too, thin as a pencil. Smith spoke first.

He had heard rumours, he said, that Knighton might be planning to leave Old Trafford in the not too distant future, that he might be joining another Football League club. Would Knighton like to make his intentions clear?

It was not so much what Smith was saying as the arrogance with which he tossed words in his direction. If Knighton was intending to stay around for the next few years or so, would he please say so or, if not, it might be helpful, in view of the impending flotation, if he would consider leaving very soon.

'Cut to the chase, Roland,' was Knighton's response.

'It appears,' Smith said, 'to some of my City friends that your continued presence on the football club's board, Michael, may be a disincentive to certain institutional investors.'

Knighton was furious but did not permit his smile to flinch.

After all this time, after all his loyalty to Manchester United, after all his disinclination to claim fame and fortune, still the myths prevailed, still the Maxwell newspaper shit hit the spot. If he had taken the money two and a half years ago, if he had taken Green's millions on offer, or the Arab money, or even the Bank of Scotland money in the first place, he would have been a legend in the City and not some kind of pariah figure as implied now by Smith.

Knighton's expression did not change. He eyeballed Smith long enough for the big man to feel uncomfortable. He wanted Smith to understand his unpredictability, his volatility, his violence of feeling. He moved one step closer to Smith so that the bigger man felt the heat of his breath.

'Bollocks!' Knighton said.

Smith blustered and blushed, stumbled over words that would not come.

'Look, you know as well as I do, Roland, that any value in the share offer that might attract investors into Manchester United will have everything to do with bottom line profit and nothing to do with my continued presence here. So, cut the crap and stop spouting your usual bullshit.'

Surely Smith must have had some comprehension that it was Knighton's ideas that had driven and produced the greatly improved prospects for a highly priced sale. Knighton, for good measure, before he left the two's company, three's a crowd room, told Smith to go fuck himself, but not to enjoy himself too much while doing so. Edwards smiled a goody-two-shoes smile at the naughty boy who had dared to challenge the teacher.

'God,' says Knighton, 'I was livid with that pompous, arrogant man, and with all his bullying crap.'

After the game, Knighton decided he had unfinished business with Smith and sought him out. 'This time, it was my turn to beckon Smith with my crooked index finger.'

Smith came into the video room and stood and waited.

'Get your fucking tanks off my front lawn,' Knighton said.

His words were echoes of Smith's own famous words to Tiny Rowland of Lonrho during resistance to the takeover of the retail group, House of Fraser. 'Otherwise, I shall shove a Kalashnikov

AK-47 so far up your fat arse you will never feel like taking another seat in any fucking boardroom.'

Smith never troubled him again, never spoke to him again, which suited Knighton just fine. It was true that Knighton was thinking of leaving Manchester United, but he would not be driven out by a bullying Smith, or by anyone else, until he was good and ready to leave on his own terms. He had some fruits of his labours to enjoy first.

* * *

His accidental alliance, for example, with Ferguson was producing serious results.

It was a silent symbiosis, this discrete connection between the football club manager and the man with the ideas that minted the money. They almost never spoke, their paths almost never crossed, but there was an understanding alright.

Fergie was no fool and knew the difference between no money and money, always had and always would. According to the *Guardian* in December 2017, Ferguson had been 'the Glazer family's winning ticket, a dream of frugal, orderly success'.

In the Knighton years at Old Trafford, the manager attended all board meetings and knew the score. He remembered, too, who it was who had approved the expenditure on Pallister. In turn, Knighton admired Ferguson, willed him to succeed. They had something else in common – an eye for a player.

Pallister was raw when he arrived, hopeless for the first few games, yet both Ferguson and Knighton knew he was the perfect player, graceful and quick, to complement Steve Bruce, a traditional English centre-half. One would play, the other would stop others playing.

Fergie was loyal, too, in the right circumstances. Knighton recalls one board meeting at which Brian McClair's ability to score goals was questioned. Everyone, fans and directors, were on the player's back for his glaring lack of form, lack of strikes.

'The boy can play,' said Ferguson. 'We'll keep him on the pitch and say bollocks to the fans and everyone else who's chastising the boy.'

If Knighton had spoken to the manager at that point, he would have said to Fergie, you keep picking the team, and I'll keep shaking the money tree for you.

It was not all about finances with Ferguson, however, and Knighton knew and applauded that, too. Since his arrival at Old Trafford in 1986, Ferguson had rebuilt the club in his own image, transforming the youth set-up as well as the first team and introducing a Protestant work ethic into the Catholic club. He was first to arrive in the morning, last to leave at night.

The money sure was useful, though.

For the 1991/92 season, more cash was made available to strengthen the United squad ahead of another push for the league title, last won in 1967. In May 1991, Andrei Kanchelskis arrived from Shakhtar Donetsk for £1m and Paul Parker, the England right-back was signed from Queens Park Rangers for another £1m, while Peter Schmeichel was purchased from Brondy for £625,000. These were significant fees for significant players and there was no longer the need to balance outgoing fees with sales of outgoing players.

This was something Knighton was proud of, and he enjoyed the further progress of the team in his final season at Old Trafford. They rose from sixth to a second-place finish in the former First Division, won the League Cup at Wembley against Nottingham Forest 1-0 and also won the European Super Cup at Old Trafford by beating Red Star Belgrade, again 1-0.

These were Ferguson's – and Knighton's – third and fourth trophies, the natural result, Knighton believed, of the beginning of the new and efficient commercial exploitation of the Manchester United brand and the club's status around the world. This coming together of profit and trophies, this convergence of new men and new ideas, this overhaul of both finance and football, was either luck and guesswork, mere random coincidence, or something really was going on here.

Knighton, naturally, said it was mostly down to money, and making that money, so that success could be purchased, not exactly off the peg, but by judicious investments in players and management, commercial infrastructure, sponsorship and television deals.

'It was all there in the *Blueprint* that I gave to Martin Edwards when I joined the club.'

* * *

And it was not just Knighton that said so.

Some journalists had come around to Knighton's way of thinking, too.

One of the first writers to recognise the true origins of the revolution taking place inside Old Trafford in the 1990s was Richard Kurt, prolific expert on all things United and author of unofficial and alternative histories of his beloved football club.

In 1998, Kurt hinted at Ferguson's indebtedness to Knighton.

*Long after he'd ceased to be a United director, Knighton's ideas were still paying off for the club and fuelling Ferguson's V12 super team.*

One of Knighton's favourite journalists was Martin Johnson of the *Daily Telegraph*. How could he not love the man that wrote of Knighton, 'You will find him fun, intelligent, and utterly charming.'

That was all very well, very frothy, very pretty, very nice to be nice, but where was the substance in Knighton?

Tim Rich of *The Independent* was a subscriber to the Knighton schools of both charisma and accomplishment.

'He makes other football chairmen look thick,' Rich wrote. Knighton laughed out loud. 'He never hesitates, he doesn't have to search for facts, he has his arguments brilliantly marshalled,' the journalist continued. 'He is a fantastic performer.'

Mark Ogden of the *Daily Telegraph* was another convert. 'Knighton had the United supporters in the palm of his hand ... Here was a man with a plan, a charismatic tycoon ready to modernise Old Trafford and allow the United brand to generate the huge income streams it provides today. It was a visionary plan, one which has now been adopted by football clubs across the globe.'

Ten years after Knighton left Old Trafford, Michael Crick's biography of Alex Ferguson, *The Boss*, appeared in bookshops and contained the first and most important revisionist statement concerning the Knighton years that had so far appeared in hardback form.

Crick, a former journalist with *Channel 4 News* and, in 2002, working for the BBC, had the following, startling words to say about Knighton and his time at Old Trafford.

*There is a strong case for saying that Michael Knighton had a more influential role in the recent history of Manchester United than many of the club's managers, directors or footballers.*

Crick's was red meat writing and prescient in its overturning of prejudice against Knighton.

In August 2009, Knighton felt almost total vindication when a copy of the *Manchester Evening News* was forwarded to his address in Sark, one of the smaller of the Channel Islands, a location to which he had retreated in order to abandon the world and rediscover his interests in solitary contemplation and art.

An unofficial team of friends and well-wishers had been keeping Knighton in touch with his past by sending press cuttings whenever his name cropped up, which it still did a tad too often for Knighton's liking. Mostly, it was the same, tired old regurgitated guff about how Knighton never had the money to buy Manchester United or how he could not complete the deal, blah, blah, blurgh, blurgh. Today's post, however, contained a true gem of an almost apology from the newspaper that had begun it all with its apparent exposé of the men behind Knighton's bid.

It was the *Manchester Evening News*, remember, that had spilled the ruinous news of the chairman elect's imbroglio with Thornton and Cohen all those years ago, which began the song and dance that ended with Knighton abandoning his dream of ownership of the Old Trafford club.

The back-page banner headline asked the most pertinent question.

KNIGHTON: FOOTBALL'S GREATEST VISIONARY?

'How will history remember Michael Knighton?' asked James Robson. The answer was still ambiguous but the question at least raised the issue, broke the taboo.

Robson warmed to his theme and talked of 'overwhelming evidence that this was not your average chairman ... that it was his vision for the future of the club and football as a whole that truly distinguished Knighton from just about anyone else in the sport at that time.'

Robson continued, 'He was able to see beyond the doldrums of a football world still shaken by hooliganism, Heysel and Hillsborough, able to see the potential to capitalise on the innate loyalty of fans and turn clubs – United in particular – into global brands.

'The commercialism so reviled by a hardcore of United supporters today is a realisation of the future Knighton predicted ... and [shows] that his predictions for the club's commercial potential were proved correct.'

When he read this Knighton sighed and sank deep into the enfolding arms of his favourite chair. It was a vindication, a rehabilitation of sorts, a new beginning at the end, a possibility of a paradigm shift in the way his universe might be viewed from now on, and all this while he had abandoned the world and its ways.

* * *

It was not only journalists, however, who ought to have been capable of a spot of historical revisionism.

It is a shame – and somewhat shameful – that Edwards has never come clean about his extreme good fortune in making the fortune he never ever dared to dream of in his early days at Manchester United. The former chairman and chief executive still maintains a strict silence about these affairs.

Once, Edwards almost opened up, admitting to the press that, yes, Knighton had proved he had the financial backing to do the deal. Go on, Martin, thought Knighton, tell them that it was Michael Knighton's generosity of spirit, his twin gifts to you, the return of the contract that was lost and gone forever, and the *Blueprint* of financial ideas and strategies that made you all your money.

Instead, the restored majority shareholder of Manchester United turned away and added an invention of his own, something along the lines of yes, Knighton had the money, but he fell out with his other two partners, and they would have sidelined him anyway at some point.

Knighton smiled at Edwards' ignorance.

Or cleverness.

Either way, it was crass untruthfulness on Edwards' part. The man was certainly cute enough to ensure Knighton was the fall guy in their partnership and from that day hence, until the publication of *Red Glory* in 2017, Edwards kept his counsel concerning these affairs.

Not all Manchester United directors were as mean spirited as Edwards.

Michael Edelson, self-made multi-millionaire, and still a current director at Old Trafford, a man Knighton never knew well, was more forthcoming.

In 2004, twelve years after Knighton's departure from Manchester United, the former rag-trade man who by then was a successful entrepreneur specialising in the creation of shell companies for stars such as Damien Hirst, Alan Hansen and Angus Deayton, said this in an interview with Martin Baker of the *Daily Telegraph*:

'Knighton did something good for me and for United. Because we pretty much followed the plan that he'd laid down.'

The plan Edelson referred to was Knighton's famous *Blueprint*, the one he'd given to Edwards fifteen years previously and had never seen again.

*WE PRETTY MUCH FOLLOWED THE PLAN HE'D LAID DOWN.*

This was the document – the version of Knighton's *Blueprint* – that can be read in full in the appendix section of this book. It is also the document whose existence has been denied time and time again by Edwards whenever questioned by journalists over the years.

Edwards' own copy, given to him by Knighton before a board meeting at Old Trafford, has never resurfaced. Knighton thinks Edwards will never admit that he ever set eyes on the *Blueprint*, if only to protect his claim of the last few decades that Knighton's intervention in the history of Manchester United was nothing more than a temporary embarrassment.

So, it was fortunate indeed, for the sake of historical truth, that Knighton recently reclaimed from storage a copy of the *Blueprint*, produced for the appraisal and approval of David Murray, Sir Angus Grossart and the Bank of Scotland.

As Knighton said about Edelson's admission, 'That was truth-telling at last.'

It was, indeed.

And it had come from a much respected Manchester United insider, who had been in the thick of it at the time, a man who had known the heat of battle against Knighton and a man with the brains and the balls to see the truth and admit it in public.

It was not Edwards who made it all happen. It was not even Ferguson, although Knighton is the first to admit that they played their parts, too. It was Knighton's plan, his *Blueprint*, that made the difference and it was a shame that Edelson's comments on Knighton's role in the financial revolution at Old Trafford were not more widely reported at the time.

Somewhere, Knighton imagines, inside the walls of Old Trafford, inside some filing cabinet or on some forgotten shelf, is the original copy of the *Blueprint*, or at least the copy he handed personally to Edwards as opposed to the one given to Knighton's bankers which included his secret plans to float United on the Stock Exchange.

It will now be gathering dust, having been fingered and thumbed, passed from hand to hand, read until eyes were midnight-sore, its back broken, perhaps, from overuse all those years ago.

Sometimes, when he thinks of Edwards fondly, Knighton accepts his former friend may have been innocent of deliberate falsification. He knows from interviews with Edwards reproduced in books – such as Jim White's *Manchester United:*

*the Biography* – that the former chairman may have been mixing up the due diligence report on the club produced for Knighton with the original *Blueprint,* which at one point was appended to the accountants' document. It is a generous interpretation of Edwards' constant denials of the Knighton masterpiece.

* * *

Knighton cannot remember the moment he decided he would leave Old Trafford.

It was always tempting to stay one more year, to live a little longer, to see a league championship, to see even more commercial success.

To this day, he does not understand his closeness to Edwards, this one-sided closeness.

They were an odd couple: the privileged and pampered Edwards and the working class hero Knighton, the unacceptable face of old, exploitative, corrupt and shoddy-goods capitalism, and the shiny-faced and brand new capitalism of property and money. Knighton still feels they would have made a good team at Old Trafford under his ownership, if only outsiders had not intruded on their deal.

They were never really close, except perhaps for a few moments around midnight at Killochan Castle, and perhaps when Edwards cosied up to Knighton to whisper at half-time about Ferguson's future at the club. Yet, Knighton will almost never say a really bad word about Edwards, bounder, cad, rat that many think his behaviour suggested he was.

Edwards might well have grinned all the way home after hearing of Knighton's departure.

He had all that he wanted, returned contract, *Blueprint* and now Knighton's leaving date, big ticks for the removal of embarrassment and the constant reminder of embarrassment. It was enough perhaps to celebrate with his wife with a bottle of something bubbly, enough to draw a line under all proceedings since the summer of 1989, enough, almost, to pretend none of it had ever happened.

'He never even asked me why,' Knighton says, but then Edwards had only ever been truly interested in Edwards. In any case, Knighton knew why he was going. He had achieved what he set out to do – to set Manchester United on the path to success, and not just ordinary success but phenomenal success.

In August 1989, Knighton had said to Ferguson, 'Give me a trophy every year.' There had been four fallow years prior to this so the chairman elect's insistence had been a bold one. Ferguson delivered on Knighton's demand, and in spades and subsequently Knighton thought to himself, I have been to Wembley five times in three years as a director of this great club after never having set foot in the place previously.

Lady Destiny has been so good to me.

In addition, the *Blueprint* was being implemented. Everything was there, including the proposed flotation of the company on the Stock Exchange, the credit cards, the consumer goods, the shirts, the shorts, the underwear, the pay-per-view television channel, the foreign markets, mainly Ireland then but pointers were there for the Asian markets, too. Edwards, his board and his commercial men were doing exactly what Knighton had planned to do himself. Knighton felt he was no longer necessary.

In 1991, the privately owned Manchester United FC was floated on the London Stock Exchange for £47m and most of Knighton's *Blueprint* was included in the prospectus. It was after the successful flotation that Knighton told Edwards of his decision to leave.

The proceedings to progress towards flotation, however, were held up temporarily through several frustrating board meetings.

Charlton was the problem in that he kept on voting for himself to be a director of the plc board to be headed by Roland Smith and the election of new directors was unable to proceed without unanimity.

Around the table, vote after vote was carried, and the result was always the same. Eventually, all patience was lost. A senior executive of the stockbroker, Henry Ansbacher, the nominated advisers to the board on the pending flotation, cut through the crap.

'For Christ's sake, Bobby, you can't be on the board, you're just a fucking ex-footballer, you have zero fucking experience of being a plc director, so stop fucking voting for yourself each time, it's just plain stupid and just plain wasting time and money. For fuck's sake, let's all move on.'

Time to go, indeed, thought Knighton.

* * *

The judgements of historians – especially concerning revolutions – have to be based on starting points clearly identified. In the case of Knighton's influence on Manchester United, and on the football world in general, the summer of 1989 was the starting point.

The judgements, in turn, have to be based on differences made and differences still being made. By the summer of 1992, three years on from Knighton's arrival at Manchester United, the club had millions of pounds in the bank, had made a profit every year since 1989 and would continue to do so every year right up to the Glazer takeover. The stadium was being rebuilt. Knighton's influence on the fortunes of Old Trafford continued long after his departure from the boardroom.

Judgement needs to incorporate not only his sixty-two days as chairman elect and his time as a director, but also the years that followed. In the five seasons after the launch of the Premier League, 1992 to 1997, United produced a turnover of £249m and a profit of £66m, and won four out of the first five Premiership titles, two more FA Cups and a League Cup. In 1999, they won the European Cup for the first time since 1968. The man who was chairman elect for a mere sixty-two days could rest his case.

* * *

Edwards and his family, over their thirty-five-year custodianship, deserved more credit than they received, Knighton believes.

For one, there was Edwards' appointment of Ferguson and secondly, there was Edwards' funny story of the pursuit of the great man. Edelson was part of the plot and borrowed a Scottish accent to talk to the chairman of Aberdeen.

'Hello,' said Edelson, 'it's Alan Gordon here, agent to the stars and to Gordon Strachan, one of your players.'

The secretary let it pass and the Manchester United director was through to Dick Donald, Ferguson's employer.

'Actually,' Edelson said, 'it's not Alan Gordon, but Martin Edwards wants a word with you.'

Edwards admitted his interest in Aberdeen's manager and displayed his lack of morals and his lack of shame with words of disarming frankness: 'We needed to find out if Alex was prepared to come, because the last thing we wanted to do was sack Ron Atkinson and then find out we were without a manager.'

Third and last there was Edwards' loyalty to his managers, his failure to act, his benign paralysis at times of crisis. He worked with only three managers in his twenty-four years at the helm and appointed only two of them, the second being Ferguson himself. He stood by his man, even if there was the occasional dalliance with change such as when whispering to Knighton during that 1989 half-time break. Stability, Knighton says, has to be beneficial.

By 1992, however, Knighton suspected that there were aspects of his creation that were beginning to smell bad. He knew all about the secret meetings between the Big Five clubs, Manchester United, Liverpool, Everton, Arsenal and Tottenham Hotspur, about their plans to break away from the Football League, to form a self-perpetuating elite they would call the Premier League.

It would effectively be the Greed Is Good League, or the Fuck The Rest Of You Smaller Clubs League.

Knighton was appalled by the callous greed of those running the big clubs. He was astonished at their lack of empathy with the other 87 professional football clubs that made up the English footballing industry. He understood that this may have been all his fault, though accepting only a small part of the blame would be less egotistical. He knew all about the laws of unintended consequences, but Knighton still did not approve, did not want to be a part of it. He was beginning to be haunted by an image of himself as Dr Frankenstein appalled at the monster he had made.

He had watched with helpless dismay through the Thatcher years the destruction of the idea of community, of solidarity, of the brotherhood of man, the blowing away, as if they were no more than heaps of slag, specks of dust from the raised coal, of Britain's mines and miners. He would not stay long enough at Manchester United to be party to the same vandalism of the football industry he loved. He suspected, knew in fact, that smaller clubs, without their fair share of the spoils from the upper reaches of the Football League, would nearly always struggle to survive. There was a battle to be fought but it could not be fought from within the fortress walls of Old Trafford.

Of course, the commercialisation of the game was necessary, but it did not have to be accompanied by the naked avarice and rapacity of the Premier League.

He was ready to begin the rest of his life.

Knighton announced to the board that he would be leaving the club at the end of the 1991/92 season and was genuinely touched when Bobby Charlton spoke.

'Michael, we're all very sorry you're going. We'd like to thank you for what you've done for the club. We've enjoyed having you here and we'd like to wish you well for the future. We'd like you to know that you'll always be welcome here at Old Trafford.'

Knighton could hardly believe his ears.

Charlton's words had been spoken with obvious sincerity and Knighton thought this was just one more side to the complex enigma that was the World Cup winner. He whispered thanks to Charlton, rose from his boardroom seat for the final time and left Manchester United for good.

He has never returned to Old Trafford.

Chapter Twenty-Three

# Fergie Time and Final Whistle

## *1992 and Onwards*

KNIGHTON SAYS his time at Manchester United was exciting, revolutionary, fun, traumatic and cathartic. He left because his work was done, or was being done.

In early 2019, reviewing his departure from Old Trafford, Knighton said: 'Commercially, the infrastructure was in place. Manchester United, from then on, would be an unstoppable juggernaut in the financial stakes and the results on the pitch would reflect this commercial strength.

'I wasn't really one for the boardroom and the champagne, I was happy to leave that to others who enjoyed that sort of thing – it wasn't really my style.'

In 1992, Knighton tried to insist that rumours that he left because of conflicts within the boardroom were completely out of order.

That was partly true but it was also disingenuous. There were no arguments – save for his deconstruction of Sir Roland Smith – but that was because Knighton was a loner, a sole trader, and a man who avoided crowds in small places, not because there had been no disagreements, vitriol, petty jealousies or plots behind closed doors.

He left Old Trafford because he believed his job was done.

* * *

Manchester United went on to win thirty-eight trophies in the next twenty-seven years and enjoyed almost complete Premier League domination between the years 1993 and 2013. Through those years, the club became perhaps the greatest sporting brand in the world, just as Knighton had predicted. There really had been an unacknowledged axis of revolutionaries working in tandem at Old Trafford when Knighton was chairman elect and then a director.

Knighton and Ferguson.

Ferguson and Knighton.

Sadly, when Fergie time was eventually up in May 2013, when the final whistle blew on the great man's time at Old Trafford, when he wrote that, *the Glazer family have provided me with the platform to manage Manchester United to the best of my ability,* he appeared to have forgotten not only Edwards but also his earlier partner in the unacknowledged axis of United revolutionaries of 1989.

When questioned, Knighton felt it would have been nice, appropriate even, if Ferguson had remembered the man who, in Knighton's opinion, provided him with the tools to start the successful work of his era; nice, too, if he had given Edwards and his fellow directors some credit, as they, at least, had the wisdom and commercial acumen to implement those revolutionary ideas in Knighton's *Blueprint*.

Knighton knows Ferguson has had kind words to say about him in private, but a public acknowledgement was maybe a step too far for the legendary manager.

* * *

In the football universe, Knighton's greatest accomplishment was his work and his legacy at Old Trafford. There were some additional achievements, however, that should be considered when appraising his time in the football industry.

Knighton was the first to write to former Football Association CEO Graham Kelly, in 1996, urging the FA to immediately introduce goal line technology. He was the first to adopt the term director of coaching rather than team manager. He used that term in Old Trafford board meetings during discussions about Ferguson.

Knighton was the first – in the 1980s – to talk of building a national museum of football, and in 1992 he produced a brochure and discussed plans for such an institution with Stuart Roy Clarke, one of football's greatest photographers. Clarke's own exhibition, *Homes of Football*, is now displayed in the National Museum in Manchester, and has so far attracted over 550,000 visitors. The photographer is another true football man who has recognised Knighton's contribution to the game. When Knighton retired to Sark, Clarke described him as 'a talent lost' to football. In March 2019, Clarke wrote to Knighton and said, 'Michael, in my years curating my exhibition, you have been one of the most wonderful and engaging characters I have come across, intelligent, idealistic, caring, warm, and a little bit mischievous.'

As a character reference, I have seen a lot worse.

Knighton was also the first to talk of having football academies at every professional club. He even visited FA headquarters to discuss the idea with FA officials. Again, he produced a brochure at his own expense, left it with the FA and, shortly after his visit there, it was announced that each club would indeed create their own youth academies.

Knighton was the first to advocate full-time professional referees. He was the first to use the term *brand* in association with football clubs.

Visionary indeed.

Maverick, too, but visionary beyond a doubt.

* * *

Ferguson, of course, is rightly lauded for his achievements. This Glaswegian firebrand socialist dabbled with the sport of kings, knelt before the English Queen to be knighted, and has a stand at Old Trafford named after him. He is a blessed and a lucky man, even more so since his wonderful recovery from the brain haemorrhage he suffered in May 2018.

Remember, though, the black-dog days at the end of 1989 when Ferguson was on the cusp of dismissal by Edwards, when Fergie himself admitted to experiencing 'the darkest period' he had 'ever suffered in the game' when he had become 'something of a hermit, driven into self-imposed hiding by failure' and when Joe Harper, the Aberdeen striker who had known Ferguson in happier times, said, 'the club and the job are too big for him'.

Recall, too, how Knighton told Fergie four months earlier to go ahead and smash the British transfer fee record to bring to United the new players he needed to transform the team.

Lucky indeed.

Blessed that Knighton appeared on the scene at Old Trafford in 1989.

Knighton, though, has always claimed Fergie deserved every bit of his good fortune.

'I said it all at my initial press conference in August 1989, when many were already calling for Alex's head, when I reminded my audience of Fergie's credentials. He has gone on to become the most successful football manager of all time while remaining, in my opinion, a kind and generous, right-thinking human being, and it is those latter qualities that really count in my book.'

Oh, lucky man.

* * *

Edwards has become the rich man, unburdened by debt and apparently unburdened by guilt that he always wanted to be.

In addition, in 2003 he achieved his lifetime ambition of selling on his father's ownership of Manchester United when he offloaded a 6.7 per cent rump of shareholding to Harry Dobson.

Edwards is a blessed and lucky man.

And what of Charlton and Edelson and Watkins?

They have all enjoyed basking in the reflected glories of a golden age for Manchester United. And it has worked well for them financially, too. Knighton doubts whether they ever think of him. Or recall his *Blueprint* and bless the day its ideas were implemented at Old Trafford.

At least Edelson had the decency, Knighton says, to give credit where credit was due when he went public with his acknowledgement of Knighton's significant contribution to the Manchester United success story.

*We basically followed Knighton's plan.*

*We basically followed Knighton's plan.*

*We basically followed Knighton's plan.*

These words of Michael Edelson, vice chairman of Manchester United, spoken while the *Blueprint* was being implemented, hammer the final nail in the coffins of Knighton's detractors and deniers.

Even so, Knighton knows, some critics will never be convinced.

* * *

For someone whose public persona remains one of arrogance and egotism, Knighton does a nice line in self-deprecation.

One of his favourite quotations from among the thousands – possibly millions – of words written about him since the late summer of 1989 is from a book by Jim White, *Manchester United: the Biography*. White described Knighton as a 'small, tubby bloke, the sort of chap you might mistake for a commissionaire'.

Knighton likes to say that appearances can be deceptive. He would like to be judged by results and by the contrast in the Edwards years before and after his involvement.

There is undoubtedly a question to be asked here: what, if not Knighton's dramatic and decisive arrival on the Old Trafford scene, if not his energy and ideas, provoked the unprecedented success of the years that followed? It is the task of historians to provide answers, and to remember Cicero's dictum.

*Who does not know that the first law of historical writing is the truth?*

* * *

*Visionary* is an attempt to correct all those unhelpful, inaccurate and unhistorical conclusions provided by the many previous accounts of these times, and to recalibrate and reassess the impact of one man on a sport he loves. Until now, Knighton has been a victim of the words and silences of ill-informed critics and ill-spirited insiders who should, perhaps, be ashamed.

Of course, one reason Knighton is still viewed with suspicion and derision is that for almost three decades he has refused to tell his side of the story in any detail. He has refused multiple offers from publishers and journalists to ghostwrite his tale.

In September 2017, Sam Wallace, the chief football writer of the *Daily Telegraph*, described Knighton's aborted takeover at Old Trafford as *one of the great football stories of our time*. Even Wallace, though, rehashed many of the tired and baseless clichés associated with the events of 1989.

For example, the lies that Knighton was dependent on backers who withdrew their support, that he 'failed to raise' the money needed to complete the deal, that he tried to 'flip the deal' and that he was 'hawking around' confidential information about the Old Trafford club. Wallace was reviewing Edwards' book, *Red Glory*.

Many keen observers of Manchester United will have viewed Edwards' book as specious in the extreme, malicious in parts, too. Knighton knows what is true and what is untrue and this is his tale.

There was one especially interesting suggestion in Wallace's article.

*Michael Knighton's failed takeover of Manchester United in 1989 has never been given the cinematic treatment but it might just be due consideration, a story so remarkable that even now it bears retelling.*

'A film would be wonderful,' I said.

'As long as it told the truth,' Knighton replied.

* * *

Knighton's reputation within the football world and beyond is well overdue revision. His place in the football firmament is far too important to be left to ignorant or prejudiced critics, journalists who have failed to take the trouble to understand the magic of the man, or failed to study the facts behind the story.

Perhaps the title of this book should have remained *The Truth Game*.

*Visionary*, though, will have to do for now.

## Chapter Twenty-Four
# Judgement Days

KNIGHTON IS a stickler for the truth and always has been. He understands the sadness and the wrongs perpetuated, sins passed down from generation to generation, all because history, all of history, is written and rewritten by winners and for the eternal benefit of winners.

Opinions on Knighton have been shifting in a positive direction over recent years, yet, in the ill-informed eyes of some of the football world and its watchers, he is even now seen as a mere footnote in the pages of Manchester United's history. He's been the chancer who never had the money, he's been the victim of lies and he's seen the history books written by the screechers and the hollerers. He's seen the back pages and the front pages, all of them full of malicious, possibly unthinking, but certainly uncaring nonsense.

* * *

An earlier history, Edward Thompson's *The Making of the English Working Class,* set out *to rescue the poor stockinger, the Luddite cropper, the 'obsolete' hand-loom weaver, the 'utopian' artisan ... from the enormous condescension of posterity.*

Although Knighton always says he is in need of no rescue whatsoever, that his achievements speak for themselves, still his reputation demands a reappraisal, if not a rescue.

* * *

There is no doubt the Manchester United project has been a brilliant success. In January 2018, the Old Trafford club signed Alexis Sanchez from Arsenal and, according to the *Daily Telegraph,* were paying this twenty-nine-year-old reject from Barcelona a staggering £400,000 a week.

One day later, the same newspaper claimed Sanchez was to become the first Premier League footballer to earn £600,000 a week, once a £20m signing-on fee, bonuses and image rights were factored into the equation. The fact that the player has not so far been a success at Old Trafford is irrelevant to the argument.

His was a statement signing, pointing out that Manchester United was able to challenge clubs financed by oil-rich nations, that nouveau riche noisy neighbours awash with cash from Abu Dhabi might still be outbid for the world's best players, that Manchester City might have won the Premier League in 2018, but United would leave no banknote unfolded in their bid to reclaim the prize the following year. Again, the fact that Manchester City were champions once more in 2019 does not disprove this thesis.

And neither does the fact that Sanchez was a disappointment at Old Trafford and has been loaned to Inter Milan in August 2019.

The fact, however, that the Chilean international will still make the second highest demand upon United's wage bill, even though he will be unable to play for them, does illustrate the stupidity and perhaps the irresponsibility on the part of the Old Trafford hierarchy in agreeing to such extortionate wage demands in the first place.

In 2019, under the new management of Ole Gunnar Solskjaer, the Old Trafford club were still intent on making assertive purchases of expensive footballers. Aaron Wan-Bissaka arrived in June for £50m from Crystal Palace and was followed in August by the reported £80 million purchase of Harry Maguire from Leicester City. The latter was a world record fee for a defender and was all rather reminiscent of Knighton's determination in 1989 to secure Gary Pallister from Middlesbrough.

It was also what Knighton said would happen all those years ago.

## Chapter Twenty-Five

# Season's End

IN DECEMBER 2017 I travelled to Wakefield for one of the series of final interviews with Knighton. I was hoping he would reflect on the twenty-five years since our first meeting. I had the matchday programme from that day, the one with the scribbled autographs of Bruce and Pallister and other names I can hardly decipher but treasure nevertheless.

Inside there is an article that looks forward in hope.

*By the start of season 1993/94 Old Trafford is likely to have changed more over a 5-year period than at any time during the club's history.*

This cannot be a coincidence, this promised root and branch transformation of the club, this five-year time span commencing in 1989 with Knighton's arrival on the scene.

By the outset of 1992, Edwards could surely sense that reformation was on the way, in the balance sheets and in the plans for redevelopment of the Stretford End, and in the fact that he no longer needed to borrow or sell to contemplate these changes. In ways perhaps Edwards could not quite comprehend, the failure of 1989 had turned to success, an ugly duckling into a swan.

At the same time that Knighton was about to leave, Edwards perhaps realised there was a possibility that, when the titles came, he would be able to claim them all as his own work. It did not matter to Knighton at the time, but perhaps it matters now, this question of ownership of ideas, this responsibility for change, this apportioning of credit where credit is due and not due.

In the twenty-five years that followed Knighton's departure, what began as a trickle became a flood, an unstoppable monster of money, to the extent that under the Glazers, Manchester United earnt enough to pay out in excess of £550m in interest on the money the Americans had borrowed to buy the club and its burgeoning business domains.

In November 2017, the club announced record first-quarter revenues of £141m, up seventeen per cent on the July to September 2016 figures. One year previously, United had become the first British football club to top the half billion pound mark in terms of revenue and, in 2017, increased that annual income from £515.3m to £581.2m.

In spite of their absence from the Champions League, United were top of the 2018 European money league put together by accountants Deloitte, ousting Real Madrid from the top spot for the second year in succession. Real returned to the top in 2019 with Barcelona second, but United were in third place with a reported revenue of £590m.

Manchester United are now one of the biggest cash cows in world football and the club divvies up the world according to sponsorship potential and brand growth, just as Knighton suggested, so that the club can continue to dominate the English game although there does remain the shadow of an outstanding debt of £487m incurred as a direct result of the Glazer takeover.

* * *

Naturally enough, in a world that spins about an axis of money and in which the creation and redistribution of wealth from middling and poor to the already wealthy is a priority, there are also losers.

Willie Layton's Wednesday, Knighton's Wednesday, is one of them.

In 1992, Sheffield Wednesday was a traditional power in the national game and had been so since Layton's time, yet, since the Big Bang, they have fallen from grace, fallen from prosperity, and now reside in the murky depths of the second tier of English football.

What if this club had opened the door when Knighton knocked?

Wednesday's demise coincided with the arrival of the money-making men of the Premiership. At the end of the 1991/92 season the club seemed set fair, were third in the former First Division and heading for European competition and a place in the new Premiership. From then on, however, their decline was steady and occasionally spectacular.

The nineties for the Wednesday were years of overspending and underachievement, three seventh places being highlights of a sort. Relegation to the second tier in 2000 was the inevitable consequence of debt, mismanagement and failure by the club's leadership to come to terms with the new, brash and harsher terms of trade in the brave new world of football finance.

In the new millennium, Wednesday became a boomerang club, alternating between the second and third tiers of English football, and in May 2013 only just clung on to the second ranks. They have spent the last six years slumming it in the English Football League Championship.

* * *

It is noticeable that there have been fewer and fewer winners since globalised finance in football arrived and many more losers of one kind or another. In England, realistically, only the two Manchester clubs, Spurs, Arsenal, Chelsea and Liverpool can challenge for what really matters.

Two of these six English clubs have enjoyed the backing of US dollars, one the support of a Russian oligarch, another the petrol dollars of the UAE, leaving Arsenal and Spurs hoping that new 60,000-seater stadiums will make up for lack of investment in players by wealthy owners. In fact, as 2019 unfolded, there was a creeping fear among fans that in England the six was becoming two, Manchester City and Liverpool.

In January 2018, the Chelsea manager, Antonio Conte, seemed to have ceded to the financial muscle of the two Manchester clubs. In a press conference prior to a League Cup semi-final against Arsenal, he said, 'In this moment, there are two teams who are top. The others have to fight for a place … We'll have to make a success not with money but with work. These big teams continue to improve and invest a lot of money, and there is this gap.'

All this, after years of English crowing about the competitiveness of the higher echelons of Premier League football, and of invidious comparisons with Spain and Germany, where, it was said, championships were utterly uncompetitive beyond a small charmed circle of elite clubs.

Even UEFA is concerned about this trend and its president, Alexander Ceferin, has suggested a luxury tax and fines for overspending clubs. However, with Financial Fair Play rules in at least partial ruin, his words seemed empty.

What hope is there now for teams such as Ipswich Town, winners of the former Division Three South in 1957, champions of the Second Division in 1961 and First Division champions in 1962? Or of Nottingham Forest who under Brian Clough were promoted from the Second Division in 1977, won the First Division championship in 1978 and the European Cup in 1979? Or, indeed, of Knighton's beloved Derby County, also once under Clough's tutelage, who were promoted from the Second Division in 1969 and won the top title a year later?

Ipswich, Forest and County today are a trio of losers in the battle for money that now is the football industry. In 2019/20 Forest and County will play in the Championship and Ipswich in the third tier of English football. What chance, too, of Manchester United ever being relegated as they were in 1894, 1922, 1931, 1937 and 1974?

Elsewhere, only Real Madrid and Barcelona in Spain, Bayern Munich in Germany and Paris St Germain in France have realistic chances of winning their respective leagues. Where is the spice, where is the all-important sporting element of surprise? It is a shrinking world, this world of money, the one that Knighton predicted in his *Blueprint*, the one that was the inevitable consequence of the policies of marketisation that he advocated as the salvation of Manchester United in 1989.

* * *

My train arrived late at Wakefield Westgate, and I apologised to Knighton who laughed.

I was grateful for his greeting and the meeting, and the transport to his home which was once owned by the former textile magnate and Victorian philanthropist John Wainhouse. It is somehow typical of Knighton that he lives in this statement-of-success house. He lives and breathes the past, does Knighton, not in a sentimental, nostalgic way, but as an inspiration, a means to make the future.

We sat in Knighton's study and I showed him the match programme from the day of our first meeting.

'What about these characters here?' I asked.

'The directors, you mean?'

'Edwards,' I said, 'what about him, how do you feel about the man now?'

I guess, as a writer, I wanted Knighton to say how much he hated them all, especially Edwards, the apparently grasping, greedy, accumulator of wealth, the luckiest man alive when Knighton returned the contract to purchase Manchester United in the autumn of 1992.

Somehow, though, I wasn't that disappointed when Knighton said he wished Edwards well, congratulated him on his good fortune, and credited him with recognising a gift horse when it hit him in the mouth, and for overseeing the commercial developments at United in the 1990s. What does need saying, however, is that Knighton's arrival in a blaze of publicity, his early declaration of intent with the signings of Pallister and Ince, made Edwards look dull and unimaginative by comparison, a grey man in a grey period of Manchester United's history. Knighton's frenetic burst of transfer market activity on his accession to power within the club, his first ten days, made the previous ten years of Edwards' reign seem dull and dreary by comparison.

Knighton was Mozart to Edwards' Salieri, Cantona to Neville – Philip probably – and Blair to Major. No doubt, Edwards would point out the inestimable value of conservatism, consistency and careful stewardship, that Mozart was dead at thirty-five and that Knighton was gone from Old Trafford within three years, after one brief flirtation with fame. That Tony Blair's reputation was ruined beyond repair by his reckless intervention in Iraq, just as Knighton's was holed below the waterline by his shenanigans in the autumn of 1989. And that Eric Cantona was a loose cannon – like Knighton – and that the Neville brothers between them played almost one thousand games for Manchester United. That loyalty was an incalculable good and that fact should not be forgotten.

The truth of the matter is, however, that Mozart, Cantona, Blair – and Knighton – were all game-changers, movers and shakers of history. No one could ever tag Edwards as exciting or innovative or a maverick, or as a turner of the page in history.

* * *

I pulled from my bag a copy of Edwards' book, *Red Glory – Manchester United and Me* published just three months earlier.

'Ah,' Knighton said, 'that does rather change things, doesn't it? Some of the comments, the lies Edwards writes, well, perhaps not knowing lies but, let's say, a confused understanding of certain facts and certain issues relating to myself, well, that section of his book is hurtful, it's simply inaccurate, and the pomposity, of course, is ridiculous.'

I respected the silence that followed, the sadness. He picked up the programme and flicked through the pages.

'And Charlton?' I said.

Knighton smiled. He knew the score and thought I might be after another story to counter the squeaky clean Charlton image.

'I've mellowed, and maybe Bobby has too, I wouldn't know.'

'What do you mean?'

'Well, just that Bobby is Bobby and I think I've come to accept that.'

Knighton paused. 'He's a complex character, Bobby, but let's just say that what you see with him, his public, his television personality, is not what you get with the real thing.'

I felt something coming, some revelation, some story that trumped the one about Charlton telling Knighton to get off the grass at Wembley in 1990.

'I'll say no more than that,' Knighton said. 'I prefer to remember him as one of the greatest footballers I have had the pleasure and privilege to watch.'

'You mean you've forgiven him, Michael?'

'There's nothing really there to forgive.'

'But there were unkind words between you, Michael?'

'Yes, it's true, Bobby can be quite cruel sometimes, it's true he's said some unpleasant and unnecessary things to me, but he also spoke well of me at the conclusion of my final board meeting. I still have enormous respect for the man.'

We moved on, perhaps to safer ground.

'Fergie,' I said, 'now he's finally made up his mind to retire, do you think he ever looks back to 1989 and thinks on the Knighton phenomenon?'

'He should do, you know, he really should do.'

Knighton was laughing again, partly at himself, but only partly.

'He ought to remember who authorised the signing of Pallister, and it certainly wasn't Edwards.'

We had talked before about the unacknowledged partnership between the two new boys on the block, Ferguson and Knighton, the outsiders, the revolutionaries, the bringers of new ideas, new worlds. We revisited that idea now. Knighton was reluctant to assess his own contribution but it needed saying, spelling out, repeating even.

Once the contract was back in Edwards' hands, Knighton and Ferguson spoke only rarely, but there was an undeniable chemistry at the club, a new spirit in the air, a reaction from the combination of new people, new money and new players purchased with the new money.

Ferguson and Knighton, in their separate spheres of influence, were the catalysts for all this change.

How would Knighton like to be judged? More sinned against than sinning? I can't remember now whether that was my suggestion as an epitaph or Knighton's.

How had he coped with the way some people had judged him then? He bridled ever such a little at this implication of failure.

'I mean,' I said, 'the way you are viewed by the world at large.'

He acknowledged that it was not easy.

'We live in a world where perception is all, where labels, once attached, remain fixed.'

I expressed the hope my book might shift some lazy ways of thinking.

'It takes a lifetime to build a reputation,' he said, 'and only a moment's thoughtlessness or animosity to destroy what has been painstakingly constructed.'

Knighton's words distracted me, and I thought, momentarily, of Charlton and the iconic status he had so assiduously cultivated. He had been a hero of mine, too, in my youth. I did not want to bring him down, but I was interested in the truth about the man behind the myth, behind the image.

I recalled seeing Charlton on the day of my first meeting with Knighton at Old Trafford. He had walked past our table in the restaurant without a word of acknowledgement of his fellow director and it had seemed to me a deliberate snub from a man with ice in his heart.

In the end, I felt there was more Knighton might have said about Charlton, but I respected his determination not to reveal all.

I reclaimed my souvenir programme from Knighton's hands, and changed the subject.

'It's Thatcherism gone viral,' I said, 'this football world.'

'It's actually exactly as Marx predicted a century and a half ago,' replied Knighton in his self-proclaimed role of socialist millionaire. 'Big fish eating little fish, international capitalism, money without borders, without controls, imperialism, wars, it's all there, including the seeds of its own destruction.'

'And football,' I said, 'that's a perfect model of your Marxist theories come home to roost.'

'Except for the socialist revolution at the end of it all, although that may come, too.'

'Yes,' I said, 'with possibly more restrictions on unlimited spending by the big boys being implemented by UEFA, that's socialism of a sort.'

'More than that, much more than that.'

Sometimes, I think Knighton is at his best when he is enigmatic.

'Whole nations, too,' he added, 'rising and falling, just like football clubs.' I smiled, and encouraged Knighton to continue. 'Oh, to be a true revolutionary. How I would love to be a latter day Wat Tyler, 1381, the Peasants' Revolt, and all that.'

'Tyler was nearly stabbed to death, then decapitated, and his severed head was then displayed for all to see on London Bridge,' I said.

'Well, of course, with a better result for my rebellion,' Knighton replied, and roared with laughter.

'What about your idea of promotion and relegation, of leagues for nations?'

'Okay, Manchester United are like the USA, rampant, dominant in most markets, mopping up most of the prizes, but there are new challenges to face, there always are in this Darwinian – and Marxist – struggle for survival, for domination. There's Manchester City, the oil-rich kingdoms of Arabia, the coming force, if their natural resources hold out. There's Chelsea, the former clunking Soviet Union, now liberated by swathes of alleged looted cash and poverty, still a major player. There's even your Tottenham, one of the rising stars, India, maybe, but I think I prefer to see Spurs more as Brazil.'

'China?' I asked.

Knighton laughed.

'China is whichever football club makes the next Great Leap Forward, becomes the Manchester United of the later twenty-first century.'

'They'll need another Knighton to inspire another Big Bang for that.'

We fall about, laughing.

'So, what about England, then?'

'It's interesting, this country, isn't it?' Knighton said. 'I rather think it's Sheffield Wednesday, just enough clout to make a noise but not enough to make a difference.'

'Terminal decline, then, if it's the Wednesday.'

Knighton chose to ignore the cheap joke. Sheffield Wednesday is, after all, a club close to his heart.

'Yes,' I rather think that is England now,' he said, 'the destruction of the traditional industries, like coal by Thatcher, textiles, steel, shipbuilding, the potteries, all could and should have been supported or, at the very least, their communities should have been cared for, assisted through their troubles. Those industries are akin to our traditional football clubs, ones that were in the old First Division when we were kids, like the Wednesday, like Wolverhampton Wanderers – although the Wolves have recovered with the help of Chinese money – Portsmouth, Bolton, Blackpool, Blackburn – the list goes on and on, the traditional trades and crafts on which English strength was once based, and now all we have is financial deregulation in both the City and in the governance of football.'

Knighton, though, had suddenly had enough of playing games. He wanted to talk about judgements.

'It's end of book time,' I said.

'Okay, then it's your shout, what you say, I mean.'

* * *

So, what I want to say is this. Like all geniuses, Knighton's creativity was flawed; there was a destructive element to most of his work. Someone I interviewed from Knighton's time at St David's School said Knighton never finished what he began.

This book, born as *The Truth Game* in 1992, is almost a perfect example of that. Its completion has come about only because of a certain persistence on my part, as well as a change in Knighton's circumstances – his becoming a grandfather, for example.

There are other examples, too.

Eknath Easwaran, an Indian teacher of meditation and Hindu philosophy who moved from Kerala to California in the latter part of the twentieth century, said that desire is the motive force behind all achievement, but that great accomplishment is only possible when desire is focused as sharply as the sun's rays through a magnifying glass, when it is unbroken in its persistence, when man is consumed only by one single goal, one burning hunger.

Knighton's focus, however, is splintered, like light bent and divided into the colours of the rainbow as it passes through a prism. He, perhaps, has too many things he is passionate about.

He is right, though, to jib at the suggestion of failure.

He transformed a school, was hugely successful in the property market, has produced breathtaking art, and revolutionised Manchester United and the wider football world.

There remains, however, the accusation of choking, bottling, call it what you will, and the return of the contract to Martin Edwards remains the greatest conundrum of Knighton's career. At least, through these pages, the lie of never having the money has been finally nailed.

The question of why he let the prize slip through his fingers, however, is still unanswered.

Some will believe that the pressure on Knighton through the late summer and autumn of 1989 was simply too much to bear, and would have been so for anyone unable to divorce themselves from the tides of human emotion, the push and pull of family, the core values of principled behaviour. However, when asked whether her husband bowed to the forces, the pressures of circumstance, Rosemary Knighton laughed.

'If you think that for one moment about Mike you really don't know him at all.'

For what it is worth, I believe Knighton was simply telling the truth when he said he was happy to hand back the contract to Edwards because his integrity was intact, he had his seat in the Old Trafford boardroom and he had a firm promise that the ideas contained in his *Blueprint* would be implemented.

It is the sole explanation that fits all the facts.

* * *

It is Knighton's art, though, for which he should most be remembered.

Yet his masterpiece, a crucifixion triptych, remains in storage inside huge wooden crates. There is, though, a five-minute film on YouTube from the time of Knighton's exhibition at King's College, Cambridge.

Watch it.

'Michael,' I said, 'it's got to have a permanent home, it's got to be out there, it's got to be seen by people, it's a masterpiece.'

'I know,' he said. There was a shrug of the shoulders and a tacit admission that this great work of art that once lit up the university chapel might never again see the light of day.

That's Knighton for you, something destructive amid the creativity. Unfathomable, even for someone who knows him as well as anyone is allowed to know him.

* * *

As for me, I never really wanted to write this summarising stuff, this judgemental, conclusive guff. I never set out to be a judge, still less a hanging judge. In an ideal world, the story tells its own truths, comes to its own halfway house. But it had to be done.

Knighton's mind seems to set him up to fail in the eyes of the world because he will not, cannot, perhaps, see things through. In addition, he is a bundle of impossible contradictions. Is he a publicity seeker or a recluse? He swings both ways on this one.

To be fair to Knighton, it has taken him almost thirty years to agree to anyone telling his stories, and I know, over that great span of time, he has refused hundreds of requests for interviews, for appearances on prime-time TV shows, and dozens of offers to tell his tale from big-time journalists.

He is a millionaire with socialist and republican leanings but also, and this may be important in terms of his football legacy, a romantic conservative in the utopian lineage of the nineteenth-century lit by William Cobbett and Orator Hunt, and in the twentieth by historians Edward Thompson and Eric Hobsbawm. That tradition was also favoured by Arthur Scargill and Michael Foot, both radicals and populists who yearned for power for the people, but only so that the almighty and overweening certainties of capitalism might be overthrown.

These men all began as revolutionaries, just like Knighton.

What Knighton helped to birth in the football world he later came to see as something to stand against. Ultimately, he believes in the powers of tradition, family, roots and values. He still loves football and watches regularly at Hillsborough, the ancient home of Sheffield Wednesday, the place where disaster and tragedy forced Knighton to understand something had to be done.

He is different now, softer, more mellow, perhaps content, although he is still capable of radical bursts of opinion, still open to more change if and when it comes. He is less inclined, these days, to try to make it happen himself.

'Come on,' he said, 'let's take Lola for a walk.'

The ears of Knighton's beloved boxer pricked up.

We climbed a steep hillside which recently had been covered in snow and were too breathless to talk. At the summit, we paused, inspired by the rolling panorama of man's interaction and fusion with the natural world, the landscape of the Industrial Revolution, the scars and the healing of time, the setting rays of the falling sun.

'Do you know that poem by Hopkins,' Knighton said, 'the one about the grandeur of God?'

*The world is charged with the grandeur of God.*

I knew it by heart.

*It will flame out, like shining from shook foil;*

*It gathers to a greatness, like the ooze of oil*
*Crushed. Why do men then now not reck his rod?*
We recited together the ancient verities.
*Generations have trod, have trod, have trod;*
*And all is seared with trade; bleared, smeared with toil;*
*And wears man's smudge and shares man's smell: the soil*
*Is bare no, nor can foot feel, being shod.*
We shouted it now, alone at the top of the scarp.
*And for all this, nature is never spent ...*

It was a moment of communion, remarkable in its naivety and its intensity. It could not last and we descended the path, began again to talk of football, ambition, money, and of football's captive men.

Knighton returned me to Wakefield Station. We exchanged promises that the book would be finished this time. And I knew then what it was I needed to say.

* * *

Knighton is the creator and author of two works of true genius.

One is his crucifixion triptych, *Hand of God, Foot of Man, Heart of Eternal Life,* which reflects his revolutionary conservatism, a manifesto for the return to the traditional values of representational art and to the preaching of the eternal and the moral values of mystery and faith.

To stand before this work is to stand before the glory of God and to tremble in its presence.

Knighton is not conventionally religious, yet his masterpiece is a meditation on the relationship between God and Man, a commentary on the heart of life, Christ's heart, rich and reddened by 120 rubies, an image rendered almost tawdry by its omnipresence inside Catholic churches throughout the world. It is Roman theological orthodoxy with a mere twist of artistic licence and a giant projection of artistic genius.

'If you believe in me,' said Knighton, 'you will receive eternal life.'

I was taken aback by the force and commitment and attack of his words.

'I come to bleed for you.'

Knighton told me that when he was creating this triptych he worked through many days and nights, absorbed by, obsessed with the project.

He was impossible to live with.

His obsession with his artwork probably cost him his marriage to Rosemary, although their friendship remains as strong as ever.

'These sculptures,' he said, 'these different colours, the different colour skins of the Christ, if there is a God, he has to represent all men, white, brown, and black.'

This crucifixion triptych, this baring of Knighton's soul before God, rightly shared sacred space at King's College Chapel with Rubens' masterpiece, *Adoration of the Magi*.

It took the installation team three and a half days to put the work in place. It had been delivered to Cambridge in a pantechnicon. There was one case for each panel and each one weighed a fraction under one ton. It cost around £25,000 to set up, just so the men who mattered at Canterbury could see what they were being offered.

They had seen the photographs and they were mad for it, but it was fair enough, Knighton thought, to appreciate the sheer scale of the work, to see it in its proper setting, within the walls of an iconic, internationally renowned and sacred building that would marry magnificence with significance, which would speak the language of the glory of God and greet similar echoing words from the stones of its surroundings.

Knighton was present at the exhibition in 2008 but pretended to be part of the back-up team headed by his curator, Ioannis Goss-Taylor, a fine art specialist. He watched and he listened as the dean and his cathedral team from Canterbury swooned over his triptych. He had always wanted this artwork to go to Canterbury, the place where St Thomas Becket sought sanctuary from the soldiers of King Henry in 1170, the place where the archbishop's brains were spilled on and stained the cathedral stones, so he was pleased that the clerics from Kent seemed to approve so wholeheartedly of his creation and of his intended gift.

The only minor irritation for Knighton was the cathedral dean's continuing insistence on the artist's name. The teachings of Jesus of Nazareth, he muttered to himself, would still have possessed the same power, the same truth, if the Son of God had been given no name. He heard his curator politely but firmly reiterate the instructions he had been given, his insistence on no publicity, no names.

It was not that Knighton expected to expiate all of his sins with this one gift to God or that he expected to go to heaven as a result, or even that he believed in a place called paradise, but he did remember Christ's injunction to pray in private, to give in private. The men who did these things in public, Christ said, had already received their reward on earth.

It was a private viewing for Archbishop Rowan Williams' team and it was a good time to hold it, because the Cambridge students were still enjoying their summer vacation and random visitors to the chapel were being discouraged by college servants. He was buoyed by the enthusiasm and appreciation of the Reverend Ian Thompson, Dean of Chapel at King's, who said he would love the installation to remain in place in his college for a few days more, so that the triptych might be available for viewing by the general public.

The following day, however, the second day of the exhibition of the crucifixion triptych, Knighton received a disturbing call from Goss-Taylor.

'Stay away, Michael,' he said, 'the place is swarming with press, and they all want to know who the artist is.'

Later, the curator called Knighton again.

'It's become a tourist attraction, Michael, the punters are pouring in.'

'Oh, my God,' was Knighton's response.

He was on his way.

He was angry because he had been told the chapel would be closed and only the archbishop's colleagues would be allowed to see the artwork. When he arrived and tried to push his way through the crowd, he thought, *It's a football mob.*

'Okay,' Knighton said to Goss-Taylor, 'how has this happened?'

It turned out it was accidental.

The college had allocated eight porters – effectively college security officials – to maintain order while the triptych was in the chapel. But the previous day, among the occasional tourists, there had been a freelance journalist on holiday with his girlfriend who sensed there might be a story to sell. He began to dig with an over-talkative porter who told the hack that the triptych was the work of a recluse known as the Pearlman, because the artwork was covered in pearls.

Another porter was being pestered without respite by the public.

Who is the artist? How much is it worth? Who is the artist? How much is it worth?

Most of the tourists had paid their entrance fee and most had come to see the magnificent Rubens masterpiece but had ended up ogling Knighton's triptych. To keep them quiet the porter decided to spin them a tale.

'Oh, yes, worth more than the Rubens, you know,' he said.

The buzz began.

Someone good at maths and someone who knew about art world values put their heads together and came up with £75m. Others talked to the freelance journalist who spoke to his editors.

Meanwhile, Knighton's curatorial team was negotiating with the lay authorities at Canterbury. Yes, the archbishop was impressed, yes, the dean and chapter would love to accept this generous gift, and, yes, the triptych would look splendid in the cathedral. But it was just a shame that the artist would not come forward, accept the accolades, acknowledge the grateful thanks of the Church.

In addition, a professional fundraiser, Heather Gambril, had been employed by the archbishop to raise cash to stop the cathedral from falling down.

She needed £50m.

'Can we sell it?' she said, within two minutes of sitting down with Knighton, a man she assumed was the artist's agent.

He was knocked back, stunned by this philistinism, used as he was to the tough currency of international art trading. Subsequently, emails were exchanged, although Knighton was careful to remain untraceable.

Here's the deal, he wrote to cathedral staff.

The crucifixion triptych must stay for a minimum of twelve months in Canterbury Cathedral and after that it could be sold with two conditions: that one third of the proceeds went to the Caritas Community, a charity Knighton's friend, Richard Bellinger, a Franciscan from Sark, had founded in the Channel Islands to assist in the rehabilitation of young offenders; that another third went to the King's College Chapel Restoration Fund; the remaining third could go to Canterbury, to do with as the cathedral saw fit.

Gambril's fundraising eyes should have been popping at the prospect. If the £75m valuation was correct she would raise half her fundraising target overnight.

To be fair to Gambril, however, it is possible to see how her reservations about Knighton's artwork might have arisen, the valuation based on gossip and the lack of knowledge of the triptych's provenance.

Still, it was not Knighton's problem that the real market value of his piece was a probable maximum of between £10m and £15m. He knew this because he had already been offered £8m by an investment banker from the USA. It might make more at auction, Knighton pondered. Damien Hirst had recently sold the contents of his one-man show, *Beautiful Inside My Head Forever,* for £111m at Sotheby's.

However, the cathedral rejected his conditions. Gambril said that if it was a gift, the cathedral should be able to decide on the use of the entire proceeds from any sale. Knighton was livid. He sensed the same greed he'd seen in football.

'Tell them,' Knighton wrote, 'that this is unacceptable to the artist.'

The *Telegraph* reported that the Church of England had declined a gift of £75m. Gambril possibly thought it might have cost the cathedral money in the long run as it would have had to have been displayed for a whole year. Another cathedral spokesperson said it would have taken up a lot of space. Heaven help us, Knighton thought.

Meanwhile, in a Knightsbridge hairdressing salon, Knighton's friend, Koo Stark, who had been the one time serious girlfriend linked with Prince Andrew, and who also knew the identity of the mysterious artist whose triptych was on view at King's, was sitting next to Lady Hambro, one of the trustees of Canterbury Cathedral.

'Such a shame, isn't it?'

'What is, darling?' said Stark.

'You know, this gift to the cathedral from that mysterious artist up in Cambridge. Such a shame we had to turn it down.'

'Jolly mysterious, though,' said Stark, repressing her desires to tell all and to giggle her way through the entire conversation.

'I wonder who the artist could be?'

Stark managed – just – to hold her peace.

Someone else sad to see the gift refused was the Reverend Richard Lloyd Morgan, chaplain of King's College, Cambridge, whose organisation stood to make a killing on Knighton's triptych.

'I can't imagine that if someone was to receive a cheque for a third of £70m they would refuse it,' he said to a *Church Times* interviewer.

Knighton greeted the £5m depreciation in the value of his work with a salutary smile and read on.

'It's here for three days, and then packed up in crates and put into a truck. I have no idea where it's gone to. It's bewildering in so many ways.'

The triptych almost went to St Mary's RC Cathedral in Edinburgh. The authorities there were desperate to provide Knighton's work with a permanent home, would place it within the chancel, and wanted it installed in time for the visit of Pope Benedict in September 2010. Unfortunately, however, the cases containing the triptych would not go through the door of the nineteenth-century Gothic cathedral, and dismantling part of the sacred building, brick by listed brick, was never a realistic option. Instead the triptych went to a warehouse in Yorkshire, where storage currently costs Knighton about £150 per week.

'It's a travesty,' I said, 'it's sacrilege.'

* * *

Knighton's second work of genius, another attempt at a bequest to humanity, is also nowhere to be found – until now, in the appendix to this book.

It is, of course, the revolutionary *Blueprint* given to Manchester United in 1989. It has been out of sight and out of mind for decades, packed away in storage boxes. Just like the triptych.

In fact, Knighton produced several variations of his *Blueprint* – one for bankers, one for Bob Thornton, one that he gave to Edwards. It is the bank's copy that is here reproduced in full.

For those reading the *Blueprint* for the first time, it is important to understand both the state of the football industry in 1989 and the revolutionary impact this document had, its influence on Manchester United and on the football world beyond Old Trafford. Before Knighton – BK if you like – was the Dark Ages. Afterwards – AK – was not all sweetness and light by any means, but the changes were staggering, the contrasts stark.

For comparisons with the revolutionary changes in the football world since 1989, perhaps imagine the world prior to the innovations of Steve Jobs and Steve Wozniak at Apple. Or think of what Walt was to Disney, what Richard Branson and Mike Oldfield, in their different ways, were to Virgin Records, of what Stephen Hawking was to black holes and the understanding of the universe, of what Edison was to electricity. Only then can you appreciate what Knighton was to Manchester United and Martin Edwards.

Comparisons, too, can be made concerning the remarkable but publicly, and even privately, unacknowledged partnership between Knighton and Ferguson: think Laker and Lock in cricket, spinners who routed Australia in 1956; think of the collaboration between Muhammad Ali and his trainer Angelo Dundee; think Gareth Edwards and Barry John, and Clive Woodward and Martin Johnson in rugby union; in racing think Arkle and Pat Taaffe, Dancing Brave and Pat Eddery, Enable and Frankie Dettori; and in football think Clough and Taylor.

Some were teams designed in heaven, some were accidental alliances, but surely the greatest fluke of them all was the uncanny symbiosis of Knighton and Ferguson. Without Ferguson, Knighton's innovative ideas, and the money generated by them on behalf of Manchester United, might have been squandered. One has only to look at the cash splashed without success at Old Trafford since Ferguson's retirement in 2013, and the sad sequence of failed managers that has followed, to understand this fact.

Without Knighton, without the initial signings of Pallister and Ince, for example, Ferguson might have been removed long before his own revolution on the playing side at Old Trafford had borne fruit.

* * *

Knighton also tried to provide the football industry with a moral framework, something I have christened *the new model chairmanship for the future of football.*

Knighton may have been football's greatest visionary, ripping up the old rule book about how to run a halfway successful football club and ushering in a new age of commerce and capital at the end of the last millennium.

There was, however, more to it than that.

Until 1989, the role of the football club director had remained relatively unchanged throughout the history of the game.

This role was filled by local men made good – the butchers of Manchester United, the bakers of Bolton Wanderers, the meat-pie-and-two-veg men, the builders and the local worthies up and down the country. They may have known little about football but at least they thought they knew all there was to know. They rubbed along, they rubbed shoulders, they shook hands, they greased palms.

Some of these business worthies may also have exploited, ripped off their workers, cheated customers and regarded football players as riff-raff and chattels – all under the shameless cover of custodianship of the local football club.

Knighton does not believe that all leaders of football clubs should be thus categorised.

But think where all the money went. A crowd of 84,584 watched the 1907 FA Cup Final at Crystal Palace when the Wednesday beat Everton 2-1. Gate receipts were £4,302, the equivalent today of £335,000. At the time, Willie Layton, Knighton's great-grandfather, was paid the maximum weekly wage of four guineas. There were ten other players to pay plus a few reserves who would not have been on the top rate of pay.

Where did all the money go?

It's arguable that Edwards worked the same financial ploy of extracting money from the sport he claimed to love, albeit, perhaps, in more subtle ways than the owners of 1907's edition of Sheffield Wednesday. Edwards, for example, borrowed money to buy the rights issue shares of Manchester United with the club effectively paying him, through salary and dividends, the cost of his shares, and repaying his borrowings.

Yes, the deal was more sophisticated than the sheer daylight robbery of the early 1900s, but it might be argued that it was turning the same party trick: you, as director or chairman got to preen and ponce, strutting your big-shot stuff about the boardroom, and the poor punters paid you handsomely to do so. It was certainly how football club ownership operated in the past and you have to make your own mind up whether that still applies today.

That was not Knighton's mode of operation, however. At Old Trafford, he took not one penny in salary or even expenses throughout his three years as a director. His revolutionary idea, for *the new model chairmanship for the future of football* was to make a profit through the exploitation of new streams of revenue and then to spend it on the team, not on dividends to shareholders. This had never been done before and has not been done since.

The model for football club owners in the twenty-first century has involved the substitution of nineteenth- and twentieth-century hypocrisy with a naked dash for cash. Football clubs, especially those in the Premiership, are now viewed unashamedly as vehicles of commercial exploitation, personal profit, prestige and power.

Manchester United's owners, the Glazer family, are an obvious example but the extent of their brazen pursuit of personal revenue streams from the club's commercial outreach is, in the opinion of most United fans and serious financial commentators, breathtaking in the extreme.

In the financial year 2011/12, United paid £50m to service the ongoing debt leveraged on to the club in the aggressive Glazer takeover. The same year, the Glazer family paid themselves a £10m dividend to pay off their £10m loan of the preceding year, and £1.6m, in addition, for each of Malcolm Glazer's six children. The club also paid a £3m management fee to the Glazers. On top of all this largesse, Kevin Glazer, one of the lucky inheritors of his father's wealth, earned £558,484 in interest, after buying some of the United debt for himself, a cast-iron investment guaranteeing a sumptuous return.

A report in *The Independent* newspaper in May 2015 suggested the Glazer family had taken out £1bn in personal profits from the club in their first ten years of stewardship. In 2017, the Glazers were paid a dividend of £18.3m. A report in *The Guardian* in October 2019 claimed the Glazers had 'drained' more than £1bn from the Old Trafford club. Mere fans may only dream of such riches and be horrified at such rapaciousness.

United's owners are not the only profiteers, however, although they may be the least apologetic. At Arsenal, there is now an absentee landlord in charge of affairs – the silent American Stan Kroenke, who pays himself, via his company, Kroenke Sports Enterprises, an eye-watering annual fee of £3m for 'strategic and advisory services'. Previously, other Arsenal directors had cashed in: in 2007, David Dein sold his 14.58 per cent shareholding for £75m and in 2011, Nina Bracewell-

Smith sold her 15.9 per cent shareholding for an undisclosed sum that was sufficiently large for her to file a lawsuit for £11.6 million against law firm Linklaters and accountants Deloitte for allegedly failing to provide her with sufficient advice on her tax liabilities consequent upon her sale to Kroenke. Bracewell-Smith has consequently moved to Monaco.

At Liverpool, where the Moores family had been custodians and majority shareholders for over half a century, David Moores, heir to the Littlewoods Pools empire, broke an unwritten agreement with Sheikh Mohammed and the Dubai Investment Corporation in order to trouser an additional £10m when he sold the club to Americans George Gillett and Tom Hicks for a clear profit of £89 million. The custodianship of Hicks and Gillett at Liverpool was a living nightmare and ended in October 2010. Martin Edwards, with his hundred-plus millions in liquid cash, was merely the first in a distinguished line of former owners who most fans now refer to as greedy bastards.

Neither is the old model of rapacious ownership confined to the Premier League, of course.

The latest example is to be found in the behaviour of the ownership of Ken Anderson at Bolton Wanderers. The administrator, tasked with saving the club from extinction in August 2019, described Anderson as a man who had 'used his position as a secured creditor to hamper and frustrate any deal that did not benefit him or suit his purposes'.

Knighton's methodology offers a different route to salvation. The problem is that *the new model chairmanship* requires protagonists to be in love with football, to be, at the very least, more in love with football than with money. Excess over expenditure has to be ploughed back into the football club, to help to create a virtuous circle of varied and profitable income streams all contributing to the creation of further sources of income which then fund the team's success on the field in terms of additional wages to attract top players and top quality management, which in turn further increases revenue.

It's a sure-fire winner, as proven by Knighton's time at Manchester United and in the years immediately after, and by the ability of the club to withstand even the most fantastical raids on their profitability by the Glazer family in the current and last decade.

The problem is that *the new model chairmanship* is rather too much like Christianity or socialism. It requires altruism, commitment and energy far too often lacking in the quick buck, bang a buck culture that prevails at present, not only in English football but also in British art and in English society in general since Thatcher, Major and Blair pronounced the death of the post-Second World War consensus that brought about a managed economy and a managed and caring society. As such, Knighton's way, like true Christianity, like true socialism, has hardly been tried.

To be fair, there are football club owners who work hard, who do their best by their local clubs, their local communities. Unfortunately, though, these men – and football club ownership is still, sadly, almost exclusively male – are thin on the ground and mostly to be found in clubs outside the Premier League and English Football League.

Knighton's genius, however, is that he has offered an alternative operational model in both football and in art, the very two spheres of human endeavour that he loves best. The key to it all, the one that unlocks Knighton's character, is that, for him at least, it was never about the money, not even when he was buying property.

At that time it was about providing for the future of his son Mark and later his other children and the rest of his family, and also about winning, about beauty, and about owning and living in glorious architectural visions – Victorian mill owners' houses, castles, and Georgian grandeur, all of which defied mere functionalism. It was about creativity and altruism, too, and every property Knighton bought set out its blaze, its brick, its stone and tile, in a gesture that said, look, this is what man can do, this is what God can do.

Most certainly it was not about money when Knighton was playing his football games at Old Trafford, or enjoying other games that life had to offer. There is an open-hearted generosity of spirit about Knighton that only those who know him well can truly understand. What Knighton does these days is provide for the care of his ailing father. For the rest of the time he offers his commercial expertise *pro bono* to deserving causes.

* * *

When we returned from our walk, Knighton disappeared then reappeared clutching sheaves of papers. They formed a typed and stapled diary from August 1989, which was old and faded but detailed his encounters with the press during that seminal month.

It's too late, Michael, I thought.

The damn book's finished now.

Of course, I couldn't help reading the stuff. It was headed *Michael Knighton – the rise and fall and sort of rise again of a 62-day media phenomenon*, and in the top right-hand corner of the first page was a handwritten scribble: *My copy!* It was big on the sheer exuberance and joy of the first day of the season, the romping win over champions Arsenal, and his ball juggling in front of the adoring Stretford End.

The diary included several cuttings including one in which *The Sun* told its readers *What he's got for his dosh*, with Peter Fitton describing the chairman elect as 'the high roller and the power broker'.

In others, Ted Macauley of the *Mirror* described United's new owner as 'a shy millionaire' and Colin Wood of the *Mail* suggested Knighton was 'the man from a working class background in Derbyshire who has succeeded where the Czech-born international publishing magnate Robert Maxwell, David Whelan, Richard Branson and the Lebanese multi-millionaire Amer Al Midani failed in the past'.

There were classic examples of the sub-editor's art, such as the headlines 'Knighton in Shining Armour' from the *Sunday Mirror* and, especially wonderful from *The Sun* when announcing Knighton's charity challenge to fellow chairmen, '£5m if you juggle your balls like me, says United's Mr Big'.

It was all rather touching, naïve, and understandably egocentric, of course.

There were days later in the month when the chairman elect had typed, *Nothing for the Knighton family scrapbook.*

The darkness was yet to come.

'Okay, Michael,' I said, as I was returned to Wakefield Station, 'I promise I'll put some of it in the book.'

* * *

Knighton is different now.

He's been reviewing his past and it's a long time ago.

He wants to see things straight, set things straight, get things right somehow.

It's been a long time coming, this book, all of thirty years, and all of us have changed, and not just Knighton.

Charlton, Edwards, and all the heroes, and all the villains in all these stories.

Time, great leveller, changes everything, always has, always will.

Mark Knighton, the son who inspired the father to achieve, is now a high achiever himself. He is a Master of Arts and Master of Philosophy, and is working on doctoral research at Cambridge University. Already, he is a leading expert on fine art and architecture.

The boy, whose traumatic birth in 1977 began this story, has come through the fire and flown high.

His father has too.

If Michael and Mark Knighton have both changed with the journey, so have all the characters in these tales.

Edwards has become wealthy beyond his dreams of thirty years ago. He has suffered, though, too, and Knighton is sorry for his pain, still thinks, if things had turned out differently, they might have made a winning team.

Charlton watches now, possibly ponders much upon the past, remains a national treasure, respected, valued, a man perhaps who has seen more change than changed himself, and Knighton thanks him for the memories.

Ferguson has escaped with his life after his brain haemorrhage.

Like Charlton, the former manager has a stand at Old Trafford named in his honour. Like Charlton, too, he surely must relive the times of a glorious past. Knighton says Ferguson is still the greatest manager of all time, and smiles at his own small part in making that a possibility.

I, too, wish them all well, and send them on their ways as hopefully happier and wiser, as well as older men.

It is only what I would wish for myself as I note my own aging and changing.

So, what I want to say, need to say, before all these stories become part of the past once more, part of a revised history, is that I have come at last to understand that all men and women have goodness at their heart, all strive and struggle to do their best, even if, to outsiders, they may appear to be doing their worst, may appear to be the villains of the piece.

Knighton, Edwards, Charlton, Watkins, Edelson, Burrows, Ferguson, Gambril, even Roland Smith, all are heroes to the extent that all have been doing the best they could at the time, for themselves, for their families, for their employers, for their football clubs, all good people travelling the lines of life.

This journeying is what *Visionary* has come to be about, even if it has taken the thirty years of the telling of all these tales for me to realise that.

What was it the Sufi mystic, Rumi, said?

*Do not permit yourself to get lost in your pain,*
*Know that one day*
*Your suffering will become your cure.*

There is both pain and wisdom in the past, but Michael Knighton has walked on, loving the paths he has travelled, and rarely looked backwards until now.

The pages of this book are autumn leaves, the words the beginnings of the gathering and the harvesting of time, of truth, and of the healing, transformative suffering of us all.

# Appendices

## *Appendix One*

**MICHAEL KNIGHTON**
**OUTLINE PROPOSALS FOR**
**INCREASING COMMERCIAL REVENUE**
**AT**
**MANCHESTER UNITED FOOTBALL CLUB Plc**
**A BLUEPRINT**
**1989**

**MICHAEL KNIGHTON** is of the firm view that by following the commercial initiatives and recommendations outlined in this document MUFC can develop into a successful leisure/ commercial vehicle which could one day have a base value of some circa £150m+ as a trading Company.

MK believes that this goal could be achievable within the next decade.

Together with creating a successful, wide-ranging leisure company whilst at the same time developing MUFC into a truly global sporting brand is the target. MUFC could develop into a brand that would be recognised across the globe as the world leader in its specific sporting sector. These are the twin aims and the core raison d' etre of this document.

MK appreciates that the opening claim of this blueprint paper will of course sound a tall order and a grossly over ambitious statement to many observers especially when one considers that MUFC filed accounts for Year End 1988 that show a loss on the Profit and Loss Account of £1.2m.

However, MK is confident that these strategic goals can be reached with the right planning.

The route to achieve this transforming level of success and arrive with the concomitant fiscal and branding status for the Club is for MUFC to implement enthusiastically the commercial proposals and recommendations that are outlined in this blueprint document.

In this blueprint the content will describe proposals for increasing revenue at M.U.F.C. from commercial activities currently undertaken by the Club, but, more importantly, to explore commercial opportunities that should be harnessed and developed to increase the all round profitability at MUFC.

A solid and sustainable year-on-year profitability is the only way that the Club will be able to compete to attract the best players in the world. Therefore, ipso facto, with financial success will come success on the field of play and the latter position is all the supporters of the Club want to see being achieved.

This blueprint will recommend a number of trading initiatives which the Club should have researched / tested with a view to adoption in the future. MK is determined that such innovative commercial ideas should be implemented once he has gained full control of the club via his offer to acquire the majority shareholding via his Company, MK Trafford Holdings Limited.

The proposals and initiatives described herein are drafted in outline form and are designed to be considered as developments of MUFC's current commercial activity programme together with promoting new and hitherto under exploited (and even ignored) commercial opportunities which MK believes must be examined in order to promote the Club onto a much higher commercial plane – a platform that will aim to use MUFC's current supporter base and capitalise on this potential. Such a strategic development should be the aim of any forward thinking ownership and management.

The areas addressed in this blueprint document are as follows:-

1. CLUB SPONSORSHIP AND PREDICTED FUTURE TV REVENUE
2. MATCH SPONSORSHIP AND OTHER SPONSORSHIP OPPORTUNITIES
3. MATCH-DAY V.I.P. CORPORATE AND PUBLIC HOSPITALITY
4. M.U.F.C. BOX HOLDERS, EXECUTIVE CLUB, SEASON TICKET HOLDERS
5. M.U.F.C. MEMBERSHIP SCHEME
6. OLD TRAFFORD STADIUM – NON-MATCH DAY FACILITIES
7. MEDIA ADVERTISING OPPORTUNITIES
8. PUBLISHING OPPORTUNITIES
9. M.U.F.C. PLAYING STAFF
10. MERCHANDISING – RETAILING AND MAIL ORDER
11. TRAVEL AND TOUR OPERATORS
12. EUROPEAN SUPER LEAGUE

**1. CLUB SPONSORSHIP**

OVERVIEW

It is a fact that Corporate sponsorship of professional football clubs, particularly those in League Division One, is the most overt and generally considered the highest revenue sector of all commercial activities at club level.

The 'benefits' of team strip (shirt) endorsement coupled with perimeter advertising, corporate hospitality and programme advertising, are the usual reciprocation for annual club sponsorship fees. The greater the T.V. appeal, the greater the sponsorship fee – thus clubs such as Liverpool (Candy), M.U.F.C. (Sharp), Spurs (Holsten), Arsenal (JVC), Everton (NEC) etc., who are perceived to have more T.V. appeal, attract the major brands. The additional benefits to sponsors of replica strips marketed throughout the U.K. and Europe increase considerably the level of brand exposure for club sponsors.

The real media value of this cumulative brand exposure is difficult to evaluate accurately since the level of T.V. exposure cannot be guaranteed at this current time by the clubs concerned but that situation may change in future.

Consequently, at this current time, sponsorship fees tend to be computed by comparison with previous fee agreement and a fairly unscientific formula often related to 'perceived market value'.

FUTURE CONSIDERATIONS

Given that the exposure of endorsed football strips during televised matches directly influences the level of sponsorship fee paid to the club – the following developments should be borne in mind.

A) TELEVISION PROGRAMME SPONSORSHIP – SPORT

For the writer of this blueprint, earlier this year, the date of 5th February 1989 at 6:00pm, was a very special and important day. This was because it signified the launch of satellite television. MK strongly disagrees with those observers, especially those leaders within the football industry, that say this form of broadcasting will not compete with terrestrial TV broadcasting and is therefore doomed to fail. In fact, the writer believes that this form of broadcasting, due to its potential of instantly having a global reach and on an hitherto unforeseen scale, will transform the current football audience.

MK predicts that this form of broadcasting will lead to revenue streams that may well be the most significant aspect of all such future revenue streams for the football industry. The current £44m TV deal could one day be worth as much as heading towards half a billion pounds in the not too distant future. That may sound like a bizarre prediction in 1989 but MK believes such future revenue streams are entirely possible.

This development together with other recent and pending changes to broadcast legislation has enabled T.V. contractors to exploit the revenue opportunities in the area of sponsored programming. Granada T.V. paved the way forward in sport programming by screening an ice hockey match, which G.T.V. arranged to be sponsored by Heineken.

It should be noted that the programme was sponsored by Heineken NOT the match.

A comparison of two similar sports programmes will highlight the potential revenue loss to football clubs: – the BBC screen a programme called Ski-Sunday – familiar to most viewers.

Sky Television screen a programme (transmitted throughout Europe via Eutelsat) called Ford Ski World. The Ford Motor Company sponsor this programme and it is evidenced by a massive exposure of the Ford logo and product propositions in both audio and visual form. The supplement to spot advertising within programme breaks of Ford endorsed 'title sequences', 'bumper breaks' and more importantly by data captions, clearly gets over the sponsor's message – to the exclusion of others.

It is predictable that English football programming will be the subject of programme sponsorship proposals to national and international brands. The cumulative brand exposure by programme sponsors may ultimately diminish the visibility and recall of club sponsors' brands on the player shirts and perimeter boards. The effect of this new initiative by T.V. contractors will, at one level at least, be a reduction in value of club sponsorship and commercial revenue unless and until the 'product' of football itself becomes the principal brand that attracts greater levels of sponsorship by and from the TV companies themselves.

MK believes this MUST be the way forward if the game of football is to benefit from the latest developments that are transforming the way that T.V. contractors look at what may attract national and international TV audiences. MK considers that the 'brand' of football per se is currently greatly undervalued by the football industry itself as a potential major TV sponsorship vehicle. MK predicts that the brand ( that is the game itself and in particular the MUFC brand as a leading club ) of football will shortly attract significant T.V. sponsorship revenue via selling the transmission rights to the highest bidder from the competing T.V broadcasting companies – a market that is growing very quickly and yet is virtually ignored by the football industry.

B) <u>PROLIFERATION OF THE MEDIA</u>

The introduction into the U.K. of Satellite T.V. (Sky and BSB) with the existing transmission 'footprints' of Intelsat and Eutelstat, will present British T.V. views with 30-60 channels from which to choose programmes. There will be a huge choice of live and recorded sport – all types of sport.

There is now an opportunity for principal football clubs in the Football League either as a co-operative or unilaterally, to derive substantial financial benefit from the situation described above. As has already been cited in this blueprint MK believes there will be an explosion in T.V broadcasting values which may well one day, sooner rather than later, reach even unimagined billions of pounds rather than the comparatively modest sums that are paid today – such is the global attraction of the sport. Few in the football industry see this potential hence the industry's reluctance to embrace satellite TV more readily. Indeed, in the writer's view, the product of football as a broadcasting rights vehicle is massively undervalued by most Club chairmen and especially by those that govern the sport at the FA and the Football League. This will change in time as the satellite TV phenomenon becomes more established.

Since T.V. Agreements are contracted between the Football League/Football Association and television contractors under the current rules of the I.B.A. it is essential that an "initiative" is taken by senior influencers, without delay. It is understood that a four year television agreement is currently operative terminating in 1992. The next TV deal should see a substantial increase in revenue if the powers that be wake-up to the global attraction of the football game as a universal product for TV audiences around the world.

C) PUBLIC PERCEPTION OF PROFESSIONAL FOOTBALL – THE EFFECT OF BRAND ASSOCIATION

Those tasked with custodianship of corporate brands pay particular attention to brand images and their perception by the customer market.

When a brand is linked to a quite separate entity for the purposes of media exposure it is important that neither image is in any way impaired at any stage in the relationship.

Professional football over recent years has suffered from a catalogue of incidents that have attracted media coverage which in turn have adversely affected the general public's perceptions of the sport. The horrific events of the Hillsborough and Heysel disasters are tragic examples. This must and will change. The comfort and safety of supporters MUST become paramount considerations if the game is to be in a position to fully exploit the new opportunities that a global T.V. network could offer a global sport like top class professional football club games. This is a key prerequisite of the writer. MK wants such high standards of comfort and safety for MUFC supporters at Old Trafford that this stadium should/will become a showcase for the whole industry.

The consequence of this general current view of English Football is an increasing concern of big Corporations when considering any form of commercial association with the sport. Manchester United FC, however, stands well above the general perceptions of other football clubs in terms of acceptability primarily because of;

- The credibility of its famous heroes – Bobby Charlton, Dennis Law, George Best, etc
- The superb stadium facilities which MK is determined to see improved still further to enable Old Trafford to become the best stadium in the country if not the world over the next ten years of ground development
- MUFC initiatives over the years in security, safety, crowd control, are also seen to be of a very high standard, etc.

The current perceptions of the sport tend not to adversely influence those companies seeking an association with MUFC and there continues to be many unsolicited enquiries for club sponsorship and, business associations.

<u>OUTLINE PROPOSALS</u>

Consideration should, however, be given to the following observations.

1. Sharp do not appear to be using the sponsorship of M.U.F.C. in their media Advertising programme, i.e. associating the Club with their product range, why not? This should be developed.
2. The M.U.F.C. playing staff do not appear to be enthusiastic about involvement with Sharp activities either in the club or outside. Is this because they do not derive any meaningful material benefits from the sponsorship agreement? This MUST and WILL change under the control of MK.

3. These days companies wish to be 'involved' in the organisation and administration of the events which they sponsor. Does M.U.F.C. invite Sharp to be pro-active in their association with the Club? If not, then this activity must be fostered and encouraged at every opportunity without delay.

If the situation arises that M.U.F.C. wish to explore alternative club sponsors for future seasons, there must be a fresh attitude towards structuring the relationship. Sponsorship in sport and the arts is an exercise undertaken by companies as part of their overall marketing strategy. Sponsorship fees are usually funded out of companies' marketing budgets as are media advertising, sales promotion, P.R. and business entertaining activity. It follows that the decision by a company to sponsor M.U.F.C. will be heavily influenced by its marketing management. For this reason a professional prospectus of the marketing opportunities created by sponsoring the club should be produced in order to attract the interest of major brands. There are many major brands that will want to be seen to be associated with the major brand in sport. This must be one of the key aims of MUFC.

The construction of the reciprocation package is clearly the most important element of the prospectus, often referred to as the 'Sponsorship Package'. An understanding of prospective sponsor companies' own marketing strategies is vital in order to compile a suitable sponsorship package and it follows that this task should be undertaken by a professional marketing team.

RECOMMENDATION

Retain the services of a Marketing Consultant or consultancy firm to act on behalf of M.U.F.C. with the following brief.

* Identify suitable national / international companies / brands and obtain detailed information concerning their business, particularly their marketing objectives and senior management attitude towards an association with M.U.F.C.

  N.B. The emotive issues of supporting M.U.F.C. must be considered.

* Produce a prospectus document / A.V. designed to illustrate in detail the marketing opportunity in a

style that is highly informative and compelling. The contents must cover every aspect of the reciprocation package and allow for tailoring to suit the needs of any sponsoring company.

* Accept the principle that by considering club sponsorship - companies would be entering into a business partnership with M.U.F.C. with the objective of developing MUTUAL, TANGIBLE, COMMERCIAL AND MARKETING BENEFITS, not simply providing revenue to M.U.F.C. and inflating the egos of the sponsor company's principals.

To progress this course of action, M.U.F.C. should produce a documented brief describing both the fiscal and marketing objectives of the Club in seeking sponsorship, then invite consultancies to tender with their proposals for engagement in respect of this project.

## 2. **MATCH SPONSORSHIP**

The M.U.F.C. stadium facilities ideally provide the venue for quality corporate hospitality programmes, an integral part of current match sponsorship packages. However, the distinction between match sponsorship and match-day VIP hospitality packages is the added media and sales promotion opportunities available to a company.

Over the years M.U.F.C. have provided a high quality match sponsorship package, the main ingredient of which has always been the pre-match hospitality event. In order to increase revenue from this activity it is necessary to create further additives to the package and establish a disciplined targeting procedure for attracting new match sponsors.

RECOMMENDATIONS

* Create a prospectus document detailing a new and enhanced match sponsors package, particularly in the area of media exposure.
* Consider additives to the 'package' which involve activities outside of MU.F.C. e.g. hotel accommodation, entertainment in the City, transportation.
* Attempt to integrate match sponsorship with companies' plans for product launches, exhibitions, con-

ferences etc planned to take place at M.U.F.C. or in Manchester.

* Set up a hit-list of companies that have NEVER experienced sponsorship at M.U.F.C., e.g. those based in the areas of the visiting team.
* One season in advance, make contact with the sponsors of all First Division football clubs, they are all potential match sponsors at M.U.F.C. on the appropriate match day.
* Ensure that the standard of service is nothing short of five star in every area under the Club's control.
* Establish in advance a bank of 'short-term local sponsors' to take up match sponsorship opportunities when the lead time is limited i.e. re-arranged or special matches at Old Trafford, and particularly successful cup runs.

### 3. **MATCH DAY V.I.P. CORPORATE AND PUBLIC HOSPITALITY**

The appeal of a VIP day out at M.U.F.C. on a match day is such that with correct marketing, the service could deliver substantial revenue. The target customer ranges from season ticket holders and ordinary fans, to the general public supporting either team participating.

RECOMMENDATIONS

* Create a prospectus document – with details of the package.
* Allocate a marketing budget to promote the facility by media advertising and direct mailing to companies.
* Ensure that promotion takes place in the localities of all the other First Division football clubs.
* Offer the facility, well in advance, to the commercial managers of visiting football clubs, with a commission built-in to the price structure.

### 4. **M.U.F.C. BOX-HOLDERS, EXECUTIVE CLUB, SEASON TICKET HOLDERS**

The Club holds data concerning this sector of M.U.F.C.

spectators and the information is valuable as a communication medium for sales propositions.

RECOMMENDATION

M.U.F.C. should investigate revenue opportunities from establishing a direct marketing programme to all the people / companies held on computer by the ticket sales office. Positive exploitation of data information of this type is essential if MUFC is to achieve the aim of gaining maximum benefit from the Club's in-house profit centre opportunities that are/will be innate in respect of its own current and extended supporter base.

* A 'Club' could be created offering all kinds of purchase advantages – leisure related products and services etc.
* These additions could stimulate the demand for season tickets etc (if required) but more importantly create additional revenue.
* The mailing list could be sold to a listing broker – who would market the facility to users of direct marketing techniques.

5. **M.U.F.C. MEMBERSHIP SCHEME**

If the government initiative / legislation comes into force, M.U.F.C. will establish a high data bank of fans / members. Accepting the rules of usage described in the Data Protection Act, an opportunity will present itself to 'commercially exploit' the members' list.

RECOMMENDATIONS

* Examine every legal opportunity to use the members' list as:
* A communication platform.
* Direct selling opportunities.
* Creation of 'Club' benefits – to members and outside retail / service organisations.

6. **OLD TRAFFORD STADIUM – NON-MATCH DAYS**

There is a wide range of uses of the Old Trafford stadium outside of match days some of which are well marketed, others either untried or poorly promoted.

As a conference, exhibition, restaurant venue, the Executive Club facilities are fairly well established, however the stadium is rarely used outside Football, Rugby League and the writer understands American Football is being planned.

RECOMMENDATIONS

* Explore the opportunities of staging events in the following categories:
* TENNIS
* LIGHT ENTERTAINMENT
* BOXING
* SUPERSTARS (T.V. Events)
* HOCKEY (International)
* INVITATION FOOTBALL MATCHES
* POP CONCERTS

* Stadium conducted tours (including all M.U.F.C. facilities) as a sight-seeing package, part of the North West tourism industry are a MUST. There is a ready market for this type of supporter facility. It is puzzling to the writer why many clubs tend to ignore such commercial opportunities.
* Construct an educational package available to educational institutions, schools, colleges, universities etc., using guides and playing staff.

## 7. **MEDIA ADVERTISING OPPORTUNITIES**

There are possibly further revenue opportunities from selling media advertising space additional to the existing facilities that are understood to comprise of:

* Perimeter advertising space and inner-stadium space
* 48 sheet outdoor poster sites

RECOMMENDATIONS

Consider selling advertising space on:

* Match tickets
* Season ticket books etc.
* Inside the Executive Club – tastefully
* On the outside walls of the stadium
* Inside the car park areas
* Match Programmes (space currently unsold)

## 8. PUBLISHING OPPORTUNITIES

M.U.F.C. MUST promote the publishing of a club magazine, NOT as a platform for M.U.F.C. propaganda, but as a more conventional sport / leisure publication distributed nationally through the wholesale / retail industry. MK believes that such publications will one day become a standard across the industry especially at the bigger clubs.

RATIONALE

All the leisure / sport publications currently on the market tend to reflect the opinions of proprietors, editors / journalists, couple with news items and advertising.

There is possibly an opening for a publication which is a platform for the professional sportsman – i.e. All sports / leisure.

RECOMMENDATION

* Explore the magazine market
* Establish the viability of introducing a new sport / leisure magazine – possibly in partnership with a reputable publisher.
* Produce a viability document.

## 9. M.U.F.C. PLAYING STAFF

Whilst it is clear that many professional footballers retain the services of 'agents' (some more professional than others) to handle their business activities, there is an opportunity for M.U.F.C. to create substantial revenue for the Club and playing staff by a more professional approach to marketing the players.

RECOMMENDATION

* Identify all current agreements between individual members of staff with companies / brands etc and examine restrictions.
* Employ a professional 'agent' to market the players on behalf of the Club and under the strict control of the Manager.
* Establish an equitable players pool (if it does not already exist) with a formula for remunerating individuals that are more commercially attractive.

* Seek out endorsement, advertising and sales promotional opportunities for the playing staff and establish a portfolio of business / brand associations.

## 10. **MERCHANDISING, RETAILING AND MAIL ORDER**

Together with the future potential of broadcasting TV rights, this is possibly the most valuable area of marketing opportunity for M.U.F.C. It centres around the use of M.U.F.C. as a merchantable brand name which endorses retailable products and services.

There is a clear distinction between M.U.F.C. souvenir products as sold in the souvenir shop, etc, and a M.U.F.C. branded product range. In the writer's view, every conceivable and appropriate marketable product could be MUFC branded with a view to positively exploiting the in-house existing supporter base whilst at the same time reaching out to increase the club's wider supporter appeal as MUFC establishes itself as an international brand in its own right.

RECOMMENDATION

* Retain the services of specialist consultants with a brief to examine the viability of establishing a M.U.F.C. brand for the purpose of franchising its use by manufacturers and retailers.
* Areas to be examined:

a) A range of branded products, the list is almost endless, but Clothing, Health Care, Cosmetics, Financial Services, etc, etc. are a MUST.
b) A retailing chain of shops should be established across the UK and abroad. A Superstore of MUFC branded goods should be established on site at Old Trafford
c) A mail order catalogue business could be developed
d) Licensing manufacturers to use the MUFC brand

* An in-depth business / marketing plan should be produced following the initial research and examination of the project

## 11. **TRAVEL & TOUR OPERATIONS**

The enormous following of M.U.F.C. coupled with its high level of corporate awareness in the public and private sector around the world suggests that the Club could enter into almost any business enterprise – outside of football, with an edge over its competitors. This initiative should be deployed at the Club without delay.

The travel and tour operators industry is highly volatile for two main reasons:

* It is a price led industry
* Brand loyalty is difficult to maintain

Consequently tour operators have over the years, merged to a level that two companies dominate the market – Thompsons & ILG (Intasun Group). Furthermore they are becoming more vertical – i.e. owning airlines, hotels and chains of travel agencies.

Yet, despite this dominance, there are plenty of independent tour operators and travel agency groups operating profitably in segmented niche markets within the U.K.

RECOMMENDATIONS

* Explore in-depth the opportunity of a M.U.F.C. branded overseas tour operators programme.
* Explore in-depth the opportunity of M.U.F.C. travel shops for both business travel and I.T. programmes (including tours).
* Membership of A.B.T.A., ATOL licensing etc.

Whilst the perception of football hooliganism linked with travel may inhibit initial thoughts of M.U.F.C. entering this industry – it should be borne in mind that M.U.F.C. has a good name and reputation for supporter safety

To be seen to be tackling problems, almost laterally, by establishing a new business in the travel and tour operations industry will certainly score major political points as well as provide a useful revenue contribution.

12. **EUROPEAN SOCCER LEAGUE**

Much has been aired in public about the concept of a European Soccer League in which 'major' clubs compete during the current football season – possibly extended into the summer.

The shaping of such a programme would serve to achieve a wide range of sporting, social and trading objectives and could be formatted as follows;

(a) Participant Clubs from:

UNITED KINGDOM – Manchester United, Tottenham Hotspur, Liverpool, Everton, Arsenal, Celtic, Glasgow Rangers.

SPAIN – Real Madrid, Barcelona

ITALY – Juventus, Naples, Inter Milan

PORTUGAL – Sporting Club Lisbon

BELGIUM – Anderlecht

GERMANY – Bayern Munich, Hamburg, Borussia Monchengladbach

PLUS OTHER REPRESENTATIVES from France, Holland, Greece, Sweden, Austria, Switzerland

(b) Spectators

Only home fans would be allowed to watch these all ticket matches – i.e. tickets distributed only to home supporters. Away supporters would be able to watch the match via satellite T.V. either at their homes or at stadium / cinema venues (as with boxing).

This method of spectator control should, if ticket distribution is efficiently controlled, prevent the export of U.K. hooligans.

(c) The prospect of presenting a higher standard of football, is clearly a major appeal of this tournament – a direct effect would be the improvement of British soccer skills particularly for the U.K. national teams.

**FINANCIAL IMPLICATIONS**

(a) TELEVISION LICENSES

The T.V. screening rights for such a tournament would be very lucrative since the financial consideration would reflect the size of the European Audience. Fees equivalent to those paid by each nation's nominated T.V. contracts for World Cup Screening right would be applied. MUFC MUST develop its own TV subscription channel – this development could be extremely lucrative.

(b) EUROPEAN LEAGUE AND MATCH SPONSORSHIPS

The tournament presents itself as a natural platform for a pan-European brand to become its primary sponsor. By including a T.V. programming sponsorship package into the agreement the sponsorship could be worth in excess of £10 million per season. Individual match sponsorship would also provide substantial revenue to the participating clubs – again multi-national corporations would be ideal candidates.

(c) COPYRIGHTS – TRADE MARKS – MERCHANDISING

The revenue opportunities by the merchandising of the brand representations of the European Soccer League, are enormous and comparable with the sums earned by host nations of the World Cup.

IMPLICATIONS ON DOMESTIC PROFESSIONAL FOOTBALL

* ADDED REVENUE
* CURRENT PROGRAMMES / COMPETITIONS REMAIN INTACT
* QUALITY OF FOOTBALL PLAY IMPROVES
* NO EXPORT OF HOOLIGAN 'SUPPORTER'
* VALUE USEAGE OF 1992 TRADING FREEDOM IN EUROPE

**SUMMARY**

There are several other areas that MK will promote and institute at MUFC once the acquisition of the majority share-holding process from the current owner has been finalised by MK's company – MK Trafford Holdings Limited:

* M.U.F.C. Development Association – this will be enhanced and promoted
* M.U.F.C. Video Films – MK believes this is essential – as the T.V. and broadcasting technological advances will ultimately have a massive impact on the game of professional football and how the sport is marketed and promoted over the coming years
* M.U.F.C. Museum, this is a MUST as a future spectator and educational attraction. MK is astonished that such a facility has never been fully exploited at the club. MK predicts a big future for football memorabilia collecting and sourcing of all kinds in the years to come. MUFC

are ideally placed to harness such a growing trend in this emerging market

* The Club MUST have its own subscription TV channel for its in-house supporter base and to capitalise on future world-wide interest in MUFC

* There are many other commercial activities which the writer will aim to implement once in control of the club

Ideally the Club must employ a professional Marketing Director to establish marketing strategy documents for each of the trading activities. In today's economy – marketing and fiscal planning is essential to the success of the business. As far as M.U.F.C. is concerned on-the-field performance is unpredictable and directly affects gate revenue, commercial activities should not be affected by team performance, only by trends in the market in which they operate. Market conditions are predictable by studying market trends and collaborating with specialist marketing-cum-sales experts.

It is common practice for businesses to employ experts in marketing and/or retain external consultants in this role. M.U.F.C. do not appear to have adopted this practice. MK strongly recommends that this policy be reappraised as a matter of urgency.

# FINALLY

PROPOSAL FOR FLOTATION

MK believes MUFC can be developed into a major, global sporting brand with a potential market value that exceeds £150m.

This section demonstrates a model which shows the initial de-gearing strategy.

1. ASSUMPTIONS

a) Offer take-up of 75%

b) roll-up of interest for 1 year

c) value of company on flotation of say £80 million

2. VALUE OF M.U.F.C. [ASSETS]

| | £ (Million) |
|---|---|
| 31st July 1989 Balance Sheet value | 5.935 |
| Increase in site value (Less C.T.) * | 11.365 |
| Value of players (Less C.T.) | 7.8 |
| Contingent liabilities (Less C.T.) say | (1.1) |
| | £ 24.00m |

* Assumed rate of Corporation Tax (C.T.) of 35%

3. No value attributable to brand name M.U.F.C.
PROPOSAL FOR FLOTATION (CONTINUED)

| A) Costs | |
|---|---|
| £20 per share x (75% x 1,006,821) | 15,102,315 |
| Legal, Accountancy & Ancillary costs, say | 417,685 |
| | 15,520,000 |
| Interest for 12 months at 16% | 2,480,000 |
| TOTAL COSTS | £ 18,000,000 |

B) 75% take-up by M.K. Trafford
24.99% floated worth 19,992,000
==============

C) Surplus to M.K. Trafford after repayment 1,992,000
==============

## COMPOSITION OF BOARD

| | Present | After M.K. Trafford's Acquisition | At Time of Flotation |
|---|---|---|---|
| Chairman | C.M. Edwards | M. Knighton | Non-Exec To be appointed |
| Deputy Chairman | – | C.M.Edwards | M. Knighton |
| Chief Executive Officer | C.M. Edwards | C.M. Edwards | To be appointed |
| Directors | J.M. Edelson<br>R. Charlton<br>E.M. Watkins<br>A.M. Al Midani<br>N. Burrows<br>R.L. Olive | J.M. Edelson<br>R. Charlton<br>E.M. Watkins<br>R.L. Olive<br>B. Chaytow*<br>D.E.M. Mond** | J.M. Edelson<br>R. Charlton<br>E.M. Watkins<br>R.A. Olive<br>B. Chaytow<br>D.E.M. Mond<br>C.M. Edwards |

* Former Chairman of Bolton Wanderers F.C.

** Chartered Accountant

## M.K. TRAFFORD HOLDINGS LIMITED FURTHER PROPOSALS FOR DE-GEARING

STRATEGY (A) UPSIDE

It is anticipated that between 65% and 80% of the shareholding in M.U.F.C. will be secured from the pending cash offer. Therefore, based on, say 75% take-up Trafford Holdings would immediately initiate steps to relinquish 24% of its holding in M.U.F.C. This would enable Trafford Holdings to control, and realise anticipated £6-10M.

The Directors are confident that sufficient interest has been shown to warrant such high expectations. Several potential investors have already come forward i.e. Amer Al Midani, Eddy Shah, Frank Warren, George Walker of Brent Walker, Pleasurama and others. In my opinion Mr. Midani is number one candidate already being a Director of the Club and would pay significantly to remain in that position. He already controls 10% of M.U.F.C.

STRATEGY (B) DOWNSIDE

If only, say 51% of M.U.F.C. shares are secured I undertake that the following policy would be adopted:-

(a) Within Trafford Holdings M. Knighton's personal holding would be reduced to 25% thereby relinquishing 25% of the equity for other potential investors. Again we would anticipate that this would realise between £6M-10M.

(b) As proposed in the corporate structure of this deal Trafford Holdings will have other assets available for disposal (ie. Properties secured to Bank of Scotland). These cover assets held in St. David's Prep School Limited and Edward Hotel Limited. In my opinion the potential values, not on a forced sale Bank basis, add up to a value of just under £14m (please refer to my schedule of assets and liabilities attached).

I would propose that a review date of say 30 March 1990 is fixed whereby the Directors should be in a position to take a view as to which strategy or a combination of the two strategies should be put in place. It may be that we are in a position to decide this much earlier than 30 March 1990.

# *Appendix Two*

## Special Bet Terms and Conditions

Graham Sharpe, Esq
William Hill Organisation plc
19 Valentine Place
London
SE 1

Michael Knighton
Killochan Castle
By Girvan
Ayrshire
SCOTLAND

Our ref:MK/RA/01
20th July 1989

Dear Mr Sharpe,

**Agreed Special Bet Conditions:**

**As a follow up to our meeting at your offices on 4th July 1989.** You have asked me to confirm in writing the following points which I gladly herewith provide:

1. I can confirm that I shall be 38 years old later this year, 1989.
2. I can confirm that I am not currently signed on professional football forms with a Football Association League Club and that I have not played in the Football League
3. I can confirm that I was a Youth Player on the books as a Club Groundstaff Boy with Coventry City FC in the season 1967/68 but suffered serious injury and returned

to full-time education after just 8 months as a full time professional trainee

4. I can confirm that I was a full County Cap player at aged 18 years
5. I can confirm that at the time of our meeting and at the time of writing this letter that my current body weight is 15st and 7lbs. My normal playing weight was circa 11st 7lbs
6. I can confirm that I have not played regular football at any level for the previous 12 years
7. I can confirm that I am currently following my own dieting and conditioning programme with the specific intention of regaining a degree of physical fitness which may assist my ambition to achieve my Football League debut in Season 1989-1990.

We have agreed that the format for any media coverage or public announcement will be mutually discussed and mutually agreed before wider public disclosure of any kind.

Perhaps you might confirm the betting odds that we discussed and agreed during our meeting in respect of the various playing situations, including my appearance in an F.A. Cup Final in the season of 1989-1990.

Every good wish,
Yours sincerely,

**Michael Knighton.**
**20th July 1989.**

# *Appendix Three*

## Notes on Sources, Inspirations

Most of the material for *Visionary* has come from interviews with Michael Knighton since 1992. As such, it is an intensely personal book.

This does not, however, imply a lack of rigour or intellectual curiosity in its preparation. The author is a history graduate from St Catharine's College, Cambridge, and has taught at Glasgow University. He has also enjoyed the privilege of access to Knighton's private papers and diaries, and to his collection of newspapers from the period of his involvement with Manchester United.

*Visionary* was never intended as a dry and academic text. Hence the decision of the author not to impede the narrative's flow with extensive footnotes and numbered sources. Anyone with sufficient interest is perfectly able to read the primary sources themselves at the British Newspaper Archive or at archives hosted by individual newspapers.

Some of the most important quotations from newspapers, for the purposes of the arguments advanced in this book, are from: Sam Wallace, *Daily Telegraph*, 14 September 2017; Michael Edelson, *Daily Telegraph*, 30 November 2004; and Mark Ogden, *Daily Telegraph*, 17 August 2009. Articles from the *Manchester Evening News* from the relevant times have also been especially interesting.

Important secondary sources – published books – that have been consulted include two titles by Michael Crick, *Manchester United: The Betrayal of a Legend*, written with David Smith in 1989, and *The Boss: The Many Sides of Alex Ferguson* (2002), and one by Jim White, *Manchester United: The Biography* (2009).

The author has also read Martin Edwards' 2017 book, *Red Glory: Manchester United and Me*.

The author decided at the outset that he would focus on the tales that Michael Knighton himself had to tell and, therefore, conducted no interviews with other major protagonists. As any honest historian would say, however, this methodology in no way diminishes the likelihood of arriving at a sensible and balanced view of the truth. This author has devoted his efforts to really understanding his subject.

I have known and occasionally worked alongside Michael Knighton for nearly three decades and think I now fathom him as well as anyone bar his family. I know his honesty, his commitment to the truth, even when it is not especially flattering. The methodology used is akin to the sociologist's way of working known as participant observation.

As a historian, the author has taken as his inspiration, Edward Thompson's book, *The Making of the English Working Classes*. In this magisterial work, Thompson determined to rescue the lost heroes of history – those relegated at best to footnotes – the long-forgotten and undervalued, whose stories would otherwise never have been told.

Without the publication of *Visionary*, Michael Knighton might have – unjustly – become one of those lost souls. This is why the author has given pride of place within Knighton's story to the Covenanter dead, rescued from the obscurity of Killochan Castle, to the heroes of the Blackwell Colliery disaster of 1895, whose names are also recorded within the pages of *Visionary*, and to the Hillsborough dead whose sufferings inspired Knighton to do something radical, something revolutionary.

It is the hope of the author that *Visionary* will help to correct the many untruths that surround the Michael Knighton and Manchester United story, and save him from the condescension and the forgetfulness of posterity, and that the book will play its part in the restoration of a good man to his rightful place in football history.